THE
JAMES SPRUNT STUDIES
IN HISTORY
AND POLITICAL SCIENCE

*Published under the Direction of
the Departments of History and Political Science
of the University of North Carolina*

VOLUME 31

———————— * ————————

Editors

ALBERT RAY NEWSOME

WILLIAM WHATLEY PIERSON

MITCHELL B. GARRETT

FLETCHER M. GREEN

KEENER C. FRAZER

ESSAYS IN SOUTHERN HISTORY

Edited by

FLETCHER MELVIN GREEN

GREENWOOD PRESS, PUBLISHERS
WESTPORT, CONNECTICUT

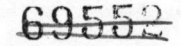

Library of Congress Cataloging in Publication Data

North Carolina. University.
   Essays in Southern history.

   First published in 1949 under title: Essays in southern history presented to Joseph Gregoire de Roulhac Hamilton, Ph.D., LL.D. by his former students at the University of North Carolina.
   Reprint of the ed. published by University of North Carolina Press, Chapel Hill, which was issued as v. 31 of The James Sprunt studies in history and political science.
      Includes bibliographical references.
      CONTENTS: Wolfe, J. H. The roots of Jeffersonian democracy.--Sitterson, J. C. Lewis Thompson, a Carolinian and his Louisiana plantation.--Shanks, H. T. Conservative Constitutional tendencies of the Virginia secession convention. [etc.]
   1. Southern States--History--Addresses, essays, lectures. 2. Hamilton, Joseph Grégoire de Roulhac, 1878-1961. I. Hamilton, Joseph Grégoire de Roulhac, 1878-1961. II. Title. III. Series: The James Sprunt studies in history and political science ; v. 31.
F209.N67 1976   975   76-49069
ISBN 0-8371-9326-5

Copyright, 1949, by
THE UNIVERSITY OF NORTH CAROLINA PRESS

All rights reserved

Originally published in 1949 by the University of North Carolina Press, Chapel Hill

Reprinted with the permission of University of North Carolina Press

Reprinted in 1976 by Greenwood Press, Inc.

Library of Congress Catalog Card Number 76-49069

ISBN 0-8371-9326-5

Printed in the United States of America

PREFACE

One of the most significant developments in the study of history in the South since the first World War has been the deepening interest of students, scholars, and the public generally in the South as a region. Interest in "Southern History" has not been confined to the South however. Courses in the history of the South are now offered in well over one hundred educational institutions, including many of the leading colleges and universities of the East, the West, and the North, as well as of the South. The foundation for this interest was laid by such distinguished historians as William Archibald Dunning of Columbia University, William Edward Dodd of the University of Chicago, and Ulrich Bonnell Phillips of the University of Michigan and Yale University.

But it was left to a second generation of historians to cultivate the southern field more intensively and extensively. Among the leaders in the second group is Joseph Gregoire de Roulhac Hamilton. He has made important contributions to southern historical interest and research by his own writings, by his collection and preservation of priceless manuscript historical materials, and by his long years of teaching at the University of North Carolina. He is the author of ten books and half a hundred and more articles and essays published in leading historical reviews and popular magazines. He has contributed hundreds of biographical sketches of Southerners to the *Dictionary of American Biography* and similar biographical directories. In addition he has edited a score of volumes of source documents.

Some twenty-five years ago Professor Hamilton conceived the idea of bringing together and making available a great body of manuscript materials bearing on the South. The result is the Southern Historical Collection at the University of North Carolina, consisting of millions of letters and papers and more than six thousand bound volumes of diaries and plantation journals. This Collection has become a sort of Mecca for students interested in southern history and is visited annually by many scholars who are writing books and articles on the South.

In his seminar on the history of the South Professor Hamilton awakened a deep and abiding interest in southern history in scores of students, many of whom wrote theses and dissertations under his direction. Hundreds of others, stimulated by his wide knowledge of and enthusiasm for southern history, continued their studies and have made contributions to the knowledge and understanding of the South.

Professor Hamilton was honored by the presidency of the Southern Historical Association in 1943. At that time some of his students planned a volume of essays in his honor but the exigencies of World War II intervened. Now upon his retirement from his professorship of history and the directorship of the Southern Historical Collection some of his many former students, wishing to bear testimony of their esteem of him as a friend and teacher and their high regard for him as a scholar, dedicate this volume of essays to Professor Hamilton.

No effort has been made to secure unity of theme in the volume; each contributor selected the topic of his own essay. It is to be noted, however, that the essays represent several well-known interests of Professor Hamilton, namely: Thomas Jefferson, the Old South, the Civil War, Reconstruction, and North Carolina state history.

The authors take this opportunity to express their appreciation to the editorial board of The James Sprunt Studies in History and Political Science for their aid in making publication of this volume possible.

THE EDITOR.

January 25, 1949
Chapel Hill

CONTENTS

	PAGE
Preface	v

CHAPTER

  I. The Roots of Jeffersonian Democracy: With Special
     Emphasis on South Carolina.......................... 1
     By JOHN HAROLD WOLFE, Professor of History, Winthrop College

 II. Lewis Thompson, A Carolinian and His Louisiana Plantation,
     1848-1888: A Study in Absentee Ownership.............. 16
     By JOSEPH CARLYLE SITTERSON, Professor of History,
     University of North Carolina

III. Conservative Constitutional Tendencies of the Virginia
     Secession Convention................................... 28
     By HENRY THOMAS SHANKS, Professor of History,
     Birmingham-Southern College

 IV. The Negro in the United States Senate.................. 49
     By SAMUEL DENNY SMITH, Professor of Social Science,
     Arkansas Agricultural and Mechanical College

  V. Public Education in North Carolina During Reconstruction,
     1865-1876 67
     By DANIEL JAY WHITENER, Professor of History, Appalachian
     State Teachers College

 VI. The Republican Party in South Carolina, 1876-1895....... 91
     By JAMES WELCH PATTON, Director of The Southern Historical
     Collection, University of North Carolina

VII. Some Aspects of the Convict Lease System in the
     Southern States.. 112
     By FLETCHER MELVIN GREEN, Kenan Professor of History,
     University of North Carolina

VIII. The Ideology of White Supremacy, 1876-1910............. 124
     By GUION GRIFFIS JOHNSON, Chapel Hill, North Carolina

ESSAYS IN SOUTHERN HISTORY

I

THE ROOTS OF JEFFERSONIAN DEMOCRACY: WITH SPECIAL EMPHASIS ON SOUTH CAROLINA

JOHN HAROLD WOLFE

So varied in nature and manifestation are revolutions that historians are tempted to call any period a revolutionary era. There are times, however, when changes occur more precipitantly than at others. This was true of the last years of the eighteenth century and the early decades of the nineteenth. While the direct connection may not have been evident, somewhat similar revolutions took place in several parts of the western world during those years. They were more than parallels—they were inter-related; and while their backgrounds varied and their results differed, they had much in common.

The changes which took place in France and in America during this age have been compared frequently. But contrasts are easily found. In every stage of their unfolding they differed in degree if not in nature. And, regardless of how they may or may not have been related in origin, the results during the decades which followed in the two countries showed noticeable contrasts. There were reactions to political democracy in both France and America. In both countries there were recurrent outbursts of popular protest. France had more internal violence during her various revolutions and less democracy afterward. In America the revolutions took the more orderly form of governmental changes through elections, in France there were street barricades and the overthrow of governments by force. Truly, the American democratic processes functioned more smoothly and consistently. It would be an exaggeration to attribute the contrasting procedure to leadership or the guidance of any one man or group of men, for obviously the two nations differed in cultural background and experience. Nevertheless, leadership was a necessary and vital force.

Thomas Jefferson did not write all the lines in the democratic revolutionary drama which was acted upon the stage of our early national existence, nor did he merely hold the script; but he contributed the more important lines and was the voice which spoke many of the others. In fact, he was the leading character. Then, as now, the roots of Jeffersonian democracy reached deep into and drew support or opposition from every layer of the contemporary culture. Truly, as Charles Maurice Wiltse recently wrote: "To understand Jefferson we must appreciate what preceded him; to evaluate him we must consider what has followed."[1] Ob-

---
[1] Charles Maurice Wiltse, *The Jeffersonian Tradition in American Democracy* (Chapel Hill, 1935), p. 5.

viously, in this brief essay, the Jeffersonian era, as well as what preceded and followed it, can be treated only in the broadest outlines.

The first thing needed is a summary of the chief ideas and practices of Jeffersonian democracy. This will be given in the words of two careful students of the subject.

Essential contributions of Jeffersonian Democracy to political life comprise confidence in majority rule, the theory of natural rights, and a system of governmental units. Of these three, belief in majority rule was perhaps the most important. But the theory of natural rights included the right of revolution and the rights to periodic revision of the constitution and fundamental laws, both stressed by Jefferson. Of the governmental units, emphasis was particularly laid on local government as the true heart of republicanism.

Contributions of Jeffersonian Democracy in the fields of economic and social philosophy perhaps were as great. The core of his economic policy was an agrarian America, with every man a landowner. The chief aim of his social reforms was the well-being of the individual. He disliked all things that smacked of oppression. His was a liberalizing influence; that Jefferson set the stamp of liberty on American life can not be denied. Among other things, he advocated free schools, free press, and freedom of religion.[2]

The second summary, written by the scholar in whose honor this volume of essays is issued, outlines Jefferson's ideas concerning the nature and mission of the American Union.

. . . Champion of State's rights he has been consistently painted, but Jefferson was in practice and largely in theory a consistent federalist, a supporter of the adoption of the Articles of Confederation, a critic of its defects, an advocate of the adoption of the Constitution, and one of its ardent defenders to the end of his days.

The close of the Revolution found him confirmed in the belief, which was presently strengthened by his residence abroad, that America offered a unique opportunity for the establishment of the most perfect system of government the world had seen, if only the dangers of the European system could be kept out. Entangling alliances must be avoided at any cost. He was even distrustful of a developing commerce because of its international implications. Manufacturing was also dangerous to American ideals. He would have preferred the United States to resemble in its self-sufficiency his plantation at Monticello. . . . Let America be an agricultural nation. "Those who labor in the earth are the chosen people of God . . . whose breasts he has made his peculiar deposit for substantial and genuine virtue. It is the focus in which he keeps alive that sacred fire which otherwise might escape from the face of the earth. . . . While we have land to labor then, let us never wish to see our citizens occupied at a work-bench, or twirling a distaff. Carpenters, masons, smiths, are wanting in husbandry; but, for the general operation of manufacture, let our workshops remain in Europe. It is better to carry provisions and materials, and with them their manners and principles." But progressive and ever ready to admit error, Jefferson was presently to favor the development of industry as a necessity in a self-sufficient nation.

Peace was an essential part of his system, war being one of the chief burdens of the human race, but he advocated a reasonable preparedness.

[2] Carrie Isobel French, The Early Political, Economic, and Social Philosophy of Thomas Jefferson (M.A. thesis, University of Chicago, 1932), pp. 43-44.

Individual liberty was the foundation stone of the Jeffersonian structure and since free government in his thinking could not exist without widely diffused knowledge, he advocated public education as a necessity. Common schools and a free press would prepare the mass of the people for civic duties and universities would train experts and leaders.

America, applying to the business of government the wisdom of all time, as adapted to its needs, would be an example and a hope to the world.

Deeply convinced as he was that America had a world mission, Jefferson was no missionary. Nowhere in him was there any fire of desire to reform the world or anybody in it other than by example. He was unsympathetic with the offer of revolutionary France to free the rest of the world, for his liberalism in addition to being tolerant, was of a sort that made him believe men fit to be free only when they were determined to be. He was as averse to forcing men's political beliefs as he was to forcing their ideas on religion and morals. Freedom in these was among the inalienable rights of sovereign men.[3]

The mere recital of Jefferson's beliefs, as summarized above, indicates their breadth and inclusiveness. Also, it seems quite clear that changing circumstances brought about theoretical adaptations which struck others as substitutions but which Jefferson, in his own flexible mind, considered only the rearrangement of minor figures in a permanent pattern. The story of the origin of Jeffersonian democracy or of Jefferson's philosophy would be the story of his life and times. Years before the American Revolution he had acquired ideas which no doubt were looked upon as odd if not revolutionary by his more conservative friends. In the original draft of the Declaration of Independence he included, along with a list of grievances against the king of Great Britain and even as a part of it, a statement of the rights of men. During and immediately after the Revolution American political leaders sought to check or even destroy the possibilities of social and economic changes, but historians know today that our struggle for independence was also an internal social conflict.

The recognition of the independence of the thirteen states by Great Britain in 1783 ended only the political phase of the American Revolution. The social phase continued. Much of this social revolution and many of its leaders became a part of Jeffersonian democracy. Soon its roots took a firm hold in the American culture—so firm a hold that it has never been broken loose.

In the changes which accompanied or followed the Revolution hardly a single institution escaped. This was true even in South Carolina, which historians until recently considered one of the early strongholds of Federalism.[4] The strong tendency toward popular control is shown emphatically in the post-Revolutionary churches. Only the influence of Francis Asbury prevented the Methodists from adopting congregationalism, the

[3] Joseph Gregoire de Roulhac Hamilton, "Jefferson's Americanism," a review of Gilbert Chinard, *Thomas Jefferson: the Apostle of Americanism*, in *Virginia Quarterly Review*, VI (January, 1930), 120-121.
[4] The late Professor Ulrich Bonnell Phillips in "The South Carolina Federalists," *American Historical Review*, XIV (1901), 529-543, 731-745, overestimates Federalist strength both politically and socially.

Catholics defied one of their bishops, and the self-governing Baptists increased very rapidly.[5] A contemporary thought that the popular doctrines of Jefferson "found nowhere a more genial soil to take root, than in the state of South Carolina. They were cherished here with enthusiasm."[6] According to Jefferson, it was Aedanus Burke who first attacked the aristocratic tendencies of the Society of Cincinnati.[7] Partly to offset and partly to deride exclusive social groups, popular organizations with such curious names as "the Free and Easy" and the "Ugly Club" were formed.[8]

The controversies during the period of the Confederation and the struggle over the ratification of the United States Constitution foreshadowed the later party divisions in South Carolina. Geographically and culturally the state was divided into two general sections known as the up country and the low country. When political lines became more clearly drawn Jefferson gained most of his followers from the former region though he was never without supporters in the latter. Many of the supporters of Jeffersonian democracy became highly dissatisfied with the aristocratic state government and its conservative economic policies during the 1780's. They attacked these forces and won partial victories. Moderate inflation was forced in 1785;[9] when this proved insufficient the agitation continued, and sometimes resulted in extra-legal action.[10] Although Charles Pinckney, who was soon to become one of Jefferson's most ardent leaders, helped frame the Constitution of the United States and led the fight for its ratification, most future South Carolina Republicans opposed it. Speaking for the opposition, Rawlins Lowndes reached his climax when he declared that he wished no other epitaph than to have written on his tomb, "Here lies a man who opposed the constitution, because it was ruinous to the liberty of America."[11] No attempt was made to prevent the calling of a convention to decide the question of ratification, but only by the narrow margin of one vote did the low country friends of the constitution

[5] David Duncan Wallace, *The Historical Background of Religion in South Carolina* (Columbia, 1916), pp. 25-26.
[6] Charles Fraser, *Reminiscences of Charleston* (Charleston, 1854), p. 49.
[7] Paul Leicester Ford, ed., *The Writings of Thomas Jefferson*, 10 volumes (New York, 1892-1889), IV, 172.
[8] Charles Fraser, *Reminiscences*, p. 57; *South Carolina Historical and Genealogical Magazine*, XXXII (1931), 77; Charleston *City Gazette*, January 4, 1797.
[9] Journal of the House of Representatives of the State of South Carolina (manuscript), September 26, 1785; Thomas Cooper, ed., *The Statutes at Large of South Carolina*, 10 volumes (Columbia, 1836-1841), IV, 712.
[10] New York *Packet*, August 28, 1786; New York *Gazeteer and Country Journal*, July 21, 1786, quoted by John Bach McMaster, *A History of the People of the United States from the Revolution to the Civil War*, 8 volumes (New York, 1911), I, 286-287; a report of the Camden grand jury, reproduced in Thomas J. Kirkland and Robert M. Kennedy, *Historic Camden*, 2 volumes (Columbia, 1905 and 1906), II, 254-256.
[11] *Debates Which Arose in the House of Representatives of South Carolina on the Constitution Framed for the United States by a Convention of Delegates Assembled at Philadelphia together with Such Notes as Could Be Procured* (Charleston, 1811), p. 52.

obtain Charleston as the meeting place.[12] Because the basis of representation gave the lower part of the state many more delegates than its population warranted, ratification was achieved by the comfortable vote of one hundred forty-nine to seventy-three.[13] Even then the delegates appended their interpretations of certain sections and instructed future representatives of the state in Congress to work for amendments.[14]

Without the rise of national political parties, local differences would have been sufficient to continue the existence of at least two strong state factions. Having settled their region first the people of the low country had established the local government. When the up country was settled later by people of different background and culture, those already in power refused to give up control even after they came to be outnumbered. When the sharing of power could be postponed no longer, concessions were made; and the subsequent internal history of South Carolina became a story of struggle and compromise between its two sections. All forms of sectionalism have never been eliminated, but the removal of the capital from Charleston to the more central location of Columbia was a step in that direction.[15] Even this, however, was a compromise for several state officers maintained headquarters in both towns. By 1790 several democratic gains had been made. Primogeniture and religious qualifications for voting were abolished, and there were easier property qualifications for the suffrage and for office holding. Nevertheless the low country still controlled both houses of the legislature and thereby the election of many officers including the governor. Fearing that its older and more firmly established social and economic institutions might not be safe in the hands of the more vigorous and democratic representatives from the up country, the low country held on tightly to its control of the state legislature. Not until South Carolina's economic interests became unified and the state grew into a kind of low country "writ large" did the more populous up country secure, through a redistribution of representation, the control of one of the houses of the legislature and the establishment of white manhood suffrage.[16] The struggles which culminated in these two victories in 1808 and 1810 were contemporary with and a part of the larger Jeffer-

[12] South Carolina House Journal, January 19, 1788 (manuscript).

[13] If the convention had been representative of the white population of South Carolina, it is doubtful whether the constitution would have been ratified. According to Orin Grant Libby, *Geographical Distribution of the Vote of the Thirteen States on the Federal Constitution, 1787-8* (Madison, 1894), pp. 42-44, the lower part of the state voted 88% for and 12% against the constitution; the middle section, 49% for and 51% against; and the upper, 20% for and 80% against.

[14] *Journal of the Convention of South Carolina Which Ratified the Constitution of the United States May 23, 1788* (facsimile), indexed by Alexander S. Salley (Atlanta, 1928), pp. 13-23. Jefferson wrote Edward Rutledge congratulating him upon the ratification by South Carolina but expressing the desire for a bill of rights. P. L. Ford, *Writings of Jefferson*, V. 41-42.

[15] David Ramsay, *The History of South Carolina from Its First Settlement in 1670 to the Year 1808*, 2 volumes (Charleston, 1809), II, 435.

[16] Fletcher Melvin Green, *Constitutional Development in the South Atlantic States, 1776-1860: A Study in the Evolution of Democracy* (Chapel Hill, 1930), pp. 105-124.

sonian movement. Clearly the roots of Jeffersonian democracy in South Carolina were deeply embedded in the local culture.[17]

In spite of the fact that the state's constitutional structure was at least potentially aristocratic and undemocratic, a majority of South Carolina's first congressional delegation were supporters of what later became known as the Jeffersonian or Republican policies.[18] Their chief departure was their support of the assumption of state debts, an action which they justified on the ground that South Carolina would not have given up the right to levy impost duties if it had not been understood that the state debt would be assumed.[19] William Loughton Smith, soon to become one of the principal Federalist leaders, was the only South Carolina representative who voted to establish the first Bank of the United States.[20] In the first Congress South Carolina began its long struggle against high tariffs. Arguing that high duties hurt the importing South especially, most of the representatives would support only moderate protection and then only to those industries which actually needed aid.[21] Most of the people in the up country and many in the low country agreed with Burke that the excise tax was "universally odious."[22] Apparently considering secret meetings undemocratic and dangerous the South Carolina legislature called upon the United States Senate to open its sessions to the public.[23]

In the election of 1792 the Republican Thomas Sumter was defeated but the election of Lemuel Benton, also a Republican, by the newly formed Pedee District prevented a Federalist majority in the state's congressional delegation. In the presidential contest George Washington received eight electoral votes, John Adams seven, and Aaron Burr one.[24] Of course party lines were still rather loosely drawn but forces and influences both within and outside of the United States were fast tightening them.

As in the rest of the nation, South Carolina Republicans and Federalists divided on the question of approving or disapproving the French Revolution. At first, however, both local groups were inclined to be sym-

[17] A comprehensive treatment of sectionalism and representation is given in William A. Schaper, "Sectionalism and Representation in South Carolina," *American Historical Association Annual Report 1900*, I (Washington, 1901), 237-463. An authoritative brief summary of early South Carolina constitutional history is David Duncan Wallace, "The South Carolina Constitution of 1895," *Bulletin of the University of South Carolina no. 197* (Columbia, 1927). The latter includes a copy of the constitution of 1790.

[18] Senator Pierce Butler and Representatives Aedanus Burke, Thomas Tudor Tucker, and Thomas Sumter joined the Jeffersonian group. One senator and two representatives supported the Hamilton program.

[19] *Annals of Congress*, 1st Congress, 2nd Session, p. 1332. Burke, Smith, and Tucker held state securities. Charles Austin Beard, *Economic Origins of Jeffersonian Democracy* (New York, 1915), p. 192.

[20] *Annals of Congress*, 1st Congress., 3rd Session, p. 1960.

[21] *Ibid.*, 1st Congress, 1st Session, pp. 112-114, 152-155, 161-167, 206, 303-305, 337-339, 349-351.

[22] *Annals of Congress*, 1st Congress, 3rd Session, pp. 1874, 1880, 1884; Charleston *City Gazette*, August 5, 1791. Only Smith voted for its passage.

[23] South Carolina Senate Journal, December 21, 1792 (manuscript).

[24] *City Gazette*, December 14, 1792.

pathetic. The news of the fall of the Bastille called forth a public celebration in Charleston.[25] While traveling in France and Great Britain during the early stages of the Revolution, John Rutledge, Jr., later one of the most ardent Federalists, praised the French and condemned the British.[26] The newspapers were flooded with pro-French letters.[27] In 1792 a French Patriotic Society, affiliated with the Friends of Liberty and Equality of Bordeaux was formed.[28] The establishment of a French republic and news of military victories occasioned many public gatherings.[29] Under such propitious circumstances Citizen Genêt, minister plenipotentiary of France to the United States, arrived in Charleston.[30] Enthusiastically received by the public and believing that he had the approval of Governor Moultrie, Genêt began arrangements for an attack upon the Spanish possessions. His journey through other South Carolina towns was a triumphal procession.[31] These activities were repudiated and condemned by both Washington and Moultrie, but the fact that an attack on East Florida was barely averted and that the movement continued for nearly a year is proof that many who did not openly support it were at least silent observers.

During 1793 another important development in party politics occurred in South Carolina—the beginning of the activities of the Republican and the Democrat societies.[32] The year 1794 was described by a contemporary as a time

> When Sansculottes and their principles had great ascendancy in Charleston—when the tri-colored cockade of France was the great badge of honour, and Ca' ira and the Marseillaise hymn the most popular airs—and "Vive la republique Francaise!" the universal shout.[33]

During this period Jefferson's association with the Washington administration had made it nearly impossible for him to promote actively the work of the Republican party. In fact James Madison was mentioned more frequently at the meetings of the above-named societies than was Jefferson. Learning from Ralph Izard that "a society under the democratic garb has arisen in South Carolina with the name Madisonian," Secretary

---

[25] John Belton O'Neall, *Biographical Sketches of the Bench and Bar of South Carolina*, 2 volumes (Charleston, 1859), I, 83.
[26] Jefferson Papers, Library of Congress, April 3, 1789. March 25, 1790.
[27] Typical examples are found in Charleston *City Gazette*, November 17 and 22, 1792.
[28] *South Carolina Historical and Genealogical Magazine*, XXXII (1931), 80; *City Gazette*, December 5, 1792.
[29] Charleston *City Gazette*, January 4, 7, 10, 15, 17, 1793.
[30] *Ibid.*, April 9, 1793.
[31] The *City Gazette* throughout April and the first part of May, 1793, carried many items concerning Genêt. Frederick Jackson Turner, ed., "The Mangourit Correspondence in Respect to Genêt's Projected Attack upon the Floridas," *Annual Report of the American Historical Association, 1897* (Washington, 1898), pp. 569-579. For the attitude of Governor Moultrie see David Duncan Wallace, *History of South Carolina*, 4 volumes (New York, 1934), II, 352; and Charles Marion Thomas, *American Neutrality in 1793* (New York, 1931), p. 120.
[32] *City Gazette*, September 7, November 6, 1793.
[33] Charles Fraser, *Reminiscences*, pp. 35-36.

8   THE JAMES SPRUNT STUDIES

of State Edmund Randolph reported the occurrence to President Washington in October, 1794. By this time the formation of such organizations had disturbed both Washington and Randolph.[34] In a message to Congress shortly afterward Washington made what Madison called "Perhaps the greatest error" of his political career when he denounced the "self-created" societies. Jefferson considered them no more deserving of presidential attack than the Society of Cincinnati.[35]

Even greater popular agitation developed when the news of the Jay Treaty reached South Carolina. The sending of John Jay to England, where Thomas Pinckney, one of the state's native sons, was already the American minister had been resented. This, together with the nature of the treaty, aroused almost universal opposition. It was felt that the South's interests had been disregarded by Jay.[36] Senator Pierce Butler was commended for voting against ratification while the Federalist supporter, Senator Jacob Read, was hung in effigy. On one occasion William Loughton Smith, John Adams, Timothy Pickering, Jacob Read, and "His Satanic Majesty," all supposedly connected with the Jay Treaty were hung in effigy "the whole day, polluted by every indignity, and, in the evening, were carried off to the Federal green, where they were burnt."[37] The opposition, however, was not confined to the Republicans. John Rutledge's very severe denunciation of the treaty was largely responsible for the refusal of the Senate to confirm him as Chief Justice of the Supreme Court of the United States.[38] A very different response greeted the more satisfactory treaty which Thomas Pinckney in the meantime negotiated with Spain. There were, however, surprisingly few letters published in the South Carolina newspapers concerning it.[39]

Although political lines had not become rigid by 1796, the elections of that year were much better measurements of party strength than any previously held. Hoping to gain votes especially in South Carolina and the

[34] Worthington Chauncey Ford, ed., *The Writings of George Washington*, 14 volumes (New York, 1889-1893), XII, 474-476.
[35] *Ibid.*, XII, 476, note.
[36] Charleston *City Gazette*, May 15, June 14, October 6, 15, 20, 26, 27, 28, December 22, 1795.
[37] Charles Fraser, *Reminiscences*, p. 45.
[38] Letter of Oliver Wolcott to Hamilton, George Gibbs, ed., *Memoirs of the Administration of Washington and Adams*, 2 volumes (New York, 1846), I, 220. In a letter to Rufus King, Hamilton sought to lay the basis for rejection on other rumors which had come to him concerning Rutledge's alleged mental condition and personal conduct, John C. Hamilton ed., *The Works of Alexander Hamilton*, 7 volumes (New York, 1851), VI, 76-77. Jefferson thought that the Senate "cannot pretend any objection to him but his disapprobation of the treaty. It is of course a declaration that they will receive none but tories hereafter into any department of the government." P. L. Ford, *Writings of Jefferson*, VII, 44.
[39] The importance of the treaty is well summarized in Arthur Preston Whitaker, *The Spanish-American Frontier: 1783-1795* (New York, 1927), p. 222; and in Samuel Flagg Bemis, *Pinckney's Treaty, A Study of America's Advantage from Europe's Distress 1783-1800* (Baltimore, 1926). An example of the newspaper comments is the letter of "An American," who thought that Pinckney would have negotiated a better treaty with England than did Jay. Charleston *City Gazette*, April 2, 1796.

South because of the supposed popularity of Thomas Pinckney and his treaty, the Federalists linked his name with that of John Adams in the presidential and vice-presidential contest. There were two electoral tickets supported in the South Carolina legislature—one for Jefferson and Pinckney and one for Adams and Pinckney. The overwhelming choice of the "Jefferson ticket" showed an obvious victory for the Republicans.[40] Charles Pinckney, who had become a Republican leader, was elected for the third time governor of South Carolina.[41] In the congressional elections the voters chose two Republicans, two Federalists, and two who had not committed themselves but who had definite leanings toward the former. Before long, however, each party had secured one of the last group.[42] In the Senate both parties continued to have one each. Thus in this initial nation-wide test of the two political parties, South Carolina had chosen Jefferson electors, a Republican governor, and a congressional delegation evenly divided. Clearly the party of Jefferson was rapidly gaining control of the state.

The excesses of the French Revolution, especially those connected with the "X. Y. Z." affair, caused a set-back for the Republican friends of France between 1796 and 1799. Since the American minister, Charles Cotesworth Pinckney was a very much respected South Carolinian, the people of the state resented his treatment abroad. William Loughton Smith and Robert Goodloe Harper, who had become the two foremost Federalist leaders in the House, were joined by their colleague, John Rutledge, Jr., in the most severe condemnation of the indignity to Pinckney.[43] Even Jefferson wrote Thomas Pinckney, brother of the American minister to France, praising the latter's conduct.[44] In the contemporary issues of the Charleston *City Gazette* and the *South Carolina State Gazette* the friends of France and England carried on a heated controversy. Thomas Sumter made one of his few recorded congressional speeches attacking a preparedness measure which he thought would grant powers to the President unwarranted by the circumstances.[45]

In the meantime members of both parties in South Carolina loyally

[40] South Carolina House Journal, December 6, 1796 (manuscript).
[41] *Ibid.*, December 8, 1796.
[42] No doubt the voters considered the uncommitted representatives Republicans. At any rate, John Rutledge, Jr., who soon became a Federalist, was Republican enough in 1796 to act as a Jefferson elector. South Carolina House Journal, December 6, 1796 (manuscript). William Smith (not William Loughton Smith, who was a Federalist member of the same congressional delegation) kept his Republicanism in spite of the efforts of the Federalists. Ulrich Bonnell Phillips, ed., "South Carolina Federalist Correspondence, 1789-1797," *American Historical Review*, XIV (1909), 787.
[43] In the *Annals of Congress* for the 5th Congress, there are many statements by these three South Carolina representatives.
[44] Jefferson Papers, May 19, 1797 (Library of Congress).
[45] *Annals of Congress*, 5th Cong., 2nd Sess., pp. 1665-1671. In this speech Sumter took sharp issue with Harper, at times showing rather thinly veiled contempt for his colleague.

supported preparedness.[46] The Federalists became confident, even defiant, and formed a military organization known as "the Federalist Club."[47] At one of its meetings, Miss Mary Legare, presenting the club with a standard, spoke of an inevitable war between the United States and France; she denounced France as "a nation of atheists."[48] The high point of co-operation among South Carolinians of both parties was the financing and the building of the sloop-of-war *John Adams,* constructed in the Cooper River shipyard, named after the President and launched on June 5, 1799.[49]

Although the Republican support of preparedness prevented the Federalists from profiting from the "X. Y. Z." affair as much as they had hoped, they did make political gains in the election of 1798. Thomas Sumter was the only Republican representative sent by South Carolina to the next Congress. This was partly offset, however, by the choice of a Republican majority in the state legislature and the election of Charles Pinckney, Jefferson's chief local supporter, to the United States Senate.[50] For governor, the legislature chose Edward Rutledge, who had been a Jefferson elector in 1796 and remained one of his closest friends.[51] Thus it was only in the congressional delegation that the Federalists made notable gains. Soon the Alien and Sedition Acts, the Jonathan Robbins case, and other incidents caused a reaction in favor of the Republicans. The earlier appointment of William Loughton Smith as minister to Portugal and the removal of Harper to Maryland in 1799 meant that the Federalists would be without their most aggressive leaders in the election of 1800.

For the campaign of 1800 the Federalists, as in 1796, chose a South Carolinian as the running mate for John Adams. This time it was Charles Cotesworth Pinckney, the chief American participant in the "X. Y. Z." affair. The break between Adams and Hamilton and the pamphlet of the latter stating a preference for the election of Pinckney as President, greatly weakened the party's chance for success.[52] In contrast, the Republicans presented a united front both as to the candidates and their relative positions on the ticket. As the campaign unfolded it became as much a contest of personalities as of issues. Unsavory rumors were circulated about Jefferson and his supporters. Newspaper correspondents made insinuating

[46] *City Gazette,* May 3-7, 22, 28, 30, June 9, 12, 21, 1798.
[47] *Ibid.,* July 9, 10, 1798.
[48] *Ibid.,* January 5, 1799.
[49] *Ibid.,* August 4, 11, 14, 1798; April 29, June 4, 6, November 15, 1799; *South Carolina State Gazette,* July 17, 1799; *Charleston Year Book, 1883* (Charleston, 1884), pp. 510-511.
[50] South Carolina Senate Journal, December 6, 1798 (manuscript). The election of Pinckney marked the suspension of the practice of choosing one senator from the up country and one from the low country. Because of this Pinckney promised to "look out for the Republican interests" of the up country. Pinckney to Jefferson, *American Historical Review,* IV (1898), 121.
[51] South Carolina House Journal, December 6, 1798 (manuscript).
[52] A copy of Hamilton's pamphlet is in Henry Cabot Lodge, ed., *The Works of Alexander Hamilton,* 9 volumes (New York, n.d.), VII, 309-356.

remarks about the public and private life of Charles Pinckney.[53] The hostility between Adams and Hamilton further divided the Federalists as the election approached. At one time Charles Cotesworth Pinckney was almost ready to recommend that Adams be replaced by another candidate.[54] Almost every device known to newspaper correspondents and pamphleteers was used by both sides. They defined their own principles favorably and cleverly attacked those of their opponents. They published many imaginary dialogues with this in mind. Especially did they seek to label their adversaries with catchy, disparaging phrases. Hardly a single issue of the Federalist *South Carolina State Gazette* or the Republican *City Gazette* appeared without several examples of such political tactics.

In no previous election had voters been confronted with such a flood of campaign literature. Not confining his activities to his own state, Charles Pinckney, wrote Jefferson, "We have Literally sprinkled Georgia and North Carolina from the mountains to the Ocean."[55] Perhaps the two ablest pamphlets were the one signed "A Federal Republican," a presentation of the Federalist cause by Henry William DeSaussure, and the one bearing the signature, "A Republican," a statement of the Republican views by Charles Pinckney. According to DeSaussure, the Federalists had saved the country during the trying times which followed the Revolution. Washington and Adams had kept the United States from going to war with either Great Britain or France and had repelled aggressions by both. American commerce had grown and agriculture had been encouraged. Furthermore, he argued, the Federalists had prevented the supporters of Jefferson from carrying the country into war on the side of France and thereby interrupting prosperity, decreasing revenues, and necessitating higher taxes. DeSaussure compared Jefferson and Adams to the advantage of the latter. Jefferson had only "shewy talents" and "theoretic learning," had been an inefficient governor of Virginia, an enemy of the constitution, had cast insinuations against Washington, was an opponent of slavery, and an open friend of France. On the other hand, DeSaussure considered Adams a tested public servant worthy of South Carolina's support. In an election as close as the one about to take place, the vote of one state might be decisive. In arguing for the election of Jefferson and Burr, Charles Pinckney attacked the commercial interests and appealed for the support of the agricultural group. In spite of all the taxes, Pinck-

[53] An especially bitter letter was printed in the *South Carolina State Gazette*, April 18, 1800. These rumors, accepted by Professor U. B. Phillips, are discounted by Dr. D. D. Wallace. Especially does the latter refute the charge concerning financial dishonesty as never having been supported "by a word of proof." *History of South Carolina*, III, 358, note. Charles Pinckney had his contemporary defenders also. The above-mentioned letter had been a reply to a very laudatory article in the *Aurora*, March 27, 1800, which had been reprinted in local papers.

[54] Letter to James McHenry, quoted in Charles A. Beard, *Economic Origins of Jeffersonian Democracy*, pp. 57-58.

[55] Several letters concerning the election of 1800 in South Carolina are printed in *American Historical Review*, IV (1898), 111-129. The letter quoted is on pages 113-114.

ney said, the Federalists had increased the public debt greatly. The direct taxes had injured the planter especially, but the business group had largely escaped. Jefferson, a planter, had to pay heavy direct taxes; but Adams, who probably owned a good deal of stock, did not. Furthermore, Jefferson did not favor the abolition of slavery in the southern states as the Federalists charged. Clearly Pinckney was stating pointedly that the agricultural South should vote for Jefferson because he was a friend of agriculture, and against Adams because he was the candidate of the "monied interest, which is by far the largest in the Northern States and the greatest favorite of the federal party." With the record open before them they could not vote for Adams and Charles Cotesworth Pinckney unless they were "content to be more oppressed and degraded and to bear heavier and more unequal burdens" than he thought they were.[56]

It was commonly believed by both parties that the outcome in South Carolina would determine the national results, so nearly balanced were the Federalists and Republicans elsewhere. With this in mind the Federalists hoped that the state's electoral votes would go to one of their candidates if not to both. Since the narrow coast section chose such a large proportion of the members of the legislature, the Republicans knew that it would require all their energies to elect enough members to insure the choice of their electoral ticket. Against them were the commercial interests, the friends of the Bank of the United States, the unpopularity of France, and the popularity of Charles Cotesworth Pinckney. In addition to Pinckney's candidacy for the vice-presidency—or according to some the presidency—the Federalists added to the strength of their local ticket by running him for the state senate also. So bitter did the campaign become that the two branches of the Pinckney family attacked each other and would not speak when they occasionally met. On election day, according to Charles Pinckney, several hundred Federalists voted who had not paid taxes. The "lame, crippled, diseased and blind were led, lifted or brought in carriages to the Poll." In order for the "Bank & federal officers & English merchants" to be sure that those under their influence voted as directed "the novel and unwarranted measure was used of voting with tickets printed on *Green & blue & red & yellow paper* & men stationed to watch the voters."[57]

It was soon discovered that two Federalist representatives in Congress would be replaced by Republicans, thereby evenly dividing the South Carolina members of the next House. And the defeat of Jacob Read, a little later, meant that both senators would be Republicans. However, the contest which attracted most attention was the choosing of the presidential electors. In order to use his influence with members of the legislature,

[56] A copy of DeSaussure's pamphlet is in the Charleston Library Society's pamphlets, series 5, vol. I, no. 6. Charles Pinckney's pamphlet appeared in the Charleston *City Gazette* and separately; parts of it are quoted in Charles A. Beard, *Economic Origins of Jeffersonian Democracy*, pp. 373-375.
[57] Charles Pinckney to Jefferson, *American Historical Review*, IV (1898), 114-116.

Charles Pinckney delayed returning to the United States Senate. After several days of vigorous political activity the Republicans won by an average majority of about nineteen.[58]

The election of Jefferson was celebrated throughout the state. At a meeting held in Charleston for that purpose, the following toast was offered: "The State of South Carolina, whose voice secured to the United States their present Chief Magistrate:—his voice should not have been a blank at the city of Washington."[59] In recognition of his leadership during the campaign, Jefferson consulted Charles Pinckney on patronage and appointed him minister to Spain.[60]

Since South Carolina had elected Republicans to high local and federal positions for several years and since no radical changes now occurred, the so-called "Revolution of 1800" was more noticeable in the nation at large than in South Carolina. Christopher Gadsden, the "conservative radical" of the Revolutionary period, thought that social and political changes already had gone too far. Newcomers had been "cajoled and imposed upon by emissaries from without, and egged on by a numerous or rather innumerable tribe of young law-followers amongst ourselves." In a letter of consolation to John Adams, Gadsden expressed disappointment and pessimism.

> Long have I been led to think our planet a mere bedlam, and the uncommonly extravagant ravings of our times, especially for a few years past, and still in the highest rant, have greatly increased and confirmed that opinion. Look around our whirling globe, my friend, where you will, east, west, north or south, where is the spot in which there are not many thousands of these lunatics.

Thus did one of the "old order" view the beginnings of Jeffersonian democracy on a national scale. But even he hoped that the new President would receive "the constitutional assistance and countenance of every citizen of the Union; and that his public actions may be judged with candor and generosity without any captious hole picking." Most of all he hoped for the restoration of harmony.[61]

Throughout the remainder of the Jefferson era South Carolina remained

---

[58] The election of 1800 has been one of the most controversial in South Carolina history. A tradition persists till today that the Republicans were so desperate that they offered to sacrifice Burr and form a ticket of Jefferson and Pinckney, a proposal rejected by the latter. The evidence does not justify this tradition. It was challenged soon after the election and several times since, but the Federalists never presented concrete proof of such an offer. This tradition and the available evidence are discussed at length and analyzed in James Harold Wolfe, *Jeffersonian Democracy in South Carolina* (Chapel Hill, 1940), pp. 157-161.

[59] *City Gazette*, March 14, 1801. On December 5, 1800, Jefferson wrote Thomas Mann Randolph that the results in other states being as they appeared to be, South Carolina would determine whether he or Adams would be President. *Writings of Jefferson*, Definitive Edition, XVIII, 226-227.

[60] Pinckney to Jefferson, January 24, February 9, March 17, 1800; Jefferson to Pinckney, March 6, 1800, Jefferson Papers (Library of Congress).

[61] Charles Francis Adams, ed., *The Works of John Adams*, 10 volumes (New York, 1865), IX, 578-580.

predominantly Republican at least politically and the more populous section of the state was Republican socially. No more Federalist governors or United States senators were chosen, thus indicating a consistently Republican majority in the legislature. With the retirement of John Rutledge, Jr., in 1803, South Carolina ceased to have aggressive Federalist leaders in national politics.[62] In the congressional elections of 1802, Republicans won in six of the state's eight districts. In spite of reverses the Federalists remained active, and the establishment of the Charleston *Courier,* a very vigorous Federalist newspaper, in 1803, frightened the Republicans for a time.[63] By 1804 partisanship had subsided sufficiently for the local Society of the Cincinnati, once extremely anti-Jefferson, to toast the President and declare—"Party Spirit: may it be kept within due bounds—we are all Republicans—all Federalists."[64] In the elections of 1804 the Republicans won in the hitherto Federalist districts. Thus, except for a few seats in the legislature and other local positions in certain areas, the Federalists were completely without offices in South Carolina.

During the second half of the first decade of the nineteenth century, foreign affairs again became an important issue. South Carolina loyally accepted the Jeffersonian policy of economic coercion as a substitute for war, but even some of the Republicans preferred armed conflict. Charging that the administration unduly favored France and discriminated against Great Britain, the Federalists had a reawakening.[65] But in 1806 and again in 1808, despite hot local campaigns, the Republicans won all major state and federal offices. The election of younger and more vigorous Republicans, including John Caldwell Calhoun, William Lowndes, and Langdon Cheves, to Congress in 1810 indicated that a new phase of Jeffersonian democracy was about to begin.[66] Dissatisfied with the policies of Madison, they had a prominent part in forcing him to agree to war in 1812. As chairmen of important committees they were active in the prosecution of the war. In spite of the many military reverses, they unceasingly preached patriotism and justified the beginning of the conflict. At the close of the war, they claimed a glorious victory, continued to preach patriotism, and actively supported the nationalistic trend of the day. To have continued this nationalistic trend, however, would have necessitated the tearing up and replanting of the roots of Jeffersonian democracy in South Carolina.

[62] Because of private as well as public difficulties, Rutledge had not been a candidate in 1802. A statement of his pessimistic view of the future is in Charleston *Courier,* February 2, 1802.

[63] The first issue appeared on January 10, 1803. Alexander S. Salley, "A Century of the Courier," *Centennial Edition of the News and Courier,* is an excellent brief sketch of this paper and others in South Carolina.

[64] Charleston *Times,* February 24, 1804.

[65] The strongest case for the Federalists was presented by William Loughton Smith in *The Numbers of Phocion, Which Originally Appeared in the Charleston Courier, in 1806 on the Subject of Neutral Rights* (Charleston, 1806).

[66] These three men, soon known as "War Hawks," joined the already aggressive David R. Williams, to make the South Carolina delegation probably the most aggressive in Congress.

This incipient nationalism had been the product of the war and war-time conditions. With the coming of peace, the people of the state soon questioned whether the interests of an area apparently destined to remain agricultural could be served best by encouraging the development of a centralized government in a nation in which they ultimately would be outnumbered in the Senate as they already were in the House of Representatives. High tariffs and other measures or policies might discriminate against agriculture and the South's "peculiar institution." An emphatic answer was soon given against nationalism, although a few leaders seemed a little slow in discovering it. South Carolina remained Republican or Democratic, as the party later came to be known, in so far as political names were concerned. The Federalist party also continued to live for many years but its members soon realized that they had little in common with the Federalists in other parts of the country.

Thus South Carolina had become an early and, at least in form, an almost unqualified convert to Jeffersonian democracy. During most of the period Republicans made up a majority of the congressional delegation and after 1800 few Federalists were chosen to either house of the federal Congress. In local politics the dominance of the Republicans was decisive but not as complete. In other matters dear to the heart of Jefferson progress was also made. In 1801 the legislature voted to set up in Columbia, the South Carolina College, an institution which later became the University of South Carolina. Several governors recommended public school systems, and in 1811 the legislature established what has been referred to by some as "the free school system." The education act of 1811 accorded with Jeffersonian principles in theory but in practice it fell far short.[67]

By way of a general summary of subsequent developments it can be said, in conclusion, that while the Republican party was evolving into the Democratic party of a later day, less immediate evolution took place in South Carolina than in the nation at large, for her particular economic system had already developed over most of her area and was fast becoming solidified. After the state had gone far toward the erection of what might have served as the political, social and educational framework of a democratic structure, economic forces delayed the work of the builders. In truth, South Carolina was inclined to return to the form, if not the spirit, of early Jeffersonian Republicanism which for the time was more to her liking than the new democratic impulses. The democratic structure in South Carolina has never been completed. But no higher testimonial to the lasting influence of Jeffersonian ideals upon the people of the state can be written than the simple statement that men still struggle for their fulfillment.[68]

[67] David Duncan Wallace in his *History of South Carolina*, III, 29, has aptly written: "This miserable makeshift, sometimes even officially called 'pauper schools,' pleased neither the rich nor the poor, the one refusing to associate with 'paupers' and the latter largely scorning to class their children as such."

[68] The last paragraph is a paraphrase of the closing words of John Harold Wolfe, *Jeffersonian Democracy in South Carolina* (Chapel Hill, 1940) p. 286.

II

LEWIS THOMPSON, A CAROLINIAN AND HIS LOUISIANA PLANTATION, 1848-1888: A STUDY IN ABSENTEE OWNERSHIP

Joseph Carlyle Sitterson

North Carolina never possessed a planting aristocracy as opulent as that of the Lower South. Yet in the rich lands of the coastal plain which stretched from Warren and Northampton counties on the north to Brunswick and New Hanover on the south there had developed by the early nineteenth century a planter society of considerable economic and political significance. A typical representative of this society was the Thompson family of Bertie County. Lewis Thompson, only a few years out of the University of North Carolina, in the early 1830's joined his fortunes to those of another Bertie family of wealth and influence by his marriage to Margaret Ann Cathcart Clark, a daughter of William M. Clark.[1] Some indication of Thompson's wealth is given by the fact that at the division of his father's estate in 1830 his share of the slaves numbered thirty-eight with a value of $8,000. On the eve of the Civil War, he is reputed to have owned close to a thousand Negroes.

As early as the 1830's wealthy planters of the Upper South, seeking opportunities for the investment of capital and a profitable employment for surplus slaves, had directed their energies to the cotton and sugar region of the Southwest. At some date prior to 1836, William M. Clark acquired from W. H. Cureton a plantation located on Bayou Boeuf in the parish of Rapides, Louisiana. In order to expand his planting operations, he purchased in 1836 from Dr. Benjamin Ballard of Louisiana a plantation located only two miles from his earlier purchase. This latter holding, bounded above by the land of William C. C. Martin and below by that of George Matthews, possessed a frontage of over 400 feet on each side of Bayou Boeuf and contained approximately 3,200 acres. At the date of purchase, the plantation was equipped with thirty-three slaves, seventeen horses, seven yoke of oxen, twenty head of cattle, and all necessary plantation implements. The purchase price was $84,000, $4,000 to be paid in cash in 1838 and the remaining $80,000 in annual installments of $10,000 plus

---

[1] The information in this article is based primarily upon the Lewis Thompson Papers in the Southern Historical Collection at the University of North Carolina Library. They cover the years 1835-1894 and deal mainly with the business interests of the Thompson family.

Mr. R. A. Urquhart of Woodville, North Carolina, a descendant of Lewis Thompson, was kind enough to furnish the writer with information about the Thompson family. The writer is indebted to Mr. H. H. Hardy of Lecompte, Louisiana, for searching in the parish records for the transfer of the Thompson plantation to William Thompson and from the latter to the Carnals.

ten per cent interest. As security for payment Clark mortgaged the property and fifty-two Negroes to Ballard. The sale had hardly been executed before William Clark died in December, 1836, leaving his son-in-law, Lewis Thompson, as executor of his large estate.

At that time the chief crop of the Clark plantations in Rapides was cotton. In the early 1840's, however, the cotton planters in the Red River region experienced several disastrous years and were "brought to the greatest depth of depression by the repeated ravages of the worm and low prices for cotton." As early as 1846 several planters in Rapides had resorted to planting sugar cane in an attempt to find some profitable substitute for cotton. Hitherto the Red River region had been considered too far north for the profitable cultivation of cane. The experiment proved to be "eminently successful" and within the following two years Thompson was growing cane on the Clark plantations.

In January, 1849, Thompson purchased from his brother-in-law, William N. Clark, his share of the Louisiana plantations for $10,000 and the assumption of William's part of the debt on the plantations. Clark's share amounted to forty-three Negroes valued at $22,080. Thompson's wife received thirty-six slaves valued at $16,200 as her share of the estate. In January, 1851, Thompson purchased from the other heirs the remainder of the two plantations without the slaves for $35,500. Payment was made out of money he had advanced to the estate since 1836. A net debt of $7,739.48 remained due Thompson by the Clark estate. The value of the plantations that Thompson had acquired is indicated by the following inventory made in May, 1850:

LOWER PLANTATION

1,980 acres of land, 800 cleared estimated at $30 per acre and the remainder at $4	$ 28,720
152 Negroes of all ages	74,345
43 head of horses, mules, etc.	4,855
	$107,920

UPPER PLANTATION

3,200 acres, 900 in cultivation	$ 42,510
213 Negroes	97,030
Livestock and equipment	4,821
	$144,361
Total value	$252,281

Thompson's large holdings in North Carolina made it impossible for him to assume personal supervision of his Bayou Boeuf property. Consequently, he left general control of the plantation (Thompson considered the upper and lower plantations together) in the hands of his brother-in-law, Kenneth Clark, who owned a cotton plantation only a few miles away. From 1851 until 1857, when plantation affairs required it, Clark assisted the overseer and kept Thompson apprised of conditions there.

From 1854 to 1857, Lewis Thompson's son, Thomas, aided Clark in the general direction of the plantation. In 1857 another son, William, went to Louisiana to assume direction of his father's interests, remaining there until 1888. The New Orleans factorage firm of Bogart, Foley, and Avery purchased supplies for the plantation and marketed its produce. Thompson paid his factor eight per cent interest for credit extended him from time to time and received the same rate of interest on cash balances kept with the firm.

An able overseer was often the difference between profits and losses to the ante-bellum planter. In the case of an absentee holding a reliable manager was doubly important. Although Kenneth Clark's assistance was invaluable to Thompson, Clark's own plantation required most of his time and attention. Nor did Thompson's extensive interests in North Carolina allow him the time for many trips to Louisiana. From 1851 to 1854 he was fortunate in having an excellent overseer, Garver by name, to whom he paid $1,000 a year. At the end of Garver's first year of management, Kenneth Clark wrote Thompson of him, "he is a safe and industrious man, has good judgment and does not abuse the negroes. There has not been one to me with any complaint against him, and I find him constantly at his post." In 1854, however, when Thompson refused to pay him extra money for taking off part of the sugar, Garver left. Thompson's inability to find a satisfactory overseer during the next few years seemed to substantiate the claim that "men of the right stamp to manage negroes are like angels visits few and far between." Finally, early in 1857 Moore Rawls, one of Thompson's Bertie County employees in whom he had considerable confidence, was sent to Louisiana as overseer. Rawls remained there until the end of 1861 and proved himself to be an able and reliable manager.

During the grinding season in the fall of the year, the sugar planter hired a sugar maker or sugar boiler to "take off the crop" and make the sugar and an engineer to care for the sugar machinery. In the case of both of these jobs, unsatisfactory men on the Thompson plantation necessitated frequent changes. In 1851, for example, the engineer was discharged for inefficiency and a new one hired while the grinding was in progress. In 1857 Thompson's New Orleans factor hired for $500 a sugar maker who claimed twenty years' experience. The choice proved to be a bad one. On December 6, Clark wrote Thompson that a large portion of the crop had been "needlessly sacrificed" as a result of the failure of the sugar maker to have the cane windrowed[2] to save it from the cold. In 1858, R. Bachemin was hired to take off the crop and apparently was satisfactory, since he was retained the following year. At the end of the 1859 season, a financial disagreement resulted in Bachemin's departure. He claimed that Thompson owed him $150 in addition to the $375 which had been paid him. Failing to get satisfaction from William, he wrote to

[2] The practice of laying cane stalks between the rows in such manner that the leaves of each stalk cover the preceding one thereby protecting it from frost.

Lewis Thompson in North Carolina, January 19, 1860: "If you don't forward me the balance of my claim I shall attach your sugar, and if I cannot recover by the court, I shall have your name publish[ed] in all the paper[s]. I promise on my children['s] head[s] to do it. Because Sir I cannot be cheated by such a Richman as you are." It would be interesting to know whether or not the threat brought forth the money.

When Thompson purchased the Clark plantations in 1859 he did not buy the slaves. Nor did his wife's share of the Negroes provide a labor force sufficiently large to work the plantation. Consequently, he hired from the Clark heirs sixty Negroes (thirty-three of whom were under ten years of age). The rate of hire was $125 per year each for men and $100 each for women, with a deduction of $25 for each child under ten years of age. In 1851 Thompson paid $2,237.50 for the use of the above hands. The same year he paid Hariet Smallwood $1,000 for the use of thirty Negroes (seventeen of whom were children). During the fifties, the labor force was increased by purchases and by the addition of slaves from Thompson's North Carolina holdings. In January, 1860, there were 194 slaves on the Louisiana plantation.

Thompson considered adequate care for his Negroes sound business policy. The slave quarters consisted of one room cabins and double cabins of two rooms which housed two families. At the time of purchase there was a shortage of slave quarters. Accordingly, in 1853 twenty double cabins were built. In order to preserve the cabins, they were whitewashed from time to time. Clothes were distributed twice each year, in the spring and fall. On many plantations shoes were not provided for summer wear, but it is interesting to note that summer shoes were distributed to the Thompson Negroes. Part of the clothing was purchased in the nearby town of Alexandria, while the remainder was made on the place. In 1852, for instance, a Negro shoemaker was busy making shoes for the plantation and in the fall of 1857 clothes were made at home. Slave rations consisted chiefly of flour, pork, molasses, and vegetables, the latter grown by the Negroes. The slaves were also allowed to cultivate small crops of cane and cotton. Generally, Thompson purchased their cash crops paying for them in money and tobacco. Chewing tobacco was greatly desired by the Negroes who plagued the overseer so much for it that after 1853 it was distributed among them occasionally.

Thomas Thompson, upon his arrival in Louisiana in April, 1854, wrote his father that he thought Louisiana a "better place for negroes than North Carolina," but further acquaintance with the country changed his mind. Indeed, the heat and dampness of the area were not conducive to a healthy slave population. Kenneth Clark, who was a trained physician, attended the sick; in 1857, he received $100 for his services. On Louisiana sugar plantations, fever epidemics were not infrequent and occasionally resulted in many deaths. In the late summer of 1853 fever prevailed in the parish and for four weeks there were on the average forty cases on the plantation, fortunately without a death. In January, 1855, "cholera of the most malignant character" made its appearance in the villages and on some of the plantations nearby, but Clark did "not fear its getting here, or prevailing on any plantations where the negroes are well cared for." Although the overseer did everything he possibly could in the fall of 1857 to prevent fever, an epidemic occurred putting as many as twenty-one Negroes in bed on some days. His description of conditions in the slave quarters is illuminating: "The negroes had around everry house, old troughs and bbls to catch & keep water in[.] I at last dug a well in the quarter and even then they did not want to clean up around their houses. I think there must have been 200 vessels of one kind or other with water in them." In spite of occasional fever epidemics it was the opinion of the physician, William A. Hardy, a former resident of North Carolina, that the diseases incident to the climate were usually not fatal and that "The mortality of Rapides would compare favorably with that of Bertie."

Work on a sugar plantation was heavy and continuous. After the planting of the cane was completed in the spring, considerable time and labor were devoted to deepening and cleaning the drainage ditches. During the cultivating season in early summer a large number of hands were employed in cutting wood to be used as fuel in the sugar furnace. During the grinding season from October to January, when it was necessary to get the cane out of the fields before cold weather, the schedule of work was usually heavier. It is not to be expected, however, that Negro drivers often set a pace that resulted in any serious ill effects from overwork. The overseer's complaint of December, 1857, that he could not get a Negro on the place to work the hands during the rain unless he stood by them, was not an isolated one. That the slaves on the place were generally well cared for is indicated by a letter of Clark to Thompson in December, 1854: "There are men here . . . that do not care for the increase of their slaves and therefore work them accordingly—Yours I am glad to say increase very rapidly and when you come to calculating you will find that your young negroes will be a figure in your favour."

Holidays were infrequent on the Thompson plantation. At the end of the grinding season, usually early in January, a few days' rest and recreation were allowed. Also, throughout the year when there was to be preaching on the place, the Negroes were given Saturday to clean themselves up for Sunday. In June, 1859, William Thompson wrote his father "I hired a Baptist preacher this spring to preach to the negroes. I could not get him to come but once a month. The negroes like him very much. He is an old man very spoken and seems to know how to preach to negroes very well."

No other duty of the ante-bellum overseer required as much judgment and ability as that of slave discipline. To handle the southern Negro slave successfully one had to be possessed of rare combination of tolerant indulgence and unrelenting severity. More important, he had to know when to be lenient, when to be stern. When Moore Rawls (overseer from 1857 to 1861) found it necessary to discipline a slave he usually wrote Thompson about the case. In July, 1857, he wrote "Wright has been pretending to be sick several weeks until 8 days ago I caught him in a dirty trick, & I give him a genteel whiping. I think that done him more good than all medicine could have been given to him." Again, in September he wrote that Old Ben "got so slack" he had to give him "a good whiping." The instances when with patience, perhaps already sorely tried, he overlooked some minor breach of behavior or made the punishment less than his better judgment dictated find no recording in his letters.

From time to time runaways were a source of considerable trouble. In April, 1857, Thad left the plantation and did not return until July. In June, Jacob ran away; in September, both Isaac and Thad left for two weeks. In the spring of 1858, Rawls found it almost impossible to keep the Negroes on the place at night. Finally, he resorted to keeping two hands on watch all night to keep a lookout for fire in the sugar house, to keep the gates shut so that the livestock could not be turned loose, and to keep Negroes and whites from coming on the place without permission. This precaution was necessitated by horse and Negro stealing which he had found fairly common in the region. Rawls found Louisiana Negroes more difficult to control than those he had supervised in North Carolina. Protesting the difficulty of his job, he wrote Thompson, May 6, 1859: "I don't get time scarcely to eat or sleep. I have not been off the plantation since the 3rd of Oct. . . . The truth is no man can begin to attend to such a business with any set of negros without the strictest vigilance on his part." That Rawls was seriously concerned with the problem of slave control is indicated by his comment on the trial of a slave for murder: "Where is it to terminate. We hear of attempts to take the lives of white men every day . . . it is time that owners of slaves should open their eyes to this matter for their lives are not more secure than that of their overseer's. But there are some slave owners who think that a white man's life is worth nothing in comparison with that of a slave because he can be easy transferred to his pocket. . . ."

Thompson's abundance of capital enabled him to keep his Rapides plantation well equipped, and as an experienced planter he realized the importance of keeping it in good order. Accordingly, in the spring of 1857 the sugar house, formerly of wood, was rebuilt with brick to make fire less likely. By that date the former house had been almost ruined by excessive heat. At the same time new kettles for the sugar mill and a crushing mill for corn were purchased. The decade of the fifties also saw the construction of additional Negro cabins, a barn, a stable, a warehouse for storing cane, and a road from the sugar house to the railroad. Thompson was insistant that his overseer keep the fences, ditches, and buildings in good repair.

Sugar plantations in the Red River region were not so highly specialized as those in lower Louisiana. This is to be explained by the uncertainty of cane cultivation that far north. In many instances, both cane and cotton were cultivated as money crops and there were frequent shifts from one crop to the other. The uncertainty of sugar cultivation found frequent expression in Kenneth Clark's letters to Thompson. At the conclusion of a poor crop year in December, 1853 he was "Thoroughly disgusted with everything connected with sugar" and declared that *"this variety of climate* which is death to sugar interests, highly conducive to the propagation of the ravenous caterpillar and favorable to visitations of direful epidemics in my opinion is the last spot than any man should hold land or risk sugar property." In 1854, he complained that unfavorable weather had produced a dryness in the cane that resulted in a small sugar output. In 1856, the plantation experienced its poorest crop. Continuous freezing weather in late January and February killed most of the cane and resulted in the unusually small crop of 122 hogsheads, no more than one-fourth as large as the usual crop.

In addition to the money crops—cotton and sugar—corn, oats, sweet potatoes, peas, pumpkins, and other vegetables were raised in sufficient quantities to supply the plantation needs. For meat, however, the plantation was dependent chiefly upon the outside and annual purchases of one hundred or more barrels of mess pork were customary. It was Clark's opinion that raising hogs in that region was an unprofitable venture. In 1855 he wrote Thompson to that effect. "My opinion is if you can get $50 per hhd. for sugar it is cheaper to buy the pork for it is utterly impossible to raise hogs here without green pastures and plenty of corn and all lands here fit for pasturage will make a hhd. sugar per acre—The great curse of this country is that we are all planters and no farmers to wind up the crops." Such supplies as pork, flour, lime, brick, nails, wagons, hoop poles, and barrels were purchased by Thompson's New Orleans factor who charged the buyer's usual commission of two and one-half per cent. Until 1854 barrels and hogsheads were made by Negro coopers on the plantation. Since, however, there was not a good cooper among the slaves the homemade barrels and hogsheads were not wholly satisfactory. On this subject Thompson's merchants complained repeatedly. In urging Thompson in February, 1854, to send an expert cooper from North Carolina, Clark remarked "It is impossible to get a passable hogshead from those you have and as for making barrels, it is throwing timber and time away." Nevertheless the hogsheads and barrels were still being made on the place in 1857 for in that year hogshead poles and barrel staves were purchased in New Orleans and from the "piney woods people" nearby.

Although Thompson raised cotton for market during a few years—in 1856, seventy bales grown on four hundred acres brought $3,613.53, and in 1857, thirty-three bales brought $1,629.49—sugar, with its by-product molasses, was the principal cash crop. The following table gives the production and gross receipts from the sale of sugar and molasses from 1849 to 1861.

Year	Sugar (hhds. of 1100 lbs.)	Molasses (bbls. of 40 gal.)	Acreage	Average Price	Gross return after deducting marketing costs
1849	261	—	—	—	—
1850	147	—	—	—	—
1851	600	1250	—	S.2½-4⅜¢ M.16-23½	$27,038.00
1852	272	400	—	—	13,428.44
1853	700	1600	520	—	c32,946.00
1854	585	824	—	—	26,581.61
1855	265	428	—	S.6⅝-8⅜ M.33-35	21,388.98
1856	122	182	250	S.8-11 M.57-62	15,768.53
1857	510	1500	—	S.3⅝-7 M-18-35	48,468.61
1858	440	860	—	—	39,165.80
1859	260	519	664	—	27,527.61
1860	265	—	544	—	—
1861	630	—	—	—	—

As can be seen from the above table, Thompson's plantation was not one of the larger sugar producing units in the state. In output, it was a medium-sized plantation. Nor was the yield of sugar per acre—sometimes less than a hogshead and almost never over one and one-half—comparable to that on the more productive plantations farther down the river. Its small yield is to be explained probably by unfavorable weather conditions, particularly cold, in the Red River region. One of the most notable trends in the production record is the variability of the yield, a fact which along with price fluctuations influenced profits considerably.

Throughout the fifties, Thompson's sugar and molasses were shipped by boat from Alexandria on the Red River to New Orleans where they were sold by his factor. Marketing costs were greater for planters in the Red River region because of higher freight charges. In addition to the usual two and one-half per cent commission for selling and the one-half of one per cent for river insurance, freight charges amounted to from $4 to $5 per hogshead on sugar and something over $2 per barrel on molasses. On a sale of twenty-eight barrels of molasses, December 15, 1851, for $236.98, $70.67 or almost thirty per cent went to pay the cost of freight and marketing. In view of this sale, Clark's comment of April 2, 1854, that "it seems to be a poor business to make molasses" is understandable. In the case of sugar where a hogshead sold for so much more than a barrel of molasses, the percentage was not nearly so high. That the sugar planters were not entirely satisfied with the marketing practices and facilities in New Orleans is indicated by Clark's complaint of January 19, 1856: "I have come home thoroughly impressed with the conviction that New Orleans is the meanest commercial port in the world. The day I landed there were 2400 bales of cotton on the levee in a most miserable condition and great quantities of sugar and molasses—parts of the wharf were breaking in from the weight and produce [was] sacrificed to get it out of the way."

Generally, it is exceedingly difficult to arrive at a reliable estimate of the profits or losses of southern plantations. Accurate records of expenditures and overhead costs were seldom kept and only occasionally did a planter record in writing the profitableness of his business. Thompson's plantation was no exception to the above generalization. Fortunately, however, the Thompson papers do contain occasional references to the financial aspects of planting.

Perhaps the most striking feature of this phase of sugar planting was the uncertainty of profits and losses from year to year. For instance, in recording the 1853 crop Thompson wrote that prices were so low that he "became disgusted, and would not keep the account any longer." Kenneth Clark's comment of April 25, 1854, was as follows: "Sugar has proved a loosing [sic] business to all this season and to those in debt perfectly ruinous—I know of several planters who have had to pay as high as forty cents on the barrel to clear the sale of molasses in the city, it [is] useless to send produce to market that does not pay." Clark's frame of mind had so changed the following year that he offered to buy Thompson's plantation for $130,000. Early in 1856 he declared that he would "rather make a sugar crop once in two years, than a crop of cotton every year"; while he admitted that operating expenses and overhead were higher in the case of sugar, so also were the profits when a good crop was made. That he was still of the same opinion a few years later is indicated by his comment of December 29, 1859, "There is no denying the fact that in the race for wealth (in which all here are enlisted) sugar planters are outstriping us who are plodding along with cotton, getting hardly one half for our crop which the same labour applied to sugar would bring." It is interesting to note that a few days later William Thompson wrote his father that he believed it would be better to shift from sugar to cotton because of the cheaper operating costs. Apparently, we have here an example of the not unusual case of each planter thinking the crop that he did not cultivate the more profitable one. That Lewis Thompson himself questioned whether the profits of sugar planting compensated for the disadvantageous features of the culture is indisputable. In December, 1858, while looking for a cotton plantation in Louisiana for his son, Thomas, he remarked: "most of my friends here urge the purchase of a sugar place as being the most *profitable,* but unless as a *dire resort* it does not strike me as being the most agreeable to the owner who wishes to enjoy himself in a more quiet manner, and be more steady and regular in the pursuit of his business— It is trouble enough to have to manage negroes in the simplest way, without having to overlook them in the manufacture of sugar and management of machinery." Moreover, he declared that if he could get a suitable offer he would sell his plantations and slaves and remove himself and his children to "a healthy country outside of all the troubles and cares of a slave population."

Even before the outbreak of war in 1861 the condition of political affairs in the nation had had considerable adverse effect on the Louisiana sugar industry. In New Orleans, as early as November, 1860, northern buyers were driven from the city. In a letter of January 23, 1861, Kenneth Clark wrote that "all commercial interests are entirely destroyed. Cotton and sugar cannot be sold. No discounting by the banks, and merchants of the highest standing are suspending every day." Although affairs were "very quiet & prosperous in Rapides" during the early months of 1861, and planters were "Persuing the calm & even temper of their way very delighted & joyous in the pleasing prospects of an abundant crop," the disruption of trade produced by the war was soon to destroy such tranquility. Those planters without adequate supplies by June found provisions exceedingly expensive and difficult to get as both had "quite run out." A friend wrote Lewis Thompson that "Money is a thing hardly to be had, no one seeming to have it, to know where to get it, or where it has gone to." Although Thompson produced a bumper crop of 630 hogsheads in 1861, in January, 1862, he was finding it difficult to sell sugar even at such low prices as 1½ to 4¾ cents per pound. At this date, the letters relative to Thompson's Rapides Parish plantation cease completely until 1865. But it is not difficult to imagine what happened during the war. Very probably little sugar was raised or marketed. William Thompson, in charge of the plantation, probably had difficulty in raising sufficient food crops to keep himself and the Negroes supplied.

Conditions at the end of the war are best described by a letter of William Thompson to his father, dated June 15, 1865. It reads as follows:

I have never left the place and have endeavored to take care [of] everything as well as I could, but I assure you it was more than I could do to save much and keep the place in very good order.... I tried to save as much of the sugar as I could but have succeeded in keeping only about 40 hhds.... I have about 350 acres of corn and 12 acres of cotton and a small patch of cane in cultivation this year.... There were on the plantation the 10 of June 1865, 175 negroes, 20 pretty good mules 6 good wagons and 2 good carts. I have made no definite bargain with the negroes yet. I hardly know what steps to take for I know the crop will no[t] justify paying wages this year. Still what little we have should be saved.

Writing in the same vein, Clark declared that the war had left the section "ruined almost entirely" with everybody broke and men "bewildered to find out in what way they can make the scattered remnant of a once large fortune the basis of future labor."

Generally, planters met the exigencies of the times in the following ways. Some made no attempt to make a crop the first year after the war, being content to raise enough food for their families. Others risked what little capital they had on equipment to commence operations at once in the hope of soon recovering part of their losses. Still others, either from choice or lack of capital, preferred to rent their land. William Thompson chose to farm his land, but fearing to take too large a risk decided to work only half the place the first year. Although he had some difficulty at first in getting the Negroes to work, he was able to hire a sufficient number to work the place as soon as they found out the land was not to be given to them. In fact, he reported in October, 1866, that the Negroes seemed to be "pretty well satisfied." To what extent the freedmen were satisfied in their new status is a matter of conjecture. They did not, except in rare instances, record their own reactions. As for the attitude of the planters toward the freedmen, the abundance of evidence leaves us no doubts. Few indeed were the southern planters who, amidst the dismal chaos of an overturned world, saw much hope of an early rehabilitation. In June, 1867, William Thompson despairingly wrote that he did not see how anything could be made "with this kind of labor." In October, he observed that the freedmen had "stolen nearly everything that was fit to eat in the county."

In spite of these and other disagreeable aspects of the new labor system, the problems of the new order were not insurmountable however much they seemed so to many a bewildered and disillusioned southern planter in 1865 and the years thereafter. All over the South, there were those who "dug in" and, making the best of a bad situation, began the struggle to rebuild a rural civilization. One of these was William Thompson. As early as 1867 he began expanding operations on the Rapides plantation. Mules, wagons, sugar kettles, and other supplies were purchased and early in 1868 the sugar mill was thoroughly repaired. Payment for the repairs and new equipment was made by drafts on Kader, Biggs & Co., Lewis Thompson's merchant in Norfolk, Virginia.

Lewis Thompson did not live to see the resumption of profitable operations on his Louisiana plantation. In 1870, two years after his death, at the partition of the estate, the Rapides plantation became the property of his son William. The latter paid $35,000 for the lands and $16,116 for the following equipment: 45 head of mules, 9 oxen, 22 hogs, 9 wagons, 4 carts, 40 hames and traces, 35 plows, 30 hoes, 20 axes, 24 cane knives, 4,500 bushels of corn, 8,000 pounds of fodder and hay, cooper and smith tools, shovels, spades, empty hogsheads, and all other personal property. By accepting the Louisiana plantation, William gave up all of his claims to the balance of his father's estate in North Carolina.

William retained possession of the plantation until 1888 when, according to family tradition, he was induced to sell it because his wife refused to move from North Carolina to Louisiana. On September 4, 1888, William sold the plantation to Mrs. L. Carnal and Kenneth Carnal for $20,000, $8,000 in cash and the remainder in four notes of $3,000 each bearing eight per cent interest annually. The plantation, known as "Chicarna Plantation" is still the property of the Carnal family and is still being planted in cane. With the changed conditions in the Louisiana sugar industry, however, have come changed methods of production on the plantations. On Chicarna, as on many other Louisiana plantations, the cane is no longer manufactured into sugar on the plantation, but is trucked to modern mills which utilize the cane from many plantations.

The Thompsons finally returned to North Carolina, but such was not the case with many families that left North Carolina for Louisiana in the ante-bellum period. The names of Norfleet, Carnal, Clark, Smith, Smallwood, Hardy, and Perry, not to mention the descendants of hundreds of North Carolina Negroes, in the vicinity of Lecompte are indicative of the extent and permanency of the North Carolina exodus to Louisiana.

III

CONSERVATIVE CONSTITUTIONAL TENDENCIES OF THE VIRGINIA SECESSION CONVENTION[1]

HENRY THOMAS SHANKS

Virginia, as did the other southern states, largely as a result of western influences within the state, gradually changed the conservative constitution of 1776 into the democratic one of 1850-1851.[2] In 1776 suffrage in the counties was limited to free-holders who owned a hundred acres of uninhabited land or twenty-five acres with a house, and in the towns to the owner of a house and lot. Representation was apportioned in such manner as to give the eastern propertied counties control of the legislature and, through it, the executive offices. The election of local officials was controlled by the wealthy classes and section.[3]

Soon after 1776 the Jeffersonian forces began an attack on the privileged system, but were blocked by Patrick Henry and his conservative colleagues from the Tidewater.[4] By 1829 reformers in the upcountry and the West were threatening revolt if concessions were not granted.[5] The legislature, because of this pressure, called a convention which increased the representation of the Piedmont and Valley. In addition it granted a slight extension of suffrage and established a judiciary which was more amenable to the popular will.[6]

These concessions were granted by the East as a result of the conciliatory attitude of the Revolutionary patriots, Madison, Marshall, and Monroe, much to the disappointment of Benjamin Watkins Leigh and Abel

[1] A fellowship from the General Education Board and a grant-in-aid from the Social Science Research Council for 1935-1936 made possible the research for this essay.

[2] The most satisfactory secondary account and analysis of these constitutional changes is Fletcher Melvin Green, *Constitutional Development in the South Atlantic States, 1776-1860: A Study in the Evaluation of Democracy* (Chapel Hill, 1930). See also Charles Henry Ambler, *Sectionalism in Virginia from 1776 to 1861* (Chicago, 1910); Julian Alvin Carroll Chandler, *The History of Suffrage in Virginia* (Baltimore, 1901); Julian Alvin Carroll Chandler, *Representation in Virginia* (Baltimore, 1896); James Clyde McGregor, *The Disruption of Virginia* (New York, 1922); Jacob Neff Brenaman, *A History of Virginia Conventions with the Constitution of 1867-68* (Richmond, 1902); and David Lloyd Pulliam, *The Constitutional Conventions of Virginia from the Foundation of the Commonwealth to the Present Time* (Richmond, 1901).

[3] F. M. Green, *Constitutional Development in the South Atlantic States*, pp. 87-91; J. A. C. Chandler, *History of Suffrage in Virginia*, pp. 13, 17; J. A. C. Chandler, *Representation in Virginia*, pp. 18-19.

[4] F. M. Green, *Constitutional Development in the South Atlantic States*, p. 140.

[5] C. H. Ambler, *Sectionalism in Virginia*, pp. 137-145; J. C. McGregor, *Disruption of Virginia*, pp. 31-34.

[6] F. M. Green, *Constitutional Development in the South Atlantic States*, pp. 221-223.

Parker Upshur who frankly admitted their opposition to democracy.[7] With others these two Easterners repudiated the theory of natural rights as well as the equalitarian philosophy of the Declaration of Independence itself.[8] To these aggressive leaders who after 1830 assumed control of the planter party, the chief ends of government were the preservation of order and the protection of life and property, with particular emphasis on the latter. They contended that the owners of property, by virtue of their holdings, were personally more concerned with these two goals than the laboring classes and for this reason were more successful in their control of political institutions.[9] Despite these arguments, the western forces in 1850-1851 forced concessions which made Virginia, in the eyes of the planter section, a radical democracy. The new constitution provided for manhood suffrage, popular elections of most state and local officers, and the distribution of seats in the House of Delegates and, to a less degree, in the Senate according to population.[10] Slaves over twelve years of age were assessed for taxes at $300 each.

During the fifties conservatives[11] in Virginia constantly attacked the changes of 1850-1851. Prominent writers and "fire-eaters," including George Fitzhugh, George F. Holmes, Edmund Ruffin, Willoughby Newton, and M. R. H. Garnett attempted to prove that abolitionism, pure democracy, and socialism were all a part of the same movement designed to destroy republican government.[12] Many of them advocated the formation of a southern confederacy as the only means of withstanding these "radical" attacks on the established order.[13] Others who did not openly

[7] C. H. Ambler, *Sectionalism in Virginia*, pp. 150-152; *Proceedings and Debates of the Virginia State Convention of 1829-1830* (Richmond, 1830), pp. 65-79, 151-173; F. M. Green, *Constitutional Development in the South Atlantic States*, pp. 211-212.
[8] Upshur and Leigh's attitude toward the Declaration of Independence was in keeping with the views of many other southern leaders of the ante-bellum period. See William Sumner Jenkins, *Pro-Slavery Thought in the Old South* (Chapel Hill, 1935), pp. 125-127, 303-304; Clement Eaton, *Freedom of Thought in the Old South* (Durham, 1940), pp. 144-145; William Edward Dodd, *The Cotton Kingdom, a Chronicle of the Old South* (New Haven, 1919), pp. 48, 51, 56; Avery Odelle Craven, *Edmund Ruffin, Southerner: A Study in Secession* (New York, 1932), pp. 44, 120-142. The *Daily Richmond Examiner*, July 5, 1861, carried an editorial to the effect that the Declaration of Independence was the "Grecian Horse, introduced into our citadel at the birth of the nation."
[9] F. M. Green, *Constitutional Development in the South Atlantic States*, pp. 213-214; W. S. Jenkins, *Pro-Slavery Thought in the Old South*, pp. 190-199, 303-304.
[10] F. M. Green, *Constitutional Development in the South Atlantic States*, pp. 290-296; J. C. McGregor, *Disruption of Virginia*, pp. 64-65; J. A. C. Chandler, *History of Suffrage in Virginia*, pp. 50-52; J. A. C. Chandler, *Representation in Virginia*, pp. 67-68.
[11] In this essay the term conservative is used to designate those who opposed democratic political institutions, such as popular elections, short terms of office, and universal manhood suffrage.
[12] W. S. Jenkins, *Pro-Slavery Thought in the Old South*, pp. 299-304; Clement Eaton, *Freedom of Thought in the Old South*, p. 328; A. O. Craven, *Edmund Ruffin*, pp. 132-133; Henry Thomas Shanks, *The Secession Movement in Virginia, 1847-1861* (Richmond, 1934), pp. 69-73.
[13] O. A. Craven, *Edmund Ruffin*, chapter VIII; H. T. Shanks, *Secession Movement in Virginia*, p. 72.

advocate the repudiation of Jeffersonian doctrines and who did not subscribe to the secessionists' views bemoaned the evil effects of democracy and especially the alterations made in the fundamental law in the early fifties.[14]

In 1861 after Virginia had joined the Confederate States of America and after many western delegates had withdrawn from the convention, conservative leaders considered the time ripe for making the constitution conform to their political conceptions. Alexander H. H. Stuart, a prominent Whig from the Valley, proposed on May 1 the appointment of a committee to recommend changes in the fundamental law.[15] On December 5, at an adjourned session, the convention approved amendments which were designed to create a government more like that of 1829-1830 than that of 1850-1851. The proposed changes were rejected by the voters in an election which, because of the war crisis on the voting days, carried little significance in measuring the sentiment of the state.[16] Nevertheless the amended constitution was in keeping with the political tenets common to a majority in the convention as well as to leaders in other parts of the South.[17] A study, therefore, of this heretofore neglected constitutional revision should throw additional light on the conservative implications or effects of secession itself.

The delegates of the Virginia secession convention were elected in February, 1861, while the sentiment for the Union was strong. Few "fire-

[14] The debate in the secession convention showed how widespread this criticism of the changes in 1850-1851 was. "Proceedings of the Secession Convention," Richmond *Enquirer,* February-May, November-December, 1861; January-February, 1862. A full report of the debates was published in the *Enquirer* from February, 1861, to February, 1862. Cited hereinafter "Proceedings of Secession Convention," Richmond *Enquirer.*

[15] *The Journal of the Acts and Proceedings of a General Convention in the State of Virginia assembled at Richmond . . . February 13, 1861* (Richmond, 1861), p. 228. Cited hereinafter as *Journal of Secession Convention.*

[16] See below, p. 46.

[17] Leaders in at least two other southern states tried to make similar changes in their constitutions as a result of secession. In the Georgia convention, a committee recommended no changes in suffrage and elections, but proposed the strengthening of the judiciary. It recommended the appointment of judges for the supreme and superior courts by the governor. Their terms were to be regulated by the legislature. A few minor changes in the method of electing the governor and the system of representation were made. The constitution as amended was adopted by a vote of 11,499 to 10,704. *The Confederate Records of the State of Georgia,* 6 volumes (Atlanta, 1909-1911), I, 519-541, 558, 562; II, 50-51.

In North Carolina the movement was prompted by sentiments similar to those in Virginia. Thomas Ruffin of Alamance, as chairman of one of the committees, recommending alterations expressed the feeling that "above all times this is the one . . . to give the people a sound conservative Constitution." Hillsborough *Recorder,* May 6, 1861. In the convention committees were appointed for revising the constitution. Ruffin's judiciary committee recommended property qualifications for justices of the peace of $100 and the election of justices by the county court. In the old constitution the justices were selected by the legislature and there was no property qualification. On May 10 the convention, because of the war crisis, decided by the close vote of 37 to 35 not to pass on the amendments. *North Carolina Weekly Standard,* May 14, 1862; Kemp Plummer Battle, "The Legislation of the Convention of 1861," *James Sprunt Historical Monographs* (Chapel Hill, 1900), pp. 140-141.

eaters" were selected. Less than one fourth of the delegates supported disunion at the time of their election.[18] Of the 152 chosen more than 50 per cent had been Whigs, one fourth had supported Douglas, and the remainder voted for Breckinridge.[19] The delegates, so far as the limited tax returns reveal, included many of considerable property and none without some taxable holdings.[20] After the passage of the ordinance of secession on April 17, many northwestern delegates who opposed disunion withdrew from the convention and their places were filled from the southern party in irregular manner.[21]

Before the passage of the ordinance of secession, northwestern delegates frequently tried to make the constitution more democratic. In these efforts they were thwarted on the grounds that it was an inappropriate time to alter the fundamental law. With secession, however, the convention by a vote of sixty-six to twenty-six agreed to tax slaves under twelve years of age at the same rate as other property. This was designed to placate the Northwest and to keep it loyal to the Richmond government.[22] This amendment, despite the earlier argument against making any changes

[18] H. T. Shanks, *Secessional Movement in Virginia*, pp. 150-157.

[19] An examination of tax records deposited in the State Archives at Richmond reveals the following facts about sixty-five of these delegates for whom reports were available.

(1) Twenty per cent of the Whigs and thirty-five per cent of the Democrats listed in the counties in which they resided fewer than five taxable slaves each. (Slaves under twelve years of age were not listed. I only checked the returns of individuals in the counties in which they resided.) Forty-eight per cent of the Whigs and forty-one per cent of the Democrats listed over twenty taxable slaves each.

(2) Only fourteen of the sixty-five delegates for whom returns are available listed stocks and bonds. Of these eleven were Whigs.

(3) Of the fifty-five who listed their holdings in land, thirty were Whigs and twenty-five were Democrats. Twenty-one Whigs and thirteen Democrats assessed their land at over $5,000 each.

These facts tend to substantiate the accepted thesis that the southern Whigs were the propertied classes. See Arthur Charles Cole, *The Whig Party in the South* (Washington, 1913), pp. 68-69. Nevertheless three of the largest planters of the convention were Democrats.

If the assumption that the Whigs represented property to a greater extent than the Democrats be accepted, it is well to remember that the secession convention, which was predominantly Whig, was more under the influence of property than the normal Virginia convention of that day. A later analysis of the party votes will be given.

[20] Eight of the sixty-five whose tax returns were examined had over thirty slaves each within the counties in which they lived. All except three listed slaves among their possessions for taxation.

[21] Twenty new members were appointed for various causes. Fourteen of these were from the Trans-Allegheny region. Local county officials appointed most of these. Several delegates whose places were not filled rarely attended meetings of the convention after the war began because of the duties assumed in the prosecution of the war or in the Confederate government. Jubal A. Early, R. H. Cox, J. B. Baldwin, John Tyler, W. Richardson, T. F. Goode, A. M. Barbour, John Echols, and Henry A. Wise were almost always absent. J. Q. Marr died during the period of the convention.

[22] *Journal of Secession Convention*, pp. 204-205; H. T. Shanks, *Secession Movement in Virginia*, note 199, p. 272.

during the existing crisis, served as a basis for the acceptance of Stuart's proposals to consider a revision of the whole constitution.

Stuart was made chairman of the committee created for this purpose. Serving with him were three other Whigs and three supporters of Douglas. The Breckinridge Democrats were not represented.[23] Apparently the chief factor determining the selections for the committee was geography rather than party affiliation, since sections instead of parties were more concerned in the revision. All members were owners of considerable property.[24]

The committee made its report on June 19. This was at a time of great confusion in the convention when members were constantly leaving to assume duties in connection with the war and when there was uncertainty about the course which the northwestern delegates would follow. Under these conditions it was so difficult to maintain a quorum that the convention agreed to adjourn until the middle of November when the body reconvened for the specific purpose of revising the constitution. By December 5 the convention had completed its work.

In presenting the report of the committee on June 19, Stuart made a factual explanation of the recommended changes and on November 16 in a longer speech he explained the purposes and arguments in support of the report. The two speeches will be treated together. He began by reminding the delegates that it was necessary to alter the constitution to meet new conditions and by expressing satisfaction in the fact that the members were bound by no pre-election pledges. "Governments," he said, "were instituted for the protection of the rights of persons and property." The great interest of every community could be divided between capital and labor and the control by neither should be too strong. If labor gained power the "despotism of king numbers" would prevail and its results would be "agrarianism." This condition, he continued, was already in evidence in the North as was revealed in the support given there to free schools, homestead acts, Fourierism, communism, and in "the habitual disregard of the ordinances of religion, and of the institution of matrimony . . . and most distinctly, in the form of abolitionism." He considered abolitionism a war on property. Its attack on slavery was only the beginning of a crusade against all property. Eventually these democratic tendencies of the North would inevitably lead to class war in which the masses, through universal suffrage and the direct election of officials, would allow the government to fall into the hands of demagogues and produce corruption. In the South

---

[23] George W. Summers of Kanawha County, R. E. Scott of the Piedmont, and William Boyd from the Valley were the Whigs. George Blow from Norfolk, A. F. Haymond of the Northwest, and W. M. Tredway of the Piedmont were the Douglas Democrats. At the adjourned session Samuel Price of the Southwest replaced Summers who did not return to the convention. Price was a Whig.

[24] One was a bank president. Four others owed from eight to twenty-three taxable slaves within the counties in which they resided. Two others were lawyers but their tax returns are not available.

slavery automatically kept a large class from participating in politics and thereby gave the intelligent people a larger control.[25]

The Virginia convention of 1850-1851, he continued, grafted on to the original constitution of 1776 the two great political evils of the North, universal suffrage and popular elections. It gave the ballot to a large group of men who had little interest in the state. Everyone, he said, had the right of protection from the government, but to deserve this right one was obligated to defend that government not only by arms but also by taxes. "If," therefore, "irresponsible non-tax paying voters select the Legislators who lay the taxes . . . the result must be oppression." Some of the committee, in consequence, recommended the restriction of the ballot to freeholders although the majority favored granting suffrage to tax payers. In either case the privilege of voting would be based on the "performance of public duty."[26]

As to the other "great evil" of the constitution of 1850-1851, the committee recommended that all legislative officers should be elected by the voters and all of the executive and judicial ones should be selected by intermediate agents. Stuart defended this plan on the ground that legislators made laws that concerned the general welfare of the whole; whereas executives and judges without fear of popular disfavor would enforce these laws as they were enacted. Although the people were qualified to elect legislators since their posts did not require special technical training, they were not competent to select executives and judges since their posts required special training.[27]

In conformity to these general principles, Stuart's committee proposed that the legislature serve as the intermediate agent for selecting the state administrative and judicial officers, and that the justices and county commissioners serve as the intermediate agents for selecting local officers. Judges of the Circuit Court and the Court of Appeals should serve during good behavior. Since the justices of the peace were both judicial and legislative in their duties, the committee recommended that the voters elect them but that their terms be sufficiently long to enable them to be independent after they had been elected.[28]

The debate which followed the presentation of the report centered around the following points: (1) the need and expediency of revising the constitution during the war crisis; (2) the restriction of suffrage; and (3) the method of electing and the terms of officers. The order of the debate followed this lineup, and will be the order of treatment in this essay.

In May at the first suggestion of a revision of the constitution, and

[25] "Report of the Select Committee on Amendments to the Constitution of Virginia," Document XXXIII, bound with the *Journal of the Secession Convention*, pp. 1-5; "Proceedings of Secession Convention," June 22, November 16, *Daily Richmond Enquirer*, August 1, November 20, 1861.
[26] *Ibid.*
[27] *Ibid.*
[28] In addition to these major recommendations the committee made several minor proposals which will be treated later.

thereafter when amendments were proposed in June and November, a serious controversy arose in the convention over the need and expediency of proposing amendments during the war. The press was particularly concerned over this issue. The *Daily Lynchburg Virginian* on November 21, 1861, complained that the existing fundamental law was the "patch-work of demagogues and charlatans. . . . [A] blatant democrat . . . and pure democracy are arrant humbugs." The Richmond *Examiner,* which first opposed a revision because it had no faith in the members of the convention[29] and because it thought the time inappropriate, admitted the need for changes.[30] The best Virginia constitution, its editor declared, was the one made in 1776 when republican instead of democratic principles were dominant. Every change after 1776, he continued, "without a solitary exception" has carried the respective commonwealths of the United States nearer the rocks on which popular government in every age has been wrecked.[31] The Richmond *Whig* insisted that there was no point in separating from the "'Yankees, if we retain Yankee institutions.' Universal suffrage and universal elections, both importations from Yankee land, are as vicious products as that vicious region ever gave birth to." The editor did not believe Virginians could ever stoop to the northern "standard of meanness; but if anything could effect it, it would be the retention of these baneful Yankee institutions." Twenty more years of these two evils would "render us incapable of maintaining, and unworthy of freedom."[32] Even the Richmond *Enquirer* which opposed any revision in the constitution during the war crisis admitted the need for alterations.[33]

Supporters of revision maintained that the war crisis was an opportune time for perfecting amendments. A few alterations, according to their arguments, were necessary in order to put Virginia in proper relationship to the Confederacy. While these changes were being made a complete revision could be accomplished without much excitement. In this period of stress, moreover, party politics and demagoguery were at a low ebb; and as a result significant reforms could be perfected without the usual friction.[34]

Those who held that it was inexpedient to alter the fundamental law in the war crisis maintained that the voters would not have the time or inclination to study intelligently the proposed changes. Some questioned

[29] For a picture of the *Examiner's* tirades against the convention prior to secession see Frederick S. Daniel, *The Richmond Examiner during the War; or the Writings of John M. Daniel, with a Memoir of His Life* . . . (New York, 1868) ; H. T. Shanks, *Secession Movement in Virginia,* p. 185.
[30] June 19, 1861.   [31] June 28, 1861.
[32] June 22, 1861. Many in and outside the convention agreed with the *Whig's* editor that universal manhood suffrage and popular elections were Yankee institutions. See debate for June 22 and November 16 as reported in the Richmond *Enquirer,* July 31, August 1, and November 20; *Daily Richmond Examiner,* July 2, 1861.
[33] November 20, 1861.
[34] "Proceedings of the Secession Convention," June 22, *Daily Richmond Enquirer,* July 31, 1861.

the authority of the convention to make the alterations since its members were elected for another purpose. Others felt that all energies and resources should be devoted to the prosecution of the war. In addition it was contended that soldiers who were on the march and civilians in the sections under enemy domination would be unable to vote.[35] The Northwest, moreover, was not fully represented in the convention itself.[36] Frequently during the sessions of the convention the opponents of revision tried to delay consideration of Stuart's proposals. In each effort, however, they were defeated until at the adjourned session of November 16 by a vote of fifty-five to twenty-six the revisionists won such overwhelming support that the opposition submitted.[37]

The second important issue before the convention concerned the committee's proposal of suffrage restriction. Stuart in his report advocated the return to the regulations in the constitution of 1829-1830. Universal suffrage, he began, deprived the minority of protection and gave to the majority the authority to impose unfair taxes on others. It violated the principle of "no taxation without representation."[38] "That man who cannot," the editor of the *Whig* added, "or who will not, pay his taxes, is in nearly all cases, either too indolent, or too dishonest, or too indifferent to the welfare of the community to be made a depository of political power." The exclusion of those who do not pay taxes, therefore, "should be made absolute and complete."[39] Edmund Ruffin recorded the same sentiment in his diary for April 24, 1862, when he wrote: "a government like ours of universal suffrage will always be a government of & by *the worst* of the people." Branch of Petersburg contended that there was "no earthly reason why we should make an exemption in favor of those who are too lazy to work for their living and their privilege as citizens."[40] Tredway, a bank president and member of Stuart's committee, expressed the feeling that the restriction of suffrage was the heart of the proposed constitutional changes. He would be willing, however, to grant the ballot to all who voted "conservatively."[41]

Nearly all of the delegates who spoke on the suffrage amendment supported the principle of restricting the ballot, but some felt that it was unwise to adopt such a change during the war.[42] Others warned that the inclusion of this amendment would defeat the whole constitution. Many, who paid no taxes but who under the regulations of 1850-1851 could vote,

---

[35] *Ibid.*
[36] Only four of the thirty delegates from the northwestern counties were present on June 22.
[37] *Journal of Secession Convention*, pp. 233, 279-280, 330, 331.
[38] "Proceedings of Secession Convention," November 16, *Daily Richmond Enquirer*, November 20, 1861; "Report of the Select Committee on Amendments to the Constitution of Virginia," pp. 7-8.
[39] December 14, 1861.
[40] "Proceedings of Secession Convention," June 22, *Daily Richmond Enquirer*, July 31, 1861.
[41] "Proceedings of Secession Convention," November 21, *ibid.*, December 2, 1861.
[42] Proceedings of Secession Convention," November 19, *ibid.*, November 25, 1861.

were in the army. Restriction of suffrage would, therefore, not only reduce their ardor but would also reduce future volunteering.[43] On June 24 the editor of the *Examiner,* who later criticised the convention for not going further in its conservative changes, wrote an effective editorial against the adoption of suffrage restriction at this time. "We doubt," he said, "whether the most detested monarchial Government ever, in times of war, attempted to abridge the rights of its citizen soldiers." He estimated that the proposal would deprive thirty thousand soldiers of the right to vote.

In accordance with these arguments, Sheffey from the southwestern part of the state proposed in place of the committee's amendment the retention of the suffrage provisions found in the constitution of 1850-1851. His motion carried by a vote of seventy-five to thirty-three.[44] The western delegates voted almost unanimously for Sheffey's proposal. The Valley divided on the question. East of the Blue Ridge the count was thirty-two to twenty in the affirmative. The results in the Valley and the eastern part of the state, the propertied sections, were apparently due to the feeling that it was an inappropriate time to take such action.

Several later efforts to restrict suffrage were made in the convention. Branch tried unsuccessfully to prevent foreigners without military service in the Confederacy from voting until after twenty-one years' residence.[45] Even after the convention had practically completed its work a resolution to allow the people to vote on suffrage restriction was carried by the count of sixty-one to thirty-four. On this ballot the Coastal Plain, Piedmont, and Valley voted fifty to eleven in the affirmative and the western delegates opposed the resolution eleven to twenty-three.[46] Interestingly enough in the later ratification ballot a majority of the voters favored the resolution restricting suffrage and rejected the other constitutional amendments.[47] All of which indicates that the sentiment in favor of disfranchisement of non-tax payers was dominant.

The third issue on which the debate in the convention was centered was the short ballot and the terms of officers. Stuart's committee proposed that central and local officials should be elected by the state legislature and local legislative agencies, respectively, as they were under the constitution of 1776 rather than by the voters as was the practice after 1850-1851. The *Examiner* revealed that the purpose of the convention of 1776 was to let the people elect the legislators and have the legislature select the

[43] "Proceedings of Secession Convention," November 19, 20, *ibid.,* November 25, 26, 1861.
[44] *Journal of Secession Convention,* pp. 337-338.
[45] The vote on this motion was fifty-three to fifty-six. One of the main reasons for its defeat was the feeling that Kentuckians and Marylanders who desired to enter Virginia to escape northern rule would be penalized. *Journal of Secession Convention,* p. 343; "Proceedings of Secession Convention," November 20, *Daily Richmond Enquirer,* November 26, 1861.
[46] *Journal of Secession Convention,* pp. 404-405; "Proceedings of Secession Convention," November 30, *Daily Richmond Enquirer,* January 29, 1862.
[47] See below, p. 46.

other officers.[48] Even the *Enquirer* admitted that the constitution of 1850-1851 was "not sufficiently based upon the republican principle" because of the "multitudinous elections."[49] The *Whig* agreed that the "evils of frequent elections . . . are enough to deprave any people and mar the operations of the best Government." Popular elections, it continued, were costly, engendered "idleness and dissipation and . . . [tended] to reduce people from patient and honest industry, and . . . [tempted] them to look to public offices for means of subsistence. It . . . foments . . . parties."[50] Jeremiah Morton, an ardent secessionist even before the election of Lincoln, contended that nothing disturbed the peace of society as "this continued and perpetual appeal to the people. The popular elections occurring almost every month have become a nuisance to the people themselves."[51]

The democrats from the western part of the state where the sentiment for popular elections was strongest did not debate the general value of the existing system; but when specific changes were proposed they offered a bold and almost united front. Stuart's committee recommended the election of the governor and lieutenant governor by the legislature. The debate on this amendment continued for four days and provoked the usual sectional animosities. Edmund Pendleton of the Northwest admitted that in peace time he would support this "retrogression." At the same time he warned the eastern delegates that the unionists of his section would use to advantage the efforts to curtail popular power. Lewis E. Harvie, a "fire-eater" whose influence for secession had been strong in the eastern counties, replied with much feeling that he wished to let the western leaders know that the East was tired of election annoyances and demagoguery. The Northwest, he continued, had no right to ask further concessions. The East had humored the West with a tax on slaves under twelve years of age only to have this favor repaid by treason.[52] Haymond of Stuart's committee and from the Northwest replied that there were still many in his section who were loyal to Virginia and the South, and that this loyalty was due more to their patriotism than to what the state and Confederate governments had contributed. Neither of these governments, he continued, had done anything for the defense of his people even though they were surrounded by hostile peoples.[53] Masters who agreed with Haymond's arguments threatened to work for the defeat of the whole revised constitution, even though he favored many of its proposals, if this amendment passed.[54] As a result of this sectional hostility the direct election of

[48] November 27, 1861.   [49] November 20, 1861.
[50] November 28, 1861. The Richmond *Dispatch* was in harmony with these views. *Daily Richmond Whig*, December 2, 1861.
[51] "Proceedings of Secession Convention," June 22, *Daily Richmond Enquirer*, July 31, 1861.
[52] "Proceedings of Secession Convention," November 23, *ibid.*, January 16, 1862.
[53] "Proceedings of Secession Convention," November 25, *ibid.*, January 17, 1862.
[54] *Ibid.*, January 18, 1862. Cowan and Gray expressed similar views. "Proceedings of Secession Convention," November 23, December 5, *ibid.*, January 16, February 24, 1862.

governor and lieutenant governor prevailed by a vote of sixty to forty-two, the Tidewater and Piedmont supporting the election by the legislature and the delegates from west of the Blue Ridge voting for direct election.[55] The East succeeded in securing a slight change in the method of election. In 1850-1851 a second election was necessary whenever no candidate received a majority of the votes cast; whereas in the proposal of 1861 the legislature by joint ballot of the two houses was authorized to select the governor and lieutenant governor from the three candidates receiving the highest popular vote, provided no one had received a majority in the popular election.[56]

Near the close of the convention's session, Speed of Lynchburg recommended that at the time of the vote on the ratification of the new constitution the voters be permitted to approve or disapprove an amendment authorizing the legislature instead of the electorate to elect these executive officers.[57] Garnett, thereupon, declared that he had been opposed to amending the constitution until he saw how "conservative" the convention was. He would now like to take advantage of the character of the body by putting through Speed's plan as well as other "conservative" measures. "For heaven's sake," he added, "let us not be afraid of our own shadow. Let us not be afraid of the obloquy that has been heaped upon the Convention by the press of the State."[58] Stuart expressed his agreement with the sentiment of Speed and Garnett, but he felt it was too late to bring these matters up. Cox, Boyd, Scott, and Price of the committee supported Stuart's position.[59] Speed's motion, therefore, was laid on the table although by the close vote of forty-three to thirty-eight.[60]

The method of selecting local officers caused less controversy. Here the conservatives who had thus far failed in their major proposals were able to bring about significant alterations. Stuart's committee had recommended the appointment of local executives by legislative agents such as county commissioners or county courts.[61] Under the appointive system of 1776, sheriffs, according to Stuart, never defaulted; but under the existing elective plan 117 out of 130 sheriffs in the state had defaulted. Over a hundred clerks in recent years, he continued, had also failed to do their duty.[62] In the main the committee's recommendations were accepted.[63]

The judiciary caused more concern and produced greater differences of opinion. Stuart's committee proposed the nomination by the governor and approval by the Senate of the judges of the state Court of Appeals and

[55] *Journal of Secession Convention*, pp. 371-372.
[56] *Ibid.*, pp. 375-376.   [57] *Ibid.*, pp. 436-437.
[58] "Proceedings of the Secession Convention," December 4, *Daily Richmond Enquirer*, February 22, 1862.
[59] *Ibid.*
[60] *Journal of Secession Convention*, p. 437.
[61] "Proceedings of Secession Convention," December 2, *Daily Richmond Enquirer*, February 13, 1862.
[62] "Proceedings of Secession Convention," June 22, *ibid.*, August 1, 1861.
[63] See below, p. 40.

the Circuit Courts. The term of these judges was to be for life or good behavior as in the federal system.[64] James Holcombe, professor of law at the University of Virginia, offered as a substitute John Marshall's proposal in the convention of 1829-1830. Under this plan the legislature would be empowered to create the necessary judicial bodies beyond the Court of Appeals which was established by the constitution and to make laws regulating them. The judges were to be appointed for the same term recommended in the other plan.[65] The convention accepted the committee's recommendation of the old system of courts with the selection of judges by the legislature.

The fight then centered around the length of the judges' terms. Sheffey, the ardent Jeffersonian from the Southwest, expressed the desire to restrict the term in order to prevent the judges becoming "too arrogant and independent." Stuart replied that the real tyrant in America was the "infuriated populace." There was, he contended, a need in a republic for judges "who can boldly stand up against a whole commonwealth if necessary and annul the acts of the General Assembly." If judges were elected periodically, he concluded, they would be subject to favoritism. L. S. Hall of the Northwest said that the judges selected for short terms under the constitution of 1850-1851 had proved capable and independent.[66] On November 27 an effort to limit the term of the judges in both courts to twelve years was defeated, thirty-four to seventy-four.[67] On this motion the Tidewater, Piedmont, and Valley voted eight to sixty-two; whereas the western delegates supported the measure by the ballot of twenty-six to eleven.

Stuart's committee maintained that since justices of the peace were legislative and judicial officers they should be elected by the electorate but for long terms, so as to remain free of popular caprice.[68] Stuart himself wanted them appointed for life as under the constitution of 1776 but the majority of the committee disagreed with him.[69] In the debate in the convention, Marmaduke Johnson of Richmond expressed disappointment at Stuart's concession to other members of the committee. He insisted that the delegates were there to make a "conservative constitution." The most corrupt officials in the government, he said, were the justices. With the returning "sense of security and conservatism on the part of the people," he continued, there would be no cause for alarm if the old system of 1776 were reinstated.[70] Johnson's opponents reminded him of the corruption

[64] "Report of the Select Committee on Amendments to the Constitution of Virginia," pp. 12-13; "Proceedings of Secession Convention, "November 16, *Daily Richmond Enquirer*, November 21, 1861.
[65] "Proceedings of Secession Convention," November 26, *ibid.*, January 21, 1862.
[66] *Ibid.*, January 24, 1862.
[67] "Proceedings of Secession Convention," November 27, *ibid.*, January 25, 1862.
[68] "Report of the Select Committee on Amendments to the Constitution of Virginia," p. 14.
[69] "Proceedings of Secession Convention," November 16, 27, *Daily Richmond Enquirer*, November 21, 1861, January 27, 1862.
[70] "Proceedings of Secession Convention," November 27, *ibid.*, January 27, 1862.

of the old county court system in which a few families controlled the appointments and in which the justices selected their successors.[71] The convention finally approved the committee's recommendation of popular election but instead of life tenure decided on a term of twelve years.[72]

Several minor changes in the constitution produced brief discussions. One of these pertained to emancipation. In the constitution of 1829-1830 free Negroes had been deprived of the right to vote, and in 1850-1851 the legislature was given the authority to restrict emancipation and to regulate the length of time free Negroes could remain in the state after freedom was obtained.[73] The Stuart committee made no changes in these proposals; but in the convention Harvie tried to make emancipation within the state illegal.[74] When reminded that this violated property rights, Harvie agreed but justified his stand on the ground that manumission was dangerous to the state. "We must quicken," he added, "our efforts henceforth in behalf of this institution [slavery]. It will become necessary for us not only to protect it, but we must legislate to extend it. We are, in fact, hereafter to become slavery propagandist."[75] His motion was defeated by the close vote of fifty-two to fifty-four.[76]

Another minor controversy of the convention arose over Stuart's proposal that the clause in the old constitution which required the legislature to appropriate money collected from the poll tax equally between the primary and secondary schools be amended so that the legislature would have more discretion to use the revenue for other purposes in time of a crisis.[77] Haymond speaking for the West objected to any diversion of school funds. Nevertheless Stuart's motion prevailed by a majority of fifty-five to forty-three.[78] Pendleton, a western delegate, tried unsuccessfully to eliminate the poll tax.[79] Tredway then proposed that appropriations above the ordinary expenditures should require a two thirds majority of the two houses of the legislature. In place of his proposal, the convention decided that all appropriation measures must obtain the support of a majority of the legislators elected and that the vote of each should be recorded.[80]

After the various sections of the constitution had been agreed to, Stuart's committee put it in proper form. The final vote on the revised constitution was seventy-four to ten.[81] Many delegates were away at the time and some refrained from voting. Nevertheless the final result represented a normal vote in the November-December sessions. Of the ten

[71] *Ibid.*
[72] *Journal of Secession Convention,* pp. 376, 391-392.
[73] F. M. Green, *Constitutional Development in the South Atlantic States,* p. 295.
[74] "Proceedings of Secession Convention," November 22, *Daily Richmond Enquirer,* December 4, 1862.
[75] "Proceedings of Secession Convention," November 23, *ibid.,* December 7, 1861.
[76] *Ibid.*
[77] *Ibid.,* January 13, 1862.
[78] *Ibid.*
[79] *Ibid.*
[80] *Ibid.*
[81] *Journal of Secession Convention,* pp. 441-442.

supporting the negative, eight were from the Northwest and one each from the Valley and Tidewater.[82]

The final controversy came over the schedule for ratification. It was agreed without much difficulty that the people should pass on the constitution itself and on the special resolution restricting suffrage to the tax payers; but when Gray of the Valley tried to have the ratification vote delayed until after the war, disagreement developed. Gray accused the members of having lost faith in the popular will. One third of the people at home, he contended, could not vote since they were within the region occupied by Federal forces. An additional sixty-thousand Virginians who were in the army were unable to examine the constitution.[83] Heck from the Northwest followed with a "word of warning to . . . those smooth oily friends of mine, that . . . they will find some day that the people will rise up in their might and send back to the shades of private life, those who seek to rule them with an iron hand." He did not hold, he concluded, that the constitution was objectionable to his people but he felt that they should be given a chance to vote on the changes.[84] Dulany added that not only the Northwest but also other sections were deprived of the right to express their will on the amendments. He asked the convention to consider the unfairness of ratification during the war.[85] The old sectional feelings were aroused. Fisher from the Tidewater replied that the Northeast also had been overrun by the enemy, but unlike the Northwest his people were still loyal to the Richmond government. "For my part," he declared, "I am tired of this perpetual garrulous chaunt [sic] about injustice to the Northwest." He had heard this for twenty years.[86] Cowan agreed that a disloyal party prevailed in the western counties, but he cautioned the Easterners not to strengthen that party by acts unfriendly to his people. His section, he added, had been treated unkindly in the convention. At different times in several parts of the hall while votes were being taken, "I have heard [members say] . . . 'there goes the northwest!' as though we were suspected here; as though we were here as mere machines, only to remain still in our seats and sanction whatever might be done by others, no matter how it may affect our section."[87] Woods joined in to say that some acted as though they were afraid of a fair vote.[88] Morgan from the same section predicted a division of the state if more consideration were not given to the rights of his people.[89] Dorman from the Valley expressed the desire to let the Northwest go in peace if its people preferred Lincoln to the new constitution.[90] Following this rather heated debate the convention decided by a vote of fifty-eight to twenty-three to present the new constitution to the people for ratification in March, 1862. Five of the

[82] Gray from the Valley and Dulany from the Tidewater.
[83] "Proceedings of Secession Convention," December 5, *Daily Richmond Enquirer*, February 26, 1862.
[84] *Ibid.*
[85] *Ibid.*
[86] *Ibid.*, February 27, 1862.
[87] *Ibid.*
[88] *Ibid.*
[89] *Ibid.*, February 28, 1862.
[90] *Ibid.*

negative votes came from those living in the Valley, three from east of the Blue Ridge, two from the Southwest, and thirteen from the Northwest.

The new constitution did not entirely conform to the recommendations of Stuart's committee. Nevertheless it was less democratic than than of 1850-1851. Conservatives were almost completely defeated in their efforts to restrict suffrage and to remove the election of governor and lieutenant governor from the control of the electorate. On the other hand they succeeded in reducing the number of elective officers and in making the judiciary independent of the populace. The bill of rights and the article on the legislative department were not materially altered. The members of the House of Delegates were to be elected and to hold their sessions annually rather than biennially as formerly. State senators were to be divided into four groups and these respective groups were to be elected in successive years; whereas under the constitution of 1850-1851 there were two groups each elected in alternate years. No effort was made in 1861 to change the system of representation.[91]

In the executive department, as already indicated, the changes in the method of selecting the governor and lieutenant governor were slight.[92] The attorney general, auditor, treasurer, secretary of the commonwealth, and members of the board of public works were to be selected by the General Assembly.[93]

The most significant alterations in the constitution were in the judiciary. Instead of one supreme court of appeals as formerly, two appellate ones with three judges each were provided for. One of these was designed to be a court of law and the other a court of equity. District courts were abolished. Twenty-one circuit courts were created and the legislature was empowered to increase this number from time to time. Judges of the appellate and circuit courts were to be elected by the General Assembly instead of by popular vote as in 1850-1851. Provision was made for these judges to serve during good behavior or until seventy years old. Every three years one fourth of the justices of the peace were subject to reelection by the voters. Vacancies occurring between regular elections were to be filled by appointment of the other justices; whereas in the old constitution these vacancies were filled by special elections. Justices were to serve for twelve years. The respective courts were authorized to select the circuit attorneys, court clerks, constables, and minor judicial officers. The governor was given the authority to appoint the sheriff nominated by the county court. Under the constitution of 1861 the sheriff was eligible for reappointment; while under that of 1850-1851 he was ineligible. In the old constitution all city officers were elected by popular vote. In that of 1861 only the mayor and town councillors were elected; other town and city officials were appointed by the council or hustings

[91] Copies of the new constitution were published in all the Richmond newspapers during January and February, 1862.
[92] See above, p. 38.
[93] Richmond *Enquirer*, January 3, 1862.

court.[94] Several minor changes such as the ones referred to on emancipation, the poll tax, and education were made.[95]

Upon the completion of the constitutional revision and its publication in the newspapers, the editors and political leaders began discussing the changes. Edmund Ruffin was pleased that the convention had made "some very beneficial & real amendments of the constitution—& every one of which is either a complete return to a before abrogated feature of the oldest constituion of 1776, or an approach thereto." He regretted that universal suffrage and the direct election of the governor and county magistrates were retained but these were "somewhat mitigated" by the improvements.[96] The editor of the Richmond *Examiner* found the changes an improvement over the document of 1850-1851, although he expressed disappointment at the convention's timidity in not making other needed alterations. The members were afraid, he continued, of public sentiment and demagogues. The reforms were only half reforms; and in consequence, he concluded, the constitution would have to be revised again.[97] The *Daily Dispatch* urged the voters to support the new constitution because it was conservative in character and free of the "Yankee innovations." This paper liked particularly the appointment of judges by the legislature and the sheriffs by the county courts. "The single opportunity to be rid of defaulting Sheriffs ought alone to bring every voter to the polls."[98] The day of the "downfall" of the old constitution of 1776, the editor wrote a few days later, "dates [the] beginning of our descent to an abyss from which nothing but this great revolution [secession] can save us."[99] The Lynchburg *Virginian* in support of ratification accused the "small fry demagogues" of appealing to the people to reject the constitution because it abridged "their liberties—the liberty to vote for constable."[100] From the Valley, Alexander H. H. Stuart's home, the Whig Staunton *Spectator* urged the voters to "complete our redemption from Yankeeism" and demagoguery. The state needed, the editor added, a constitution that would give "security to life, liberty and property." Although the changes did not go so far as he desired, the revised constitution was a great improvement for it "rids us of the eternally recurring popular elections of Sheriffs, Constables, Clerks, etc. It establishes a judiciary that will discharge its duties promptly, fearlessly, and impartially. It gives greater stability and dignity to the magistry, and it will we trust secure the faithful execution of the laws, and the economical administration of the public monies."[101]

[94] *Ibid.,* December 7, 1861, January 3, 1862.
[95] See above, p. 40.
[96] Diary of Edmund Ruffin, December 7, 1861, Library of Congress.
[97] December 7, 1861.
[98] March 14, 1862. The Petersburg *Daily Express,* November 28, 1861, expressed similar views.
[99] April 1, 1862.
[100] December 21, 1861.
[101] January 7, 1862.

More than any other paper the Richmond *Whig,* the organ of the conservative forces and the propertied classes, praised the new constitution. When the movement for revision began immediately after secession was accomplished, its editor wrote successive editorials in favor of ridding the constitution of "Yankeeism," which he interpreted as including popular elections and universal suffrage. "Substantial good government," his argument ran, "good laws, and good officers honestly and faithfully to administer them, are something better than the imaginary blessings of a system which contemplates only the welfare of drones and vagabonds." Although the changes did not go far enough they were an important step in the right direction. Moreover, the war crisis was the time, he continued, not only for Virginia but also for the whole Confederacy to create an ideal government based on "fundamental principles. . . . We believe it is not impossible, and that it is desirable that our Confederacy should consist exclusively of gentlemen and negroes. By a wise system of government, encouraging the virtues which make the gentleman, and discouraging the vices which constitute the blackguard, the result is possible."[102]

The most important newspapers in the Valley, Piedmont, and Tidewater supported the amended document.[103] The Richmond *Enquirer* was an exception. In June it warned Stuart's forces that the time was inopportune to amend the constitution. Later in November when the convention worked out the changes, this paper, although admitting the need for moderate alterations, opposed drastic amendments. Its editor felt that the constitution of the Revolutionary period created a government which was entirely under the control of the propertied classes. The fundamental law of 1850-1851, on the other hand, was too democratic for him; but of these two he preferred the latter.[104] By the later part of November this paper became alarmed at the drastic changes being made and warned the people to keep an eye on the convention.[105] Nevertheless this eastern organ of Jacksonian democracy endorsed many of the amendments approved by the convention. It liked especially the annual sessions of the legislature, the method of electing the governor and lieutenant governor, and the appointment instead of the election of minor officers. It disapproved, however, the independence of the judiciary, for the judges and justices would be less responsible to the public's interests. It did not like the increased patronage given to the legislature.[106] The Berryville *Conservator* agreed with the *Enquirer's* indictment of the convention, which, it said, created a constitution which vested "too much power in the hands of the few."[107]

[102] December 2, 19, 1861.
[103] The smaller newspapers in these sections gave little space to the constitution. They were too much concerned with the war itself to devote any space to the amendments.
[104] November 20, 1861.
[105] November 29, 1861.
[106] December 7, 1861.
[107] Quoted in Lynchburg *Virginian,* February 5, 1862.

In the main there was very little discussion of the amendments by the press and leaders outside of the convention from the adjournment in December until the closing of the polls on March 15, 1862. The constitution was published twice a week during this period in the leading newspapers of the state, but there were only a few editorials and articles defending or condemning the changes. From January 1 until the ratification vote in March, for instance, there was only one reference to the constitution in the Richmond *Examiner* and the Petersburg *Daily Express,* respectively, and in both papers the item was only an explanation of the method of ratification.[108] Neither side after the adjournment of the convention revealed much interest in the results. Public discussions were not held and the papers carried no accounts of resolutions of public meetings endorsing or condemning the amendments.

This was a period when the people, the leaders, and the press were concerned with invasion. The Confederacy suffered many defeats in the winter of 1861-1862. By March 13, the date of the ratification vote, the Federals held most of the Mississippi River, all of Kentucky, nearly all of Tennessee, and much of western, northern, and eastern Virginia. General George B. McClellan was in the Peninsula gathering his forces for an attack on Richmond. The Virginia legislature was debating conscription, soon to be followed in this course by the Confederate Congress. At the time of the balloting on the new constitution, March 13-15, the camps were active with preparation to withstand the expected Federal attacks from three sides. On March 10 Governor John Letcher called for the mustering of the entire state militia into service in order to comply with President Davis's emergency request for forty thousand troops from Virginia. Martial law was proclaimed on March 12 in Petersburg and the surrounding district.[109]

As a result of these factors and conditions, the voters gave little attention from January to March to the constitution and its ratification. On election days very few people appeared at the polls. In Richmond the election was "one of the tamest affairs that ever came off in this city. What with the militia muster and the crowd of frantic candidates for exemption gathered in the second story of the City Hall, the polls were deserted. . . . Commissioners and clerks sat listlessly looking at one another all the day long."[110] Similar reports came from Staunton, Lynchburg, and Petersburg.[111] The total vote for the whole state was less than 30,000 as compared with a vote in normal times of 160,000.[112] Counties north of

[108] Richmond *Examiner,* March 10, 1862; Petersburg *Daily Express,* March 12, 1862.
[109] Proclamations of the Governor of Virginia, State Department of Archives, Richmond; Petersburg *Daily Express,* March 14, 1862.
[110] *Daily Richmond Examiner,* March 14, 1862.
[111] *Daily Lynchburg Virginian,* March 17, 1862; Staunton *Spectator,* March 18, 1862; Petersburg *Daily Express,* March 14, 17, 1862.
[112] Executive Journal of Virginia, Book 202, p. 120, State Department of Archives, Richmond.

the Rappahannock River, the northern part of the Valley, the Eastern Shore, and most of the Trans-Allegheny section were either under the control of Federal forces or cut off from Richmond. Even in places not held or threatened by northern forces not one fifth of the voters cast ballots.[113]

The vote of the state was never completely tabulated, but in his proclamation of May 2 and in his message to the legislature on May 6, 1862, the governor reported the results as 13,233 for and 13,911 against the new constitution, and 16,518 for and 9,201 against the restriction of suffrage.[114] The constitution, therefore, was defeated by 678 votes. The suffrage amendment passed by a majority of 7,317; but since the suffrage amendment depended upon the approval of the rest of the constitution it did not go into effect. The governor explained that this report was offered for only eighty-seven counties, camps, and towns, but that additional unofficial returns from other countries, not within the Federal lines, indicated that the majority against the constitution was actually larger than the official report.[115] In all of the larger towns for which reports are available the vote was overwhelming for the constitution. In Richmond the results were 486 to 15, in Lynchburg 250 to 33, in Augusta County which included Staunton 428 to 174, and in Petersburg 173 to 6 in favor of the new constitution.[116] The results were not tabulated by counties and for that reason it is impossible to analyze the sectional popular vote on the constitution.

In explaining the defeat of the new constitution, the editor of the Richmond *Enquirer* rather joyfully recorded that is was an inappropriate time to alter the "fundamental document." Members of the convention, he continued, tried to go further than the people wanted to. "Theorists of the body embraced the supposed opportunity" to attach to what the people wanted, what the people did not want. "Indeed it was claimed, with some exultation, by a supporter of their proceedings, that the unpopular alterations would be buoyed through by the other. . . . It was an attempt to do away with what they called a 'Yankee Constitution' by a 'Yankee trick.' "[117]

The ratification vote cannot be taken at face value because it represented too small a percentage of the voters and because it included too limited a portion of the state. Since the largest part of the state which did not have a chance to vote was democratic in sentiment, it is safe to

[113] Lynchburg cast 283 votes compared with a normal 1,000; Augusta normally cast 3,500 ballots and in this election there were only 602 votes; Richmond with a normal vote of 3,700, cast only 601 in this election; and Petersburg with a normal vote of 1,700, cast only 179 in this balloting.
[114] *Daily Richmond Enquirer,* May 3, 7, 1862; Executive Journal of Virginia, Book 202, p. 120, State Department of Archives, Richmond.
[115] *Ibid.,* Book 202, p. 120.
[116] *Daily Richmond Enquirer,* March 18, 1862; *Daily Lynchburg Virginian,* March 17, 1862; Staunton *Spectator,* March 18, 1862; Petersburg *Daily Express,* March 17, 1862.
[117] April 23, 1862.

assume that an election under normal conditions would have resulted in a larger negative vote on the amended constitution. Despite these facts, the passage through the convention of the conservative amendments, plus the large majority in the ratification of the suffrage provision, shows the temporary if not permanent conservatism of that part of the state which was not occupied by federal troops. More important than this is the fact that the debates and votes in the convention indicate the reactionary tendencies of the leaders. It is appropriate, therefore, to summarize and analyze these votes within that body.

The votes in the convention on the following important issues were: (1) suffrage restriction, thirty-three to seventy-five; (2) election of the governor and lieutenant governor by the legislature, forty-two to sixty; and (3) life tenure for judges, seventy-four to thirty-four.[118] On these issues sixty-two per cent of the Piedmont, Tidewater, and Valley delegates against seventeen per cent of those from the Northwest and Southwest voted conservatively. The surprising thing in these results is the large number of votes in the East against the changes and the large conservative vote in the Valley. Many eastern delegates voted against the proposed changes because of their fear that the alterations would antagonize the West and impair the unity necessary for the success of the war.[119] The large conservative vote in the Valley was partly due to the fact that most delegates from that region were Whigs and large property owners, elected because of their unionist leanings.

On the whole those who voted for the ordinance of secession were not so enthusiastic about the new constitution as those who opposed disunion. Taking the votes on the three measures together it is found that fifty-three per cent of the latter group and forty-eight per cent of the former faction voted conservatively. Here again the opposition of the secessionists was partly due to policy rather than political tenets.[120] The party vote on these issues was interesting. Sixty-three per cent of the Whigs and forty-six per cent of the Democrats voted conservatively. There was little variation between the votes of the small slaveholders and large ones.[121] In

[118] The following table shows how the sections voted on these issues.

Issue	Tidewater Aff.	Tidewater Neg.	Piedmont Aff.	Piedmont Neg.	Valley Aff.	Valley Neg.	Northwest Aff.	Northwest Neg.	Southwest Aff.	Southwest Neg.
(1) Suffrage	10	14	10	19	10	10	1	17	2	15
(2) Election of governor by legislature	11	9	17	8	9	14	1	13	4	16
(3) Life tenure of judges	20	4	24	0	19	4	4	17	7	9

[119] The *Enquirer's* position illustrates this. See the issues of November 20, 29, 1861.

[120] This is illustrated by the statements of Garnett, Ruffin, and the *Examiner. Daily Richmond Examiner*, June 19, 24, 28, November 25, 27, 1861; Diary of Ruffin, November 18, 1861, Library of Congress.

[121] The vote on suffrage illustrates the truth of this statement. Here ten slave holders of one to five slaves each, twelve of five to twenty slaves each, and four of over twenty slaves each voted for restriction, against eighteen, fifteen, and six in the respective categories.

contrast to the almost solid sectional votes on issues of this type in the conventions of 1829-1830 and 1850-1851, there were many from the East and the West who broke with their section.[122]

Although it is evident that the secessionists did not originate the revision in 1861, the fact remains that secession gave the propertied sections and classes their chance to make the constitution conform to their political philosophy. Since the convention happened to be more conservative than might have been expected of a constitutional convention in normal times, such conservative leaders as Stuart took advantage of the occasion. Once this movement got under way the conservatives were aided by large propertied secessionists including Garnett, Harvie, and Ambler.[123] With the Northwest unfaithful to the East it was hoped that the conservative constitutional system that obtained prior to 1850-1851 could be reestablished.

[122] In 1829-1830 all the negative votes on the constitution as amended came from the West except one each from the Valley and Tidewater. J. C. McGregor, *Disruption of Virginia*, p. 45.

[123] These three were the largest slaveholders in the convention.

IV

THE NEGRO IN THE UNITED STATES SENATE

Samuel Denny Smith

Much has been written concerning the Negro in American life since 1865. Some writers have emphasized the great progress he has made, while others point out the mistakes he has made in his attempts to rise from the low social and economic state in which slavery left him. Both schools call attention to Negro leaders in all walks of life, but especially to those prominent in politics for a generation after the Civil War. Scores and even hundreds of Negroes held elective and appointive office in those days when the suffrage was first granted to the Negro and to a certain extent withheld from the southern white man. Very little, however, has been written and little is yet known by the general public of the most politically honored members of the race—those who were elected to, and served in, the United States Senate.

In the late 1860's and through the 1870's Negroes served as municipal, county, and state officials in great numbers. Then from 1870 on, twenty-two Negroes from the South were elected to the United States House of Representatives.[1] In 1870 Mississippi sent a Negro to the United States Senate to serve a one year unexpired term, and in 1874, the same state elected a Negro to the Senate to serve a full six year term. It is the purpose of this brief essay to present a survey of the part played by these Negro senators and other members of their race who were ambitious but unsuccessful for the honor.

A glance at the racial population of southern states of the period is necessary for an insight into the political situation. South Carolina had a Negro percentage of 60.7%; Mississippi 57.5%; Louisiana 51.5%; Alabama 47.5%; and Georgia and Florida, 47% each.[2] Yet in Mississippi alone was the Negro element politically aggressive and sufficiently well organized to win a United States senator-ship for the race. The obvious explanation is that in South Carolina, Louisiana, Alabama, Georgia, and Florida, there were capable, ambitious, aggressive white carpetbaggers and scalawags who reserved these offices for themselves and appeased the Negroes with the lesser offices. It is appropriate on the other hand to examine the situation in Mississippi that secured for the Negro these highest honors.

Mississippi, as the home of Jefferson Davis, was singled out for stern treatment by the North. The Black Code of the state, enacted before

[1] Samuel Denny Smith, *The Negro in Congress, 1870-1901* (Chapel Hill, 1940), pp. 5-6.
[2] Samuel L. Rogers, Director, *Negro Population in the United States, 1890-1915* (Washington, 1918), pp. 26, 208. The above figures are from the census of 1880.

Negro suffrage had been granted, had angered the North. Hence an effort was made to stimulate the Negro to come to the front in political affairs. In 1867 the Republican party held its first state convention and Negroes were in the majority. By 1870 when Mississippi was readmitted to the Union, the Negroes of the state were demanding a share of offices in proportion to their voting strength.[3]

In 1869, the Reverend Hiram Rhoades Revels was nominated as a compromise candidate for state senator from Adams County. He won the nomination by the narrow margin of seventeen to sixteen. Revels had not been active in politics but made a favorable impression by his short speech of acceptance. Thus was launched almost by accident a political career that was spectacular in the extreme and meteoric also in its sudden rise and wane.[4]

Revels was elected on the Republican ticket by a majority of between 1,500 to 2,000. In January, 1870, he took his seat in Jackson and opened the senate with prayer. This accident or chance may have made him United States senator. Mississippi had at last made her peace with the federal government and was to be represented in Congress again. The legislature was to fill three senatorial places—one for a full term, one for a five year unexpired term, and one for a single year unexpired term. It was agreed to give the full term beginning in 1871 to James Lusk Alcorn, a scalawag, and the five year term to Adelbert Ames, a carpetbagger. The Negroes then demanded the third member as they furnished about a third of the Republican vote on a joint ballot in the legislature. Both whites and other Negroes were considered but the choice settled on Revels as the logical man. He was nominated in a Negro conference, then in Republican caucus, and elected by a large majority in joint session.[5]

From January 20, 1870, when he was elected, until he was seated February 25, the press gave much attention to his previous career and to his main characteristics. Hiram Rhoades Revels was born free September 27, 1822, at Fayetteville, North Carolina. Removing to Indiana he studied at a Quaker Seminary and later went to Galesburg, Illinois, where he graduated from Knox College. He was ordained in the African Methodist Episcopal Church and preached in Indiana, Kansas, Missouri, and Kentucky. He was in Baltimore when the Civil War started and helped recruit the first Negro regiment in Maryland. In 1863-1864 he taught in St. Louis but left there to help the provost-marshal care for the freedmen at Vicksburg, Mississippi. Going on to Jackson, Mississippi, he organized churches and lectured. When his health failed he went north for two years until the close of the war. Then he returned to Natchez and

[3] James Wilford Garner, *Reconstruction in Mississippi* (New York, 1901), pp. 181, 187, 270.
[4] John Roy Lynch, *The Facts of Reconstruction* (New York, 1913), pp. 40, 41, 44.
[5] J. R. Lynch, *Facts of Reconstruction*, pp. 44, 46, 47.

preached to large congregations until his venture into politics.[6] He was of a very light complexion and looked little like a colored man. He had good manners and spoke with ease, fluency, and in general good taste.[7]

Some doubts were cast on his eligibility, technical and otherwise. It was held that he had not been nine years a citizen as required by the Constitution for a senator, and that he was guilty of fraud and immorality. Such charges were to be expected from Democrats but it was intimated that even the Radicals did not wish a Negro in Congress. It was said that they were playing a political game to keep the Negro vote while the whites reserved the offices for themselves.[8] These views were put to an actual test on February 23, when Senator Henry Wilson presented Revels' credentials to the Senate. Since the credentials were signed by General Adelbert Ames a long debate ensued as to the right of an army officer to certify to civil elections. Senator Henry G. Davis charged directly that Revels had not been a citizen for nine years and Senator John P. Stockton wished the credentials referred to the judiciary committee. Senator James W. Nye rejoiced that a Negro was coming to replace Jefferson Davis. The debate prevented a vote on that day.[9]

The case was considered sufficiently important to consume most of the next day in the Senate. Both Jacob M. Howard and Simon Cameron stressed the fact that Revels was to fill the vacancy left by Jefferson Davis. Cameron even claimed that in 1861 he had predicted such an outcome.[10]

On February 25, the debate was continued and concluded. Henry Wilson made the principal speech in favor of Revels. He openly exulted that Revels was coming in as a black man from Mississippi and that 800,000 Negro voters would surely be grateful for what the Republicans were doing for them. This led Stockton to rejoin that Revels was being admitted because he was black and not because he was legally qualified. It was expected that Charles Sumner would carry the brunt of the defense but he contented himself with a brief speech.[11]

Late in the day a motion to refer to a committee was lost, and then a motion was carried to admit Revels. On both motions the Democrats were overwhelmingly defeated by a vote of forty-eight to eight. Revels was then escorted to the desk by Wilson, took the oath, and was seated. For the occasion, the galleries were packed and even standing room was at a premium because of the intense interest in the affair.[12]

[6] *Biographical Congressional Directory* (Washington, 1913), p. 950; William J. Simmons, *Men of Mark: Eminent, Progressive and Rising* (Cleveland, 1891), p. 948. William Horatio Barnes, *History of Congress. The Forty-first Congress of the United States* (Washington, 1872), pp. 108, 109.
[7] Memphis *Daily Avalanche,* January 21, 22, 1870.
[8] Mobile *Register,* January 27, February 1, 15, 18, 1870; Savannah *Morning News,* February 1, 1870.
[9] *Congressional Globe,* 41st Cong., 2nd Sess., pp. 1503 f., 1513.
[10] *Ibid.*, pp. 1542-1544.
[11] *Ibid.*, pp. 1561, 1567.
[12] *Ibid.*, p. 1568; New York *Times,* February 26, 1870.

Revels was the first Negro to be seated by either house. It was almost a year before a Negro was seated in the House of Representatives. This explains the sensation caused by Revels' entrance to the august body associated with memories of Henry Clay, John C. Calhoun, Daniel Webster, and Stephen A Douglas.[13]

As the committees were already made up and the session far advanced, Revels was at a disadvantage in so far as committee assignments were concerned. Yet the Radicals were anxious to push him forward and make the most of their protegé, and he was named to the committee on education and labor. For the committee he reported adversely on the matter of teaching phonetics at West Point and Annapolis, but favorably for donating the Marine Hospital at Natchez to the state of Mississippi for educational purposes.[14]

He introduced three minor bills but all failed to pass. He was more effective in presenting petitions to the Senate. While most of these were of private nature, a few were significant. One suggested abolition of the franking privilege; another the removal of all political disabilities in Mississippi.[15]

But there was more public interest in Revels, the speaker, than in Revels, the legislator. Consequently his maiden speech was awaited with much eagerness. After three weeks of membership he spoke March 16 on the readmission of Georgia under the Bingham amendment. It was a gala occasion for his race and its friends. The speech had been well advertised in advance. The galleries were packed long before Revels rose to speak and he made good use of the opportunity. He expressed diffidence as a new member but, being the only Negro in Congress, Revels felt that he must speak for his race. He traced the conduct of the Negroes during the Civil War in order to show that they were peaceable and had no ill will for southern whites during or after the war. Revels claimed the North owed the Negroes a debt of gratitude for having turned the scale in the crisis. He charged that the Georgia whites were not reconstructed and that the Bingham amendment would leave them in control and the freedmen unprotected. Many members of the House of Representatives had come in to hear Revels and many congratulated him at the close of his speech.[16]

Revels made a major speech on May 17 on the removal of political disabilities. He had heretofore petitioned on behalf of individuals but now he advocated restoration of full rights for all loyal men, whether one or a hundred, or a whole state. He asserted that the Republican party in Mississippi was pledged to such a policy and that the legislature unanimously favored it. He said that harmony prevailed in Mississippi as much as in any state and that there was not a single report of violence or law-

[13] S. D. Smith, *The Negro in Congress*, p. 45.
[14] *Congressional Globe*, 41st Cong., 2nd Sess., pp. 1586, 1608, 2738.
[15] *Ibid.*, pp. 2234, 5076, 5114, 1607, 1676, 1817, 1856, 2285.
[16] *Ibid.*, pp. 1986-1988; New York *Times*, March 17, 1870.

lessness in the state.[17] His was a liberal attitude for his proposal would give the vote to many Democrats and probably mean his own political eclipse but he was willing to risk it. Many feared that Jefferson Davis would be returned to his old seat in the Senate if all Confederates were forgiven and enfranchised. With that fear in the background, Davis was often denounced on the Senate floor but the magnanimous Revels made not a single attack on his famous predecessor.

Revels was absent during much of this session when important votes were taken. A study of the records shows that he was usually partisan in his support of the administration. He voted for the readmission of Texas under a carpetbag government, for the seating of Ames, for naturalization to be extended to non-whites, and for enforcement of the Fifteenth Amendment, and to abolish the franking privilege.[18]

Revels had felt that he was the spokesman of 5,000,000 Negroes in the nation and that his advocacy should not be limited to the Senate floor. So many came to him for office, for jobs, or advice that he finally had to refuse to see anyone during sessions.[19]

Using the prestige of his official position Revels began to make addresses in large cities away from Washington. At Baltimore he lectured to large audiences, including many whites. With sound common sense he stressed economy and education for the Negroes. He declared that the Negroes must be true to themselves, to the country, and to the Republican party. But in Philadelphia he was refused the use of the Academy of Music. The *Nation* thought this refusal of the Republican directors was contrary to public sentiment in the city. He had better success in Cincinnati where he spoke on "The Tendency of Our Age." This lecture was delivered in many parts of the country and was largely attended.[20]

In general, Revels made a good impression on the country in contrast to his Republican colleagues from the South. The Cincinnati *Enquirer* remarked that Revels was "regarded as scrupulously honest which is a good deal to say of a carpetbagger. In point of intelligence he is a head and shoulders above the average carpetbagger."[21]

When the new session of Congress convened in December, Revels appeared a week late. He had already been placed on the District of Columbia committee. The freedmen had congregated there in great numbers and this gave Revels an additional chance to help them. But he seemed more interested in Mississippi and her protection by a good levee system than in the Negroes of the District. He introduced a bill to aid in repairs and construction of levees in Mississippi. He resubmitted several petitions on behalf of constituents. One, more important, was a joint reso-

[17] *Congressional Globe,* 41st Cong., 2nd Sess., p. 3520.
[18] *Ibid.,* pp. 2272, 2349, 3015, 3521, 5123, 4003.
[19] New York *Times,* March 7, 1870.
[20] Memphis *Daily Avalanche,* March 8, 1870; *Nation,* April 7, 1870; New York *Times,* July 11, 1870; Alexander Kelley McClure, *Recollections of Half a Century* (Salem, Mass., 1902), p. 253.
[21] Cincinnati *Enquirer,* November 12, 1870.

lution from the Mississippi legislature asking congressional aid for a printing house and for a school for the blind.[22]

On January 11, 1871, Revels spoke at length in favor of the levee bill. This was a typical, southern, cotton speech, free from partisan and racial bias. He referred to a petition he had presented from the Mississippi legislature asking for $2,000,000 and 5,000,000 acres of public lands for rebuilding the levees. In speaking of the importance of cotton he said: "By common consent, as it were, this great medium of national wealth once assumed so extraordinary a place in our political economy as to be regarded in point of commercial power as king of the industrial pursuits of the Nation. In this restricted sense may not the phrase 'king cotton' still speak of the magnitude and importance of the cotton growing interest of the whole country?" He discussed the possibilities of Egypt, Brazil, and India as rivals in cotton culture to the United States. India was the chief rival but was handicapped by uncertain moisture and climate, and more expensive labor. Yet the fertile Mississippi lands were exposed to floods and the state was too impoverished to build the necessary levees. The most fertile lands were in the Delta and if properly protected 3,000,000 to 4,000,000 acres of the finest cotton land on the globe would be opened to settlement. The bill was referred to a committee where it died.[23] His other legislative efforts were also futile. He reported a bill to incorporate the Dime Savings Bank of the District of Columbia. No doubt this would have helped the freedmen, especially, but it failed to pass. He introduced another bill to incorporate the Grand Tabernacle of Galilean Fishermen, but the name was not sufficient to carry it through.[24]

Revels' term was drawing to a close and he felt that he must get his views and principles on record. On February 8, 1871, he delivered his swan song in connection with the bill for mixed schools in the District of Columbia. Revels finally had a chance to express his views. He favored mixed schools in order to break down race prejudice which he thought was increasing. Yet he had no charge against the white race as a whole. He stated: "I desire to say here that the white race has no better friend than I. The Southern people know this. . . . I am true to my own race . . . but at the same time I would not have anything done which would harm the white race." The Negro, said he, should be built up but not at the expense of the white man. He thought mixed schools would not lead to social equality. He declared he would leave the Republican party if it passed legislation really damaging to any part of the white race. Common carriers, Revels said, were largely to blame for discrimination against Negroes. He closed his last speech in the Senate on a high plane. "Mr. President, I have nothing more to say. What I have said I have said in kindness; and I hope it will be received in that spirit." The Senate went

[22] *Congressional Globe*, 41st Cong., 3rd Sess., pp. 40, 52, 116, 367, 598, 1099, 1329.
[23] *Ibid.*, pp. 425, 426.
[24] *Ibid.*, pp. 593, 664, 1805.

into executive session and no action was taken on the education bill.[25]

In his votes in this last session Revels was with the administration in supporting a federal election law with penalties and for federal aid for steamship service to Mexico. He opposed, however, making public the proceedings of the committee on southern outrages.[26]

Thus came to a close the brief political career of the first Negro in the Senate. His term expired March 3, 1871, giving him a term of just a year and a week. Little could have been accomplished in such a short time even by a more able and experienced man. Revels was under handicaps that made his senatorial term futile. He was suddenly thrust into politics and knew in advance that his successor was already chosen. In fact he had been a name and a symbol of Negro representation rather than a real senator. Even his admirers felt that his position was abnormal and not likely to be repeated or continued. Negrophiles were glad that a precedent had been set in the Senate but admitted that his short senatorial career was ineffective. It is well known that it takes a year or more for a senator to "learn the ropes" around Washington and that a second term senator is more effective than a first termer even with upward of six years service. Hence they were not embarrassed to admit that Revels had accomplished little.

An editorial in the New York *Times* declared that Revels was competent to speak of the effect of legislation on race relations and the injury sometimes done the colored man by his overzealous advocates. Hence Revels discouraged mixed schools in the District of Columbia as the price of compulsory education. The Negro, said *The Times,* should be allowed to make his own way quietly and on his merits. "Give him fair play and do not make too much fuss about him."[27]

Revels gave an interview to the *National Republican* in which he expressed his views on various issues. In disagreement with Sumner, he favored the annexation of Santo Domingo. Revels declared that some Republican newspapers distorted facts and misquoted his speech on the school bill. The *National Republican* declared that Revels spoke with freedom and earnestness and with a degree of brilliancy that was not usually attributed to him. The colored people should be proud of their spokesman in the Senate, whose "modest and unassuming manner has commanded respect and consideration even of political opponents."[28]

A few days after his retirement Revels was interviewed by the *Independent*. He said he had been well treated by the administration. He had found George S. Boutwell, Secretary of the Treasury, especially kind. Under the cloak of friendship office seekers had besieged him for aid. Dodging as many as possible, Revels asserted he had turned a deaf ear to all except those who had treated his race honestly and fairly. After

[25] *Ibid.,* pp. 1059, 1060.
[26] *Ibid.,* pp. 1208, 1640, 1817.
[27] New York *Times,* February 11, 1871.
[28] *National Republican,* February 23, 1871.

his retirement Revels hoped to be a spokesman for his people throughout the nation.

Revels was in the prime of life and lived thirty years after his term ended, but his later career was in the realms of education and religion rather than in politics. The Negro was much in need of intelligent and sincere leadership in education and religion and Revels could qualify for such leadership. Serving as President of Alcorn College for Negroes at Rodney, Mississippi, Revels won the confidence of the whites and put the college on a substantial basis. Then he turned to religious and pastoral work of the African Methodist Episcopal Church and died in the actual performance of religious duties. When the end came at Holly Springs, Mississippi, January 16, 1901, his brief political service had almost been forgotten in the greater respect for his usefulness as a private citizen and churchman. Most white carpetbaggers left the South permanently when their political careers ended but Revels settled down as a resident and gave his best years in the South.[29]

Blanche K. Bruce, the other Negro senator, was born in Prince Edward County, Virginia, March 1, 1841. His mother was the slave of a wealthy planter. Nominally a body-servant, young Bruce was actually the pet of the plantation and suffered few of the hardships of slavery. Bruce was very light colored and the playmate and fellow student of his master's son. A private tutor taught the boys and Bruce took advantage of the opportunity and became well educated. He did as he liked, was free to come and go at his pleasure, and could have escaped at any time but did not care to. A few years before the Civil War started, he was carried to Missouri by his young master. In Brunswick, Missouri, he became a printer's devil but spent his spare time reading books and papers and laying the foundation of a good English education.[30]

When the war broke out in 1861, Bruce escaped to Hannibal, Missouri, and joined the Union Army. Instead of fighting, however, he organized the first school entirely for Negroes in the United States. Saving a little money, he entered Oberlin College and paid his expenses by sawing wood and other odd jobs. He did not graduate but returned to St. Louis and worked on a boat plying the Missouri River to Council Bluffs, Iowa. Later he went prospecting in Arkansas, Tennessee, and Mississippi. The political prospects looked good for a newcomer in Mississippi, so he settled there. A fellow carpetbagger, General Adelbert Ames, appointed him to conduct elections in Tallahatchie County and the Republican state senate made him its sergeant-at-arms. With such political support and by his own tact, shrewdness, and honesty, he obtained a number of appointive and elective offices. At various times he served as tax assessor and col-

---

[29] *Biographical Congressional Directory*, p. 950; S. D. Smith, *The Negro in Congress*, pp. 23-25.

[30] John Wesley Cromwell, *The Negro in American History; Men and Women Eminent in the Evolution of the American of African Descent* (Washington, 1914), p. 164; *Biographical Congressional Directory*, p. 507.

lector, as sheriff, member of the levee board, and county superintendent of schools. In spite of official duties he bought large tracts of land and made considerable money by raising cotton.[31]

These political jobs gave Bruce useful contacts with other politicians. This was especially true of his post with the legislature. Bruce also attended party conventions, local and state. At these meetings he became well known not only to the rank and file of the delegates but to the party leaders or "bosses" who had the influence that he needed. In these ways he established political alliances with Ames and Alcorn, two powerful white Republicans, and with John R. Lynch and James Hill, Negro Republican leaders. The alliance with Lynch and Hill was mutually helpful. John R. Lynch became a representative in Congress for three terms; Hill became secretary of state in Mississippi and federal internal revenue collector; and Bruce became a United States senator. This alliance gained control of the state party machinery. At nearly every Republican state convention Bruce or Lynch served as chairman with Hill as floor manager. Bruce became a professional politician and knew all the tricks of the trade.[32]

By 1872 Bruce had begun his campaign for the United States Senate. This was the year when party loyalty was put to the test by the Liberal Republican movement. Hill and Bruce were delegates to the Republican national convention at Philadelphia. They helped renominate President Grant and then returned home by way of Washington. They visited the Senate chamber and sat in the seats of Senators Ames and Alcorn. Hill asked Bruce if he would like to occupy the seat officially. When Bruce protested that it was out of the question, Hill replied: "I can and will put you there. No one can defeat you." Accepting Hill's offer of aid Bruce refused to accept any state office in 1873 in order to hold himself ready for the greater honor. He could have been lieutenant-governor or even governor as the Negroes furnished a very large majority of the Republican vote.[33]

When the legislature convened in January, 1874, Ames was not a candidate for reelection and it was said that he favored Bruce for the long senatorial term beginning March 4, 1875. In those years when elections of senators were sometimes long drawn out, it was the custom to start balloting long in advance of the beginning of the term. So the Republican caucus nominated Bruce on the second ballot by a vote of fifty-two to thirty-six for all others combined. On February 3, 1874, the General Assembly elected him by an overwhelming vote; he even secured some

---

[31] J. W. Cromwell, *The Negro in American History*, pp. 164-166; New York *Times*, March 18, 1898.
[32] J. R. Lynch, *The Facts of Reconstruction*, pp. 192, 193; John Roy Lynch to Samuel Denny Smith, December 14, 1928.
[33] J. R. Lynch, *Facts of Reconstruction*, p. 77; J. W. Cromwell, *The Negro in American History*, p. 166.

Democratic votes.[34] Bruce had a year before assuming his duties, during which he served as sheriff of Bolivar County. The Vicksburg *Times* gave prominence to a life sketch of the new celebrity. It declared that he had shown integrity, sound sense, and discretion in all the offices he had heretofore held. To remove the carpetbagger taint, it said that he had come to Mississippi in 1853 and lived in Marshall County.[35] A Democratic newspaper suggested that Bruce remain a bachelor. The paper understood that social life in Washington was important and that white women would object to association with a Negress. It was supposed that the Senate refusal to seat the Negro P. B. S. Pinchback[36] of Louisiana was the result of the opposition of wives of senators.

Ordinarily the new Congress to which Bruce was elected would not have met until December, 1875, but President Grant called a special session to meet in March to deal with the disturbed conditions in Louisiana. Bruce was present during this session lasting from March 5 to March 24. He was appointed to the committees on manufactures, pensions, and education and labor. He voted regular on every opportunity but made no remarks whatever, although thirty-three other members spoke at length on this troublous situation.[37]

Perhaps Bruce was suppressed by his initial experience in the Senate. He was in the first group of new senators called to the desk to be sworn in. By general custom the senior senator from a state escorts the junior member up but Senator Alcorn refused Bruce the usual courtesy because of a grudge against Ames, Bruce's sponsor. Bruce started up unattended but Senator Roscoe Conklin of New York volunteered to accompany him. Bruce was so grateful that he later named his only son Roscoe Conklin. The spectators in the galleries were most interested in picking out Andrew Johnson but next they wanted to see Bruce. What a contrast they presented! Tennessee was a border, doubtful state but had now sent a Democratic, white senator while Mississippi, a supposedly Democratic state, had sent a Negro Republican. In a way Bruce's presence seemed more unusual than Revels' had five years before. For by 1875 most carpetbag governments in the South had been overthrown and home-rule had been restored. In fact the House of Representatives was strongly Democratic. Possibly for these reasons Bruce was warmly welcomed by the Republican senators. The New York *Times* compared Bruce in appearance to King Kalakava of Hawaii. It said Bruce had a fine physique, intelligent features, and gentlemanly bearing.[38]

Bruce was present when the regular session convened in December although there was talk that Bruce, George E. Spencer, and Stephen W.

[34] Vicksburg *Times,* January 31, February 1, 4, 1874; Mobile *Register,* February 5, 1874; J. R. Lynch, *Facts of Reconstruction,* p. 77.
[35] Vicksburg *Times,* February 15, 1874.
[36] Natchez *Daily Democrat and Courier,* August 19, 1874.
[37] *Congressional Record, Spec. Sess. Sen.,* pp. 1, 8, 9.
[38] J. R. Lynch, *Facts of Reconstruction,* pp. 78-79; New York *Times,* March 6, 1875.

Dorsey, all carpetbaggers, would be expelled because of bribery in their elections. Nothing ever came of the charge; and there is no evidence that Bruce resorted to bribery. Of the seventy senators, only Timothy O. Howe, Henry L. Dawes, Simon Cameron, and Bruce had bouquets on their desks.[39] For over a month Bruce alone represented Mississippi for Alcorn remained at home until January 10, 1876; Bruce did not express himself on the floor and earned the name of "the silent senator." The only bill he introduced was one to pay bounties to colored soldiers, sailors, and their heirs. In spite of all the raids on the Treasury, this bill failed. Bruce presented two petitions which received no consideration.[40]

But Bruce did have the courage to talk in the party councils, and he gained favorable publicity thereby. He chose to make an issue of the Louisiana situation. Pinchback had again asked admission to the Senate but was again rejected. Bruce threatened that if Pinchback was not seated the Negroes should make terms with the old masters in the South. He said that if Grant and the Republicans did not care for the Negro support the latter should desert the Republican party. Bruce denounced Grant and his third term ambition and declared he would not support Grant if he were nominated. Grant invited Bruce to call on him but for a time Bruce refused to go. Party leaders were alarmed for they would need all the Negro vote in the coming presidential election. Finally Lynch joined Bruce and Pinchback in urging the Negro race not to divide on political issues. Bruce was too much a partisan to bolt, and in 1880 he was a member of the Grant bloc and stuck by him for thirty ballots.[41]

Pinchback's cause finally induced Bruce to make his first Senate speech after a year's membership. He contended that the Louisiana legislature was a legal one and therefore had a right to choose a senator. He argued that accepting Pinchback would clear up the situation for all concerned, and give to Louisiana the full representation she should have. He paid Pinchback a high tribute personally, as a father, husband, and citizen. Naturally Bruce voted to admit Pinchback but the resolution was lost.[42]

Later in the session Bruce made his first full length speech in the Senate. The election of 1875 in Mississippi had given the Democrats an overwhelming majority. That was the natural thing to expect since federal troops had been removed and since the white Democrats were well organized. A resolution to investigate the election was introduced in the Senate and Bruce found his tongue and his voice. His chances for re-election would vanish unless the Democratic trend were reversed. Bruce stated his reluctance to speak until more familiar with the routine and until he was better informed on public affairs, but silence at this time

---

[39] New Orleans *Times,* December 7, 1875; Philadelphia *Public Ledger,* December 7, 1875.
[40] *Congressional Record,* 44th Cong., 1st Sess., pp. 165, 308, 1871, 5138.
[41] New Orleans *Times,* February 11, 12, 13, 14, 1876; J. W. Cromwell, *The Negro in American History,* p. 170.
[42] *Congressional Record,* 44th Cong., 1st Sess., pp. 1444, 1445, 1558.

would be infidelity to his trust, an injustice to his people and state. He argued that free institutions were at stake in Mississippi because a Republican majority in 1873 of 20,000 had changed to a minority of 30,000 in 1875. The Negroes made up 95% of the Republican vote and nothing could have happened to change them, in a state with such limited means of communication. He thought fraud and intimidation were the only answers. Bruce quoted the Yazoo *Democrat* as saying: "Carry the election peaceably if we can, forcibly if we must." Such tactics had reduced a Republican majority in Yazoo County to a vote of seven. Most of the trouble he blamed on the White Leagues but failed to note the violence on his side or the incendiary remarks of the Radical newspapers. He traced the economic, moral, and social progress of the Negro for the past decade and urged that these gains be guaranteed by the United States. He said that a few Negroes would go into the profession, a few more would become mechanics, but the bulk of them would cultivate the soil in the South and they should be protected in their rights. He voted for the investigation and it carried.[43] In 1876 the Republicans at last proposed to clean their own house. The Senate was convened as a special court to try W. W. Belknap who had been impeached by the House for malfeasance in office. The trial lasted from April 5 to August 1 and every senator had a chance to express himself, but Bruce held his peace. His party loyalty would not allow him to denounce and it was difficult to defend Belknap. He contented himself with a partisan vote of "not guilty" on all five articles. A majority of senators voted guilty on every article but not the necessary two-thirds majority for conviction.[44]

The presidential campaign was already under way with Rutherford B. Hayes and William A. Wheeler as the Republican nominees. In spite of the rebellious talk of the year before, Bruce took an active part in the campaign in Mississippi and Louisiana. Many Republicans bolted on the reform issue; Bruce remained regular, but advised the Republicans against the use of violence.[45] When the short session of Congress met in December, Bruce was present and received the same committee assignments as in the preceding session. The November election was still in dispute and many senators were involved, but Bruce took no part in the controversy. He introduced a private bill and presented two petitions, none of which was acted upon. Discussing the "outrages" in Louisiana, Senator David M. Key denied that white men could have done the things alleged. Bruce interrupted without gaining the floor and asked if Key meant that Negroes then were guilty because the crimes were too atrocious for whites. Key denied the implication and said he meant only savages could have acted so. Bruce insisted he was surprised at such a reflection on a race that did not deserve censure. Key again said that Bruce was mistaken in taking

[43] *Ibid.*, pp. 2101, 2119.
[44] *Congressional Record, Spec. Impeachment Trial W. W. Belknap*, pp. 118-120.
[45] *National Republican*, October 11, 1876.

offense. This off-hand interchange was Bruce's only participation in the Senate debate from December to March.[46]

President Hayes called the Senate into special session the day after his inauguration. Bruce held over on his old committees but a select committee on levees of the Mississippi River was formed with Bruce as chairman. Serving under him were the veteran James G. Blaine, Simon B. Conover, a Florida carpetbagger, and two Southern Democrats, Francis M. Cockrell of Missouri and Isham G. Harris of Tennessee. This illustrates the partisanship of the committee system. Bruce deserted his party on the admission of L.Q.C. Lamar of Mississippi. There was some question of the legality of the Mississippi legislature that had elected Lamar and his seat was questioned. Bruce took no part in the discussion but in the end voted to seat Lamar which was done. In a way Bruce thus admitted the validity of the legislature whose election he had so sharply criticized a few months before. This inconsistency was a happy one for it led to goodwill between Bruce and Lamar which lasted until Lamar's death. On political issues they were usually far apart but they could at least be friendly enemies. At Lamar's death in 1893 Bruce paid a glowing tribute to Lamar and his fairness to the Negro race.[47]

During this session Bruce presented petitions from Negroes of Mississippi asking for an appropriation of $100,000 to aid them to emigrate to Liberia but they did not get it. He showed his timidity by passing up a chance to serve as chairman of the manufactures committee. Senator Newton Booth had resigned leaving Bruce the senior member and acting chairman. Bruce asked that Edward H. Rollins be made chairman and it was so ordered.[48]

In October Hayes called Congress into special session. The new House of Representatives was Democratic and intent on removing federal troops from state affairs and elections. This led to a long drawn out contest and little could be accomplished. Bruce took no part in the heated discussion. His sole contribution was to reply, when asked if he were paired with the senator from Florida: "He is not. He is paired with the senator from Alabama."[49] But he was always present to vote for administration measures. He voted against reducing the army; and for the admission of William P. Kellogg from Louisiana but to exclude Matthew C. Butler from South Carolina. Both were seated but Kellogg was to be the last carpetbag senator.[50]

When the regular session met in December, 1877, Bruce seems to have struck his stride at last and to have been more at ease on the floor. He introduced a number of pension bills that were passed and signed. He

---

[46] *Congressional Record*, 44th Cong., 2nd Sess., pp. 1, 46, 47, 679, 736, 1547, 264.
[47] Edward Mayes, *L.Q.C. Lamar, His Life, Times and Speeches* (Nashville, 1896), pp. 593, 594; *Congressional Record, 45th Congress, Spec. Sess. Senate*, pp. 1, 39, 15.
[48] Edward Mayes, *L.Q.C. Lamar*, pp. 364, 414, 423.
[49] *Congressional Record*, 45th Cong., 1st Sess., pp. 49, 50, 700.
[50] *Ibid.*, pp. 423, 712, 797.

62   THE JAMES SPRUNT STUDIES

also introduced bills to pay bounties to heirs of soldiers who were enlisted from slavery, and one to establish a national academy of education but they were defeated.[51] He presented three petitions on prohibition which received no consideration. Another petition asking for refund of the cotton tax to southern farmers gave Bruce a chance to speak briefly for his section.[52]

His more lengthy speeches were confined to racial matters. In January, 1878, the Senate held memorial exercises for Oliver P. Morton and Bruce made the longest address of his senatorial career up to that time. He placed Morton second only to Abraham Lincoln and Charles Sumner as a friend and a hero to the Negro. He admitted that Morton opposed Negro suffrage at first but later came to be a champion of fullest Negro rights.[53]

Again he spoke at length in favor of Ambrose E. Burnside's bill to recruit Negro soldiers on the same basis as whites and not as segregated Negro units. It had been the policy to have the Ninth and Tenth Cavalry, the Twenty-fourth and Twenty-fifth Infantry as units for all Negroes in the army. In the navy, naturally, no whole ships were assigned to Negroes but the crews were mixed. Bruce claimed that recruiting officers might turn down Negro applicants on such a basis but such action would be better than segregation. He thought it time for the Negro to paddle his own canoe, and to sink if unable to paddle it. No action was taken on the proposal. Senator Allen G. Thurman complained that Bruce spoke in such low tones that very little of his speech could be heard.[54]

When the final session convened in December, Bruce was on hand and served on the same regular and special committees as before. The New York *Times* noted that Bruce was surrounded by many friends at the opening of Congress as were the more noted leaders Blaine, Bayard, and Lamar.[55] Bruce as chairman of the levee committee reported a bill providing for correction, permanent location, deepening the channel, improvement of navigation and protection of alluvial lands along the Mississippi River. This would seem to include everything that could be desired but the Senate amended it, and the session ended before the House could concur.[56]

Near the end of this session Vice-President Wheeler was absent from the Senate and Bruce was called to the chair and presided for some time. It is common to pass this honor around to various members of the Senate but for a Negro to preside even temporarily over this august body was eventful. Bruce later spoke in opposition to a proposed restriction on Chinese immigration. Strong resentment against Orientals was sweeping the country and it was considered the patriotic stand to put an end to

[51] *Ibid.*, 45th Cong., 2nd Sess., pp. 1, 40, 3454, 4791.
[52] *Ibid.*, pp. 116, 1360, 1929, 2598.
[53] *Ibid.*, pp. 382, 383.
[54] *Ibid.*, pp. 2440, 2442.
[55] *Ibid.*, 45th Cong., 3rd Sess., p. 1, 12; New York *Times*, December 3, 1878.
[56] *Congressional Record*, 45th Cong., 3rd Sess., pp. 1045, 1055, 1114, 2315.

their admission. Yet Negroes were regarded in somewhat the same way. Should Bruce think then as an American or as a member of a minority race in America? He admitted the parallel between the two races and spoke against Chinese exclusion or restriction. He argued that since the Negro, who had been a citizen for only a few years had proven his worth, the Chinese should be given the same opportunity. The bill passed but was vetoed by the President.[57]

The Forty-sixth Congress was Democratic in both branches; hence Bruce belonged to the minority for three sessions, but he seemed to fare about as well as before. In spite of its Democratic majority, President Hayes called a special session of the new Congress in March, 1879. Bruce was a member of the same committees as of yore, but Lamar replaced him as chairman of the levee committee. Bruce later asked to be excused from membership on the levee and the pension committees. He gave no reason for the request but it was granted. Certainly there was no friction between Lamar and Bruce for Lamar later asked that Bruce be reappointed which was done.[58] Bruce asked for a special committee to be appointed on the Freedmen's Saving Bank. The committee was appointed, Bruce was chairman but three southern Democrats made up the majority. The committee was given authority to investigate the causes of the Bank's failure and to make a speedy adjustment of its affairs. Naturally Bruce had a special interest in the Bank since many Negroes had lost their savings by its failure.[59] A number of private claims and petitions were presented but none granted.[60]

While Bruce was absent from the Senate because of illness a bill had passed providing for a Mississippi River Commission to consider improvements on the river. On his return Bruce asked to record his vote. Such delayed voting was contrary to Senate rules but Lamar backed Bruce's request on the ground that Bruce had gone on record by his public expression of approval. Lamar had again showed a courtesy to his Negro colleague from Mississippi. While Bruce and Lamar agreed on this levee issue they were paired as opponents on many political questions and that pair was soon invoked twice. On use of troops at the polls and use of United States marshals and deputies, Bruce favored and Lamar opposed. On the latter occasion Lamar was absent and Bruce voted, forgetting the pair. He quickly discovered his mistake and was given permission to withdraw his own vote.[61]

In November, 1879, the Democrats of Mississippi again gained a sweeping majority in the legislature and Bruce knew that he was doomed. The new legislature in January, 1880, elected James Z. George to succeed Bruce by an almost unanimous vote.[62] The Jackson *Clarion* gave Bruce

[62] Jackson *Clarion*, November 19, 1879, January 28, 1880.
[57] *Ibid.*, pp. 1306, 1307, 1314, 1400.
[58] *Ibid.*, 46th Cong., 1st Sess., pp. 1, 15, 913.
[59] *Ibid.*, pp. 286, 1392, 1393.   [60] *Ibid.*, p. 1623.
[61] *Ibid.*, pp. 2103, 2226, 2227, 2437.

a left-handed compliment by saying that he had been as fair and impartial a representative of the Negroes and Republicans as could be found in the South. "If he has done no good, he has done no harm. . . . One thing we can say about Bruce, he was always there to answer roll call."[63]

Bruce attended the session of Congress of December, 1879, and introduced bills, petitions, and claims galore. Most of these were private or unimportant but some had a wide significance. Several pertained to education of the colored race, some to clearing up assets of the Freedmen's Bank, and one had international implications—that pertaining to the distribution of money under the Geneva Award for the Alabama Claims. Bruce was unable to pilot any of these through but did show his growing interest.

In the latter part of the session Bruce made three full speeches on widely differing issues. There had been a great exodus of Negroes from the South to Kansas and the Mid-West. There was a division among Negro leaders as to the wisdom of the exodus but none could deny that the refugees were in distress. Bruce did not argue whether they should have gone but insisted that they were starving and should be helped in every way possible. He pointed out that the English were sending aid and favored admitting the goods free of duty.[64]

In discussing a new agreement with the Ute Indians, Bruce insisted that the previous policy had been one of selfishness with few honorable exceptions. He supported the proposal to divide lands among the Utes on the ground that it would make them permanent settlers instead of nomads and that the Indians would settle down to civilized ways of living.[65] Two days later, Bruce had occasion to say that the whites themselves needed more civilization and Christianization. This was called forth by the report of a Negro cadet at West Point who had been mutilated. Bruce urged an investigation. He expressed the view that, under the circumstances, an appointment of a Negro to West Point would be the severest punishment he could think of to inflict on his bitterest enemy. Senator George F. Hoar argued that the act was only an incident in cadet hazing and was to be preferred to the usual ostracism of Negro cadets.[66]

Bruce had the honor of presiding over this Democratic Senate on one occasion, but it must have been uncomfortable duty since George G. Vest of Missouri had the floor and was bitterly assailing Kellogg and the Republican party in general.[67]

Bruce's career in the last session from December, 1880, to March, 1881, was an anti-climax. Serving on the same committees, he appeared to be more interested in freedmen's affairs than in anything pertaining to his state or nation. He sponsored only a few minor bills and petitions all of

[63] *Ibid.*, February 4, 1880.
[64] *Congressional Record*, 46 Cong., 2 Sess., pp. 124, 338, 693, 836.
[65] *Ibid.*, p. 1042.
[66] *Ibid.*, pp. 2195, 2196, 2249.
[67] *Ibid.*, pp. 2971, 2972.

which were fruitless. The only success that he had was in securing some discarded Senate furniture for a Home for Colored Women and Children.[68] He took no part in the Senate debates of this session.

Bruce had determined not to go back to Mississippi to live and would not need to give an account of his stewardship. He was assured of an appointive federal job, and so he need not worry about the future. He was supposed, however, to represent a sovereign state; instead he had acted as if he represented only the Negroes and the Republican party. The experience of Bruce and Revels had shown that it was difficult for a black man with limited training and preparation to win success in the Senate made up of unsympathetic whites. He may serve acceptably, however, in an elective capacity from a small constituency or in an administrative office where he was independent of the goodwill and votes of antagonistic whites.

After the close of his senatorial career, Bruce served as Register of the Treasury from 1881 to 1885; recorder of deeds for the District of Columbia, 1891-1893, and again 1897 until his death March 17, 1898. In these positions he gave general satisfaction. He was mentioned as a possible candidate for the vice-presidency, and for an appointment to a cabinet or diplomatic position. He held a high place in the party councils in the nation. He was a delegate to every national Republican convention from 1868 to 1896, and as temporary chairman presided over the 1880 convention.[69]

In conclusion it may be said that the role played by the two Negroes in the Senate was a minor and ineffective one. Both were handicapped by lack of training and experience and by opposition of the whites. They served for the most part with white colleagues who tolerated them but who were hostile to Negro participation in politics. And Revels and Bruce too often emphasized racial matters and exaggerated their importance.

It seems appropriate to mention a few Negroes who aspired to the Senate and had varying degrees of support but were not elected. The outstanding figure in this group was Pinckney Benton Stewart Pinchback. The son of a wealthy man, Pinchback was well educated. He entered politics in Louisiana at the end of the Civil War and received many honors before trying for the United States Senate. January 15, 1873, the Louisiana legislature elected him to the Senate for the six year term beginning on March 4. He was not admitted but filed a contest. This was carried over until 1875. In the meantime the legislature had reelected him on January 13, 1875. On March 8, 1876, he was finally rejected by a vote of thirty-two to twenty-nine. The Republican leaders wanted to go before the country in 1876 on a reform platform. There was much doubt of the legality of the legislature that had elected Pinchback; hence the Senate

[68] *Ibid.,* 46th Cong., 3rd Sess., pp. 1, 14, 15, 146, 477, 668, 836.
[69] *Biographical Congressional Directory,* p. 507; New York *Times,* January 20, 1881, March 18, 1898.

Republicans rejected Pinchback. He remained influential in Louisiana, but never again tried for the Senate.[70]

When the Louisiana legislature met in December, 1876, it elected another Negro to fill out a short term in the Senate. James Lewis, a colonel in the state militia, was given this honor. Since the Democrats regained control of the southern states as a result of the compromise worked out in the disputed presidential election Lewis did not press his claim on the Senate.[71]

Mississippi, having furnished two Negro senators, had another candidate for the honor. In 1870, James J. Spelman, a Negro member of the legislature, received several votes on each ballot before Revels was elected. Spelman was a carpetbagger from Connecticut who had been in Mississippi only two years. He was obscure and little is known of him before or afterward.[72]

The last member of this aspiring group and probably the ablest was Robert Brown Elliott, of South Carolina. By the end of 1872 he had already served a term in the House of Representatives but thought he saw a chance to rise higher. When the South Carolina legislature met December 10, 1872, to elect a senator there were three candidates from whom to pick: Elliott, the leading Negro politician of the state; Robert K. Scott, the retiring carpetbagger governor; and John James Patterson, a carpetbagger who had plenty of money. Patterson was elected with ninety votes; Elliott received thirty-three, and Scott seven votes. Elliott charged that the Negro legislators had been bribed by the wholesale and implied that Patterson himself had been guilty of bribery.[73]

Since 1880, no Negro has received even slight backing for the Senate. It is easy to see that the abnormal conditions of Reconstruction were responsible for the election of both Revels and Bruce. Suffrage restrictions, political shifts of the post Reconstruction years, and southern white attitudes will prevent the election of a Negro to the Senate, at least from the South, in the foreseeable future. The chief result of the election of Revels and Bruce in the 1870's was to arouse the anger and hostility of the whites, and few benefits accrued to the Negroes from the experiment.

[70] W. J. Simmons, *Men of Mark*, pp. 759-775; New York *Times*, October 12, 1888.
[71] W. J. Simmons, *Men of Mark*, p. 956.
[72] *Ibid.*, p. 928.
[73] Mobile *Register*, October 27, 1872, February 14, 1873; S. D. Smith, *The Negro in Congress*, pp. 54, 137.

V

PUBLIC EDUCATION IN NORTH CAROLINA DURING RECONSTRUCTION, 1865-1876

Daniel Jay Whitener

Three quarters of a century have passed since Calvin H. Wiley sat in his office of General Superintendent of Common Schools at Raleigh and heard the fateful news that General Joseph E. Johnston had surrendered to General William T. Sherman. With this collapse of armed resistance, the agencies of the state government ceased to function in North Carolina. During the next ten years the attempts to reestablish an acceptable state government were so inextricably bound up with the elemental passions and basic hopes of the people that this decade is one of surpassing interest. No phase of that history was more closely identified with those passions and hopes than was public education.

The two fundamental educational issues that dominated the Reconstruction era were education of the freedmen and financial support of public schools. Without a crushing military defeat, staggering debts, exhaustive poverty, and burning passions, either of these issues would have taxed to the limit the fortitude of even the most resolute statesman. All of them in combination might be expected to produce an almost insoluble social and economic tangle.

The history of education during Reconstruction in North Carolina began on October 2, 1865, when, at the command of President Andrew Johnson, a convention for the purpose of reestablishing constitutional government assembled at Raleigh.[1] After declaring the ordinance of secession null and void, the convention adopted three ordinances that affected the common schools. It repudiated the Civil War debt, ratified the Thirteenth Amendment, and declared vacant all state offices in existence April 26, 1865, whose incumbents had taken the oath of allegiance to the Confederacy.

The ante-bellum common school system was built around an endowment, called the Literary Fund,[2] of about $3,000,000 invested in the stocks of state banks, internal improvement projects, and in state bonds. From the income of this fund the common schools received about half their operating expenses; the other half came from local county taxes. Efforts during the war to use this money for military purposes generally failed;

---

[1] Joseph Gregoire deRoulhac Hamilton, *Reconstruction in North Carolina* (Raleigh, 1906), p. 120; *Records of the North Carolina State Convention of 1865* (Raleigh, 1865).
[2] Edgar Wallace Knight, *The Public School in North Carolina* (Boston, 1916), pp. 84-104; Marcus Cicero Stephens Noble, *The Public Schools of North Carolina* (Chapel Hill, 1930), pp. 97-123; Charles Lee Coon, *Public Education in North Carolina; A Documentary History, 1790-1840*, 2 volumes (Raleigh, 1915), I, 279.

only about $650,000 had, at one time or another, been invested in state bonds.[3]

Repudiation of the Civil War debt wrecked the Literary Fund and left the common schools without adequate state aid. By this action the banks and other enterprises in which the school fund was invested were bankrupt since they had invested heavily in Confederate securities. Later some of these assets were liquidated, but the amount salvaged was far too small to finance public education. Indeed, in 1866 the total income from what remained of the fund was only about $776.[4]

By the ratification of the Thirteenth Amendment, legalizing what in fact had already been accomplished by the triumph of the Union armies, the problem of the social status of the freedmen was thrust upon the state. Before the war a law made the teaching of a slave to read and write a crime.[5] While the Negro now had his freedom, which carried with it a tacit admission that he would need an education, his status in society was by no means established. Among prominent statesmen there were those who would destroy all the public schools lest the freedmen be given admittance.

The action of the convention, by ordinance, declaring vacant all the state offices in existence April 26, 1865, left the schools without a state superintendent. For some reason Wiley had never taken the oath to support the Confederacy and he now denied that the ordinance applied to him.[6] During the next six months, until the legislature in 1866 abolished the office, Wiley's official status was confused. Although William Woods Holden, the provisional governor, refused to recognize him,[7] the governor did not appoint another to fill the office. Governor Jonathan Worth likewise denied official recognition to Wiley and his repeated requests for salary.[8] In 1866 the legislature accepted his report, ordered it printed, but refused to recognize his claims.[9]

During the month following the adjournment of the convention, little or nothing regarding education was done, interest being centered on a general election and the organization of a government. Not until the special session of the legislature, which met January 18, 1866, did the subject of public schools receive state-wide attention. Here and there, however,

[3] *Report of the Literary Board, Public Documents (1866-1867)*, No. 18; E. W. Knight, *Public Schools*, p. 104.
[4] E. W. Knight, *Public Schools*, p. 104.
[5] M. C. S. Noble, *Public Schools*, p. 265.
[6] *Records of the North Carolina State Convention of 1865*, p. 63.
[7] J. G. deR. Hamilton (ed.), *Correspondence of Jonathan Worth*, 2 volumes (Raleigh, 1909), I, 512.
[8] MSS. in Board of Literary Fund Receipts, 1862-1872; J. G. deR. Hamilton, *Correspondence of Worth*, I, 522, Letter from Worth to Wiley, March 31, 1866.
[9] J. G. deR. Hamilton, *Reconstruction in North Carolina*, p. 610. Wiley appealed to the governor, to the attorney general, to the courts, and to the legislature without avail.

local subscription schools were being organized, but tax-supported schools were nonexistent.[10]

Governor Worth's message to the General Assembly expressed the noble sentiment that "Whatever may be our pecuniary distresses, our youth must be educated."[11] Newspapers of that time and even historians of the period erroneously interpreted this statement as an endorsement of the movement to reopen the public schools.[12] On the other hand, Worth was planning, along with others, a program of private education and the closing temporarily of the common schools.[13]

Worth submitted to the legislature, with the recommendation that it receive careful consideration, the last report of Wiley, who was characterized as an "able and indefatigable Superintendent of Public Schools." Wiley's report was chiefly an appeal on behalf of the common schools of the state. Differing from the privately expressed opinion of Worth, Wiley boldly challenged the legislature to take steps immediately to reopen the schools.[14] Facing courageously the problem of school revenue, he estimated that about $880,000 would be salvaged from the Literary Fund. This amount, recommended Wiley, should be divided into four equal parts and distributed one part each year to the counties on the basis of schools actually taught. Such a policy would eliminate the necessity of levying taxes and would stimulate backward districts to open schools which otherwise might not be opened. Although the remainder of the principal would be used, Wiley believed that an endowment fund for public education was an outmoded practice and that revenue from taxes would be much more desirable. "If for instance," said Wiley, "there were 2500 schools taught and $180,000 distributed, (the average distribution before the war), it will give to each school $72.00 and this a considerably larger sum than the former average amount paid each district."[15] Two plans for converting the stocks belonging to the Literary Fund were recommended.[16]

[10] *Carolina Watchman*, February 5, 1866; Salisbury *Banner* quoted in *Carolina Watchman*, January 29, 1866. "At present there is no such thing in the State as a free school house."
[11] *Legislative Documents (1865-1866)*, Doc. 7, p. 14.
[12] Raleigh *Sentinel*, January 29, February 19, March 1, 1866.
[13] In a private letter addressed to William A. Graham, January 12, 1866, just seven days before this message was delivered, Worth wrote: "I have no confidence that the condition of our negroes will be elevated by emancipation—but in our present condition I fear we shall have a Freedmen's Bureau and military rule over us, if we make discrimination—as admittance in Common Schools. I mean if we educate the negroes in like manner—and your school fund being reduced to nothing and our people impoverished, *I think the Com. School system had better be discouraged for a time, and thus avoid the question as to educating the negroes.*" (Italics mine.) J. G. deR. Hamilton, *Correspondence of Jonathan Worth*, I, 467.
[14] *Report of the Superintendent of Public Instruction, 1865-1866.*
[15] *Ibid.*, p. 30.
[16] "The *first* plan is to issue certificates of indebtedness, in sums convenient for general circulation, bearing 1 *per cent* interest, receivable for all State dues, and to be redeemed in four, five, or six years. The *second* is to convert the stocks of the fund into national securities, and establish a national bank, under the management of the Literary Board." *Ibid.*, p. 34.

Unfortunately for the children, the legislature submitted to the private counsel of such men as Governor Worth and disregarded the advice of Wiley and most of the newspapers. The Raleigh *Sentinel,* in close touch with the political leaders and familiar with their plans for the school system, uneasily exlaimed, "We hope no one entertains the idea of giving them up or allowing them to languish."[17] As subsequent events proved, this hope was forlorn. Despite all efforts to the contrary, those opposed to public schools not only refused to agree to any plan that embraced moderate financial support, but even destroyed the system by striking at its organization.

Early in March a law abolishing the offices of superintendent of common schools and the treasurer of the Literary Fund was enacted.[18] The resources of the Literary Fund were to be deposited in the public treasury. But the law did not stop with these backward steps; it destroyed even in the face of the loss of the state funds the responsibility of the county to furnish part of the school revenue. By clothing the county court with power to levy and collect taxes "at their discretion," for the support and maintenance of common schools in their respective counties, it left the public schools without prospects of county taxes. The legislature, anticipating that the five members on the county board of superintendents would now have little to do, reduced their number to one. Indicating the nature of the schools contemplated, the law authorized discretionary taxes for aid to subscription schools and empowered the district committees to permit the public schoolhouses to be used.

The motives that prompted this wanton destruction of the public system were doubtless mixed. In both houses of the General Assembly the chief argument centered around the very obvious circumstances that the people were unwilling and unable to pay taxes for public education.[19] Generally speaking, the House, being a better test of public sentiment among the average income group, showed more willingness to appropriate money for education than did the Senate. Bills were introduced in the popular branch appropriating from $50,000 to $200,000, and several of these bills were actually adopted by small majorities.[20]

The second motive for this backward step was the fear that the Freed-

[17] January 29, 1866; see also Salisbury *Banner* in *Carolina Watchman,* January 29, 1866, which advocated selling the state railroad property for the benefit of the education fund.
[18] *Public Laws of North Carolina* (1865-1866), Ch. 34, p. 87.
[19] For debates in the House see the *Daily Standard,* March 7, 8, 12, 1866, and the Raleigh *Sentinel,* March 3, 1866; for debates in the Senate see *Sentinel,* March 1, 1866, and *Daily Standard,* March 10, 1866.
[20] "A bill for the benefit of common schools of the state, reported from committee on education (the substitution *adopted*), proposes to issue for the benefit of schools $200,000 worth of certificates of indebtedness, yearly for two years, redeemable in 6 per cent bonds of the State, or in the National Currency," *Sentinel,* March 3, 1866. For other bills see the *Daily Standard,* March 8, 1866; *House Journal* (1866), p. 211; MSS in Legislative Papers, 1865-1866.

men's Bureau backed by the power of the Union army might force colored children into the public schools.[21]

Although not publicized so much as the issue of taxation, the possibility of mixed schools doubtless more than any other reason convinced even the friends of the public schools that a temporary suspension of the system was a policy of discretion. Secondary motives were hostility to the principle of public education and to Wiley personally.[22] Neither of these was the decisive factor. Two days after the passage of the destructive school legislation, in a resolution unanimously approved, the General Assembly praised Wiley for his great services in behalf of the children and tendered to him the thanks of the people of North Carolina.[23]

During the summer of 1866, the public was unconcerned about schools. Yet when fall passed into winter without the customary common schools, there arose in some sections of the state "Considerable Complaint . . . against the last Legislature for its course upon this subject."[24] In the fall campaign James F. Craige, announcing himself for the Senate, advocated the confiscation of property over $20,000 to be applied "to the soldiers and orphan children of Confederate dead . . . and that the latter may be educated."[25] Less radical individuals and many conservatives, including Wiley, never ceased to urge the reestablishment of public schools.[26]

When the General Assembly met in 1867, a resolution to instruct the finance committee to levy a tax of $200,000 "to be applied to the resusci-

[21] J. G. deR. Hamilton, *Correspondence of Jonathan Worth*, I, 467. During the debate in the Senate "Mr. Covington thought the people could not sustain them at present, moreover, under existing circumstances, the Freedmen's Bureau might force colored children into them, to which our people would never consent. For the present, therefore, he was in favor of abolishing the offices and suspending the system temporarily." *Sentinel*, March 1, 1866.
[22] During the debates in the House McAden denounced Wiley, saying: "He had been of no use on God Almighty's earth and the State was unable to pay such a salary to a man who merely wrote long essays, and drew interminable bills." *Daily Standard*, March 12, 1866. Earlier, in the Senate, Carter of Beaufort County attacked Wiley, claiming that "an officer who had made such a report as the present incumbent had done, upon the swamp lands of the State should be dismissed." *Sentinel*, March 1, 1866. The editor of the *Sentinel* denounced the senators for their criticism and praised Wiley. Indeed, all the criticisms of Wiley were quickly and effectively answered.
[23] "Resolved: that the gratitude of the people of North Carolina is eminently due to the Reverend C. H. Wiley," for services rendered to the common schools; "Resolved: that he is hereby tendered the thanks of the people of the State by this General Assembly, and the assurance that the discontinuance of the office of General Superintendent of Common Schools was not prompted by any want of appreciation of his public service, but by the present inability of the State to keep up the common school system." *Public Laws of North Carolina* (1865-1866), p. 151; M. C. S. Noble, *Public Schools of North Carolina*, pp. 280-281.
[24] *Sentinel*, November 13, 1866. "We are pleased to see that the discontinuance of our public or common schools, creates very general anxiety for their renewal." *Ibid.*, January 31, 1867.
[25] Hillsboro *Recorder* quoted in the *Sentinel*, August 17, 1866. The latter denounced such a policy as agrarianism, being a "ridiculous and demoralizing proposition . . . short of highway robbery."
[26] J. G. deR. Hamilton, *Correspondence of Jonathan Worth*, II, 833; *Sentinel*, January 25, 29, November 13 1866; *Weekly Standard*, October 30, 1867.

tation of the common Schools" was introduced in the Senate.[27] This proposal was a bold attempt to head off any real aid to public schools by the clever device of mobilizing against them the economic interests upon which the tax would fall. After some delay the whole project was ordered to lie on the table, from whence it was not recalled.[28] Yet so strong was sentiment for public education that the legislature did not dare ignore it entirely. Two laws, one of which touched the issues of taxation, were enacted.

Incorporated towns were empowered to hold special tax elections with reference to the establishment of municipal schools.[29] Approved by a favorable vote funds from the town treasury and from a special poll tax of not more than $2.00 could be used to finance a city school.[30] The second law was a puny gesture to reestablish the county organization destroyed in 1866. Called an act to protect certain interests of the common schools, it authorized the county court to appoint not more than five nor less than three county superintendents.[31] Since many of the public school buildings were being destroyed by lack of adequate protection or were being used by tenant farmers, white and black, the powers of the school committees were more specific; they empowered the committees to protect the schoolhouses. On the crucial subject of county taxes for education, the law was stolidly silent.[32]

Even before these laws were enacted the movement of events cast their shadows before them. Early in March, Congress enacted the Reconstruction acts, thus beginning the "Tragic Era." During the remainder of 1867, the issue of public education assumed progressively a political standing. The Republican leaders, heartened by the enfranchisement of the Negroes, began to lay plans to seize control. In the fall campaign they boldly appealed to class prejudice, charging that the Conservatives (former Democrats) were hostile to the economic welfare and educational improvement of poor people, white and black.[33] Many of the Republican county conventions in November adopted resolutions on education, calling for "a liberal system of free schools for the benefit of all" to be supported by an *ad valorem* tax.[34] Stunned by the enfranchisement of the Negroes and by the impending events, the Conservatives said little or nothing about public education.

[27] *Senate Journal* (1866-1867), p. 212; *Sentinel,* January 31, 1867.
[28] *Senate Journal* (1866-1867), pp. 240, 323.
[29] *Public Laws of North Carolina* (1866-1867), Ch. 14, p. 17.
[30] Raleigh *Sentinel,* January 2, 1867; *Senate Journal* (1867), p. 364. With a "local or municipal school," the issue of mixed schools could be avoided.
[31] *Public Laws of North Carolina* (1866-1867), Ch. 15, p. 21.
[32] The opinion expressed later, that these laws show a changed attitude toward public education and that this conservative leadership would have quickly launched a system of public schools based on taxation, has little foundation in fact.
[33] *Weekly North Carolina Standard,* October 30, 1867; Wilmington *Post* quoted in *ibid.,* December 4, 1867.
[34] *Weekly North Carolina Standard,* October 30, November 20, December 4, 1867.

EDUCATION OF THE FREEDMEN

Emancipation freed about 100,000 Negro children of school age in North Carolina who were almost totally illiterate. For four years after the close of the war, until the school law of 1869 went into operation, they were without any state or local tax-supported public schools. During this time the only legislation that dealt with the former slaves was an act to extend to the blacks the provision of the apprenticeship law which required the master to teach the child to read and write.[35]

As has already been pointed out, one of the primary reasons for the destruction in 1866 of the public school system was the fear that Negroes might be granted admittance. Some Conservative leaders contended that they approved of education for Negroes, and doubtless to a degree they were sincere, but the great majority of the white people regarded education for Negroes as useless if not positively harmful.[36] Probably the most commonly held attitude on the subject was expressed by William A. Graham in a letter and W. W. Holden in person to the Negroes assembled in an educational convention held in Greensboro, 1866; they advised the Negroes first to get homes and work for themselves and then to provide education for their children.[37]

Faced with the growing determination of the North to give more extensive privileges to the freedmen, the Conservatives, gradually became more friendly to the idea of education for Negroes. In their press they even began to write about a plan.[38] Upon one point the Conservatives agreed: if the Negroes wanted schools they would have to pay for them.

In the absence of tax-supported schools, two agencies, northern benevolent societies and the Freedmen's Bureau, closely cooperating and often pooling their efforts, worked to instruct the Negroes. Coming in the wake of the Union army, the American Missionary Association and the American Union Freedmen's Commission were the first and most important benevolent organizations to open schools during this period.[39] Next in importance were the Friends' schools. In 1869 these and other groups were teaching 11,826 colored children enrolled in 152 schools taught by

[35] *Public Laws of North Carolina* (1865-1866), Ch. 4, p. 100.
[36] J. G. deR. Hamilton, *Correspondence of Jonathan Worth*, I, 467. "I have no confidence that the condition of our negroes will be elevated by emancipation," Letter to William A. Graham, January 12, 1866; *Standard*, September 28, 1869.
[37] *Tri-Weekly Standard*, October 11, 1866; see also *Sentinel*, January 29, June 9, October 4, 6, 23, 1866; *Weekly Standard*, July 11, October 10, 17, 1866.
[38] In a letter to Lydia Maxwell, January 15, 1867, Governor Worth wrote: "I desire that they (negroes) be educated." *Ibid.*, II, 874; see also *Sentinel*, January 31, 1867, quoting the Wilmington *Journal* for a discussion of a plan; *Sentinel*, June 9, 1866, editorial, "Shall the Freedmen be Educated?"; *Carolina Watchman*, March 5, 1866, editorial, "Who are to Educate the Blacks?"
[39] *Report of North Carolina Superintendent of Public Instruction* (1869), p. 17.

224 teachers.[40] The total amount of money spent and the number of pupils taught for the period are not available.

The Freedmen's Bureau, an official agency of the government of the United States, was also actively engaged in the promotion of education among the Negroes. In 1865, with 63 schools and 85 teachers, about 5,624 pupils were receiving instruction. In 1869, the year the agency was abolished, the Freedmen's Bureau operated 431 schools, employed 437 teachers, and enrolled more than 20,200 Negro children.[41] These schools were widely distributed. In 1867 schools had been established in two-thirds of the counties, and plans were made to organize one or more in each of the remaining counties.[42] The Reverend F. A. Fiske, Negro superintendent of the Bureau's educational work, announced that $350 had been set apart for repairing or the erection of suitable schoolhouses for each county that did not have a school.[43]

At the outset many of these "missionary" schools were absolutely free, including food, clothing, and books.[44] The great majority of the teachers were young women from the North, who, with more courage than experience, had excitedly enlisted in this "second" war against ignorance. Perhaps no group of teachers ever labored more unselfishly; none was ever less appreciated by the white people.[45] Chiefly because of the willingness of these "school marms," as they were called, to mingle on terms of social equality with the Negroes, they were almost universally excluded from white society. Everywhere the practice of "let them alone" pre-

[40] Summary of these efforts:

	Schools	Teachers	Pupils
Under A. M. A. and Freedmen's Commission	19	68	2,840
Under Friends' Society	29	40	2,425
Under Episcopalian Commission	6	11	600
In Presbyterian Schools	16	21	1,100
In Private Schools	82	84	4,861
Total	152	224	11,826

Ibid., p. 25. The practice of these agencies and the Freedmen's Bureau of pooling their efforts led to both claiming credit for the schools taught.

[41] United States Executive Documents, 42 Cong., 2d Sess., No. 1, p. 653. For an excellent summary article see: J. G. deR. Hamilton's "The Freedmen's Bureau in North Carolina," South Atlantic Quarterly, VIII (1909), 154.

SUMMARY

Time	Schools	Teachers	Pupils
October 1, 1865	63	85	5,624
January 1, 1866	88	119	5,506
April 1, 1866	119	154	11,314
October 1, 1866	62	68	3,493
March 1, 1867	156	173	11,102
April 1, 1868	336	339	16,435
July 1, 1869	431	439	20,227

[42] Weekly North Carolina Standard, November 10, 1867.

[43] Raleigh Register, October 22, 1867.

[44] Public Documents (1870-1871), Doc. No. 6 (Report of the Rev. J. W. Hood, agent of the Board of Education), p. 270.

[45] Sentinel, June 19, October 23, 1866. "There was a yell and a howl over the Northern men and women who came South, with the termination of the war, to lend a helping hand in the education of the freedmen's children. The school system fostered by the Government, under the care of the Freedmen's Bureau, was inaugurated in opposition to the great mass of the whites, who, by education, were opposed to education for the blacks." Standard, September 28, 1869.

vailed. That the Negroes received these teachers and their schools with enthusiasm, no one would question.[46]

The educational results of these agencies would be difficult to evaluate. Many Negroes who otherwise would have remained illiterate were taught to read and write. Yet if education was primarily a process of adaptation, then the results were almost wholly harmful. Around these schools the docile Negroes, through no fault of theirs, were organized to perpetuate in Congress a party bent upon exploitation and political and economic domination. Consequently these schools quickly became political party agencies, sowed seeds of racial hatred and fanned an unattainable and unwarrantable ambition for immediate social equality. Not the least of the causes for the stubborn refusal of the property holders during the next three decades to accept the handiwork of the Republican leaders in behalf of "a general and uniform system of public schools," as outlined in the Constitution of 1868, was the evil doctrines taught and the unconventional conduct practiced by the northern school teachers who fired with missionary zeal, were unwittingly the tools for the political party in power.

The Constitutional Convention of 1868

The Constitutional Convention met in Raleigh, January 14, 1868, composed of 120 delegates, all of whom were members of the Republican party except 13 Conservatives. Eighteen of the 107 Republicans were "carpetbaggers" or men who following the close of the war had moved from the North to the South, and 15 were Negroes. No convention in North Carolina ever assembled amidst so much bitterness and ill will.[47] Early the committee on education, which numbered eleven Republicans, with the Reverend S. S. Ashley, a carpetbagger, as chairman, and two Conservatives, was appointed.[48] On March 6, the committee's report called Article IX, signed by only the Republican members, was debated.[49]

The chief disagreement on the Article centered around the issue of separate schools for the white and Negro children. As recommended by the majority, it did not, unfortunately, authorize the establishment of separate schools; neither did it command mixed schools. Silence on the race issue, the Conservatives charged, meant that the Republicans were plotting to force children of the two races into the same schools.

Efforts repeatedly made by the Conservatives to add an amendment that would authorize separate schools were successively and overwhelm-

[46] Raleigh *Register,* October 11, 25, 1867; *Weekly North Carolina Standard,* December 18, 1867.
[47] Conservative newspapers, January-March, 1868—*Sentinel, Carolina Watchman,* and *Morning Star.*
[48] *Journal of the Constitutional Convention of 1868,* p. 44; *Sentinel,* January 21, 1868.
[49] *Journal of the Constitutional Convention of 1868,* p. 341. The Republican members who signed the majority report were: The Reverend S. S. Ashley, chairman, W. T. J. Hayes, Jno. Read, J. W. Hood, G. William Walker, William T. Blume, A. W. Fisher, W. H. Logan, Allen Rose, John R. French, and W. H. S. Sweet. The Conservatives who did not sign were J. R. Ellis and John W. Graham.

ingly killed.[50] The Republican majority was determined to keep out of the constitution any reference to color or race that might be interpreted as a discrimination against the Negroes, all of whom were Republicans. No earlier constitution of North Carolina, they said, had provided for separate schools, although free Negroes within the state before the war had never attended the common schools. This issue was primarily a local problem, and, they argued, the constitution correctly placed the whole matter in the hands of the county officials. If the local communities wanted to follow a practice agreeable to them the constitution should respect, not thwart, their wishes. But, pointed out the Conservatives, in a number of eastern counties where a majority of the voters were freedmen, the Negroes would force the white children into the mixed, or into private schools. Thereupon a Negro member declared this would never happen because his race, too, wanted separate schools. Then, as the debate continued, the Republicans shifted to the more tenable position that the Article really left the issue in the hands of the General Assembly, where the white people would always have a majority.[51]

At least three elements within the Republican party accounted for its refusal to agree to a proscription against mixed schools. The carpetbaggers, most of whom were sincere, believed that such schools should be established. Just as determined were the native white Republicans, the great majority of whom would not tolerate such a plan. In between were the Negroes, who were usually suspicious of both groups, because each tried to control their votes to the disadvantage of the other. One fact was recognized by all—white Republican voters, along with Conservatives, were unalterably opposed to mixed schools. Thus, the Republican spokesmen individually declared, as did the Conservatives, that they were committed to separate schools. Consequently, near the close of the convention a resolution declaring that "the interests and happiness of the two races would be best promoted by the establishment of separate schools" was adopted.[52] Disregarding the sincerity of this Republican statement of policy, which was in no way a part of the constitution, the Conservatives, sensing the lack of unity, declared that the resolution was an admission of the inevitability of mixed schools and hastened to lay plans to carry the issue to the voters. The Republicans strove unsuccessfully to keep the issue out of the campaign for ratification.[53]

Except for the unwise and mischief-breeding omission of a clause definitely authorizing separate schools, Article IX had many excellent features. In organization the school system was superior to that of the

[50] *Journal of the Constitutional Convention of 1868,* pp. 338, 342, 343; *Sentinel,* March 7, 1868. Plato Durham, Conservative, offered an amendment: "The general assembly shall provide separate and distinct schools, for the black children of the state, from those provided for the white children." John W. Graham unsuccessfully offered a similar amendment.
[51] *Standard,* March 7, 1868; see also *Sentinel,* July 17, 1868.
[52] *Journal of the Constitutional Convention of 1868,* p. 473.
[53] Closely connected with mixed schools was the issue of compulsory attendance.

ante-bellum period. The General Assembly in its first session was commanded to "provide by taxation or otherwise for a general and uniform system of public schools, wherein tuition shall be free of charge to all the children of the State between the ages of six and twenty-one years."[54] A state board of education was created to take over the powers of the old Literary Board, and the office of state superintendent was reestablished.[55] With the county commissioners invested with control over local taxes, the county was to be divided into districts and one or more schools taught in each district for a period of four months each year. To implement the responsibility of the county, should the commissioners fail to levy a tax sufficiently large to run the schools four months, they were "liable to indictment."[56] Under the control of the board of education, the University was declared to be a part of the public school system.

The chief contributions of the new constitution to public education lay in the provisions it set forth for school support.[57] Three sources of revenue were contemplated. First, it required that the proceeds from the sale of the swamp lands and the receipts from fines, forfeitures, penalties, and certain other funds, be invested as an irreducible fund, the interest of which was to be used for schools.[58] Second, it authorized taxation as a means of support; without doubt the framers contemplated a state property tax, a new principle and the "chief contribution of the post-bellum constitution to the cause of learning."[59] Third, the "proceeds of the state and county capitation tax shall be applied to the purposes of education and the support of the poor, but in no one year shall more than twenty-five per cent thereof be appropriated to the latter purpose."[60]

The Article closed with a section on compulsory attendance. A permissive clause extended to the General Assembly the power to require all children between the ages of six and eighteen to attend school for a period of not less than sixteen months, unless educated by other means.[61]

Even before the adjournment of the convention the campaign for the ratification of the constitution and the election of state officers started. Disregarding an almost unanimous stand of the Republicans to the contrary, the Conservatives declared that the constitution not only did not prohibit mixed schools, but it actually designed them. Skillfully they interpreted the compulsory attendance clause to mean that the poor man, unable to educate his children "by other means," would be compelled to

[54] *The Constitution of 1868*, Article IX, Section 2.
[55] Called General Superintendent of Common Schools under the pre-war system.
[56] *The Constitution of 1868*, Article IX, Section 3.
[57] *Ibid.*; Samuel Hunter Thompson, The Legislative Development of Public School Support in North Carolina, pp. 165-170. (Unpublished doctoral dissertation, University of North Carolina, 1936.)
[58] *The Constitution of 1868*, Article IX, Section 4.
[59] S. H. Thompson, Development of Public School Support, p. 166.
[60] *The Constitution of 1868*, Article V, Section 2.
[61] *Ibid.*, Article IX, Section 17.

send his children to mixed schools.[62] Republican orators and newspapers ment that under the new Constitution, white children will be compelled to go to school with colored children."[64]

Another major attack on the constitution made by the Conservatives was the charge that under it taxes would be prohibitively high, especially school taxes.[65] Ratification, they said, would compel the white property holders to bankrupt themselves paying taxes to open public schools for their children and colored children whose parents, being without property, would pay little or no taxes. To obey the constitution the legislature would need to raise $400,000 in taxes, a policy that would "grind property holders to powder."[66]

On taxation the Conservatives spoke out of a real fear and from passionate feelings. While the issue of mixed schools did not so vitally concern the property holders because they could, if the worst came to the worst, send their children to private schools, they used that issue to frighten or prejudice the poor white people. A property tax for the education of white children alone would mean bankruptcy, for Negro children damnation and agrarianism.

The Republicans answered that they were not "leveling downwards" by taxation for education but were "leveling upwards."[67] Knowing the strong aversion among all classes to taxation and trying to use it to their advantage, they interestingly declared that the "Republican Party is the party of cheap, simple, just government."[68] They pointed out what the Conservatives ignored until after the election, but then endorsed with faith and charity, that the constitution imposed very definite poll- and property-tax limitations which should allay the unjustifiable fears of the property-holder that the school tax meant confiscation or agrarianism.[69]

After a vitriolic campaign during which even the most impassioned appeals of their leaders failed to bestir the Conservatives, the constitution was ratified and the Republican office holders chosen by substantial ma-

[62] *Carolina Watchman*, March 20, 27, April 3, 1868; *Morning Star*, March 31, April 7, 1868; *Sentinel*, March 9, 19, 28, April 8, 1868.
labeled this "Rebel Lie No. 2,"[63] saying, "There is no truth in the state-
[63] *Standard*, March 28, 1868.
[64] *Ibid*.
[65] *Carolina Watchman*, April 3, 10, 24, 1868; *Sentinel*, March 21, April 13, 17, 1868; J. G. deR. Hamilton, *Correspondence of Jonathan Worth*, II, 1192.
[66] "This Yankeeized agrarianism raises its grisley front in every paragraph of the Constitution, sweeps its puritanic talons around every acre of our domain and is the most rapacious of all the bloody devils of unmerciful conquest." *Sentinel*, March 19, 1868.
[67] *Journal of the Constitutional Convention of 1868*, p. 487; see also *Daily Stardard*, March 28, 1868.
[68] *Weekly Standard*, April 13, 1868; also see *ibid.*, April 19, May 7, 1868.
[69] *Sentinel*, April 8, 1868; Charlotte *Democrat* quoted in *Carolina Watchman and Old North State*, May 1, 15, 1868. The limitation on property was 66⅔ cents on the $100 valuation of property.

jorities.[70] The Reverend S. S. Ashley was elected over Braxton Craven, Conservative, to the office of state superintendent of public instruction, and W. W. Holden was chosen governor. With the constitution ratified and the members of the General Assembly certified, interest in public education shifted to the legislature.

The School Law of 1869

The Republican party in control of all branches of the state government was unreservedly committed to a program of schools supported by taxation for the children of both races. So advanced was its policy that more than half a century passed before another party tried seriously to carry it out. At the special session in July the Republican leaders promptly laid plans to enact into law the school program promised during the last campaign. The General Assembly, following the recommendations of Governor Holden,[71] quickly answered those who charged that mixed schools would be established by passing in the House by a vote of ninety-one to two a resolution authorizing separate schools.[72] When the Senate agreed to a similar resolution,[73] the answer on this issue was unmistakably clear.

In his message to the legislature that convened in the following November, Governor Holden threw his personal and official influence into the contest for public schools.[74] Although he regretted that the greater part of the Literary Fund was lost, "it is unnecessary to show how it was lost," he declared that "education is the cheap defence of nations," and that "free public schools for all the children of the State must be had at whatever cost."[75] He recommended a general and uniform system of public schools, separate for the races, but in other respects there should be no difference in character or support. After calling attention to the first report of Superintendent Ashley, the governor closed his message with an eloquent but futile plea that party differences be forgotten "in this great work."[76]

Submitted to the governor just four months after he took office, Ashley's first report reveals the scope of his activities and the enthusiasm with which he entered upon his duties.[77] Having spent considerable time investigating the investments of the Literary Fund, he estimated the value

---

[70] The election was held April 21, 22, and 23, 1868. There were 117,428 white people and 79,444 Negroes registered. The vote for the constitution was 93,084 against 74,015, leaving more than 29,000 registered voters who did not vote.
[71] *Legislative Documents* (1868-1869), No. 1, p. 8; *Carolina Watchman and Old North State*, July 10, 1868.
[72] *House Journal* (1868), pp. 50-54; *Sentinel*, July 17, 1868.
[73] *Sentinel*, July 17, 1868.
[74] The School Law of 1839 and the School Law of 1933 with the Law of 1869 make a trinity of pioneer school legislation.
[75] *Public Documents* (1868-1869), No. 1, p. 7.
[76] *Watchman and Old North State*, November 27, 1868.
[77] *Reports of Superintendent of Public Instruction* (1868-1869), November, 1868.

of the stocks and set the amount of their income at about $32,982.70[78] As this amount would be far too small to finance public education, "the people would have to be taxed for the purpose of supporting the schools." The total amount needed might seem to some people prohibitively large, but the per capita tax would be small. At least, said Ashley, whether large or small, ignorance is a far heavier tax than education. "A State can afford to be poor, but cannot afford to be ignorant."[79] Promising a complete bill later, he specifically recommended the immediate establishment of normal schools for the training of teachers, especially of women teachers.

Early in January, 1869, a bill entitled "An Act to Provide for a System of Public Instruction," prepared by Ashley, was introduced into the legislature.[80] It was the most comprehensive school bill since Archibald D. Murphey submitted his famous report to the legislature in 1817. The editor of the *Sentinel* commented grudgingly, "Whoever reads it for something new, original, striking, or startling will be disappointed."[81] However, the editor derided its author and denounced the bill because it provided that all the poll tax should go to schools and charity; he added that this tax together with a property tax which had been recommended would be used to "send every negro to school from six to twenty-one years old."[82]

In the course of the debates, the troublesome issue of mixed schools again came up, and a clause prohibiting them was passed.[83] The most stubbornly contested sections were those that dealt with taxes, especially local taxes. As prepared by Ashley, one forward-looking section gave to township trustees the power to call special elections to vote taxes for schools beyond the minimum four months. Eventually, the Conservatives, led by John W. Graham, and Thomas J. Jarvis, aided by some Republicans defeated this local tax clause.[84] "We cannot refrain," wrote the editor of the *Standard,* "from expressing our conviction that a great mistake was made in taking from the town commissioners the powers to regulate school affairs and the placing it in the hands of the county commissioners."[85]

[78] He estimated the educational fund, from the railroad stock and banks of North Carolina and Cape Fear, in the aggregate, at $1,679,600; the state treasurer's certificate due the state and drawing six per cent at $383,045; bonds at six per cent $21,584; the amount drawn from entries of vacant lands at about $1,500; and the retail tax on liquor at $6,762.50; from all of which the annual income of the educational fund would be $32,982.70. *Ibid.,* pp. 2, 3; *Sentinel,* November 25, 1868.
[79] *Ibid.,* p. 3.
[80] MSS in Legislative Papers, 1868-1869.
[81] January 11, 1869.
[82] January 9, 1869.
[83] *Senate Journal* (1868-1869), p. 703.
[84] "We (John W. Graham and Thomas J. Jarvis) believe that the township Board of Trustees, under the supervision of the County Commissioners by the Constitution, have exclusive control of the taxes to be levied, and we are unwilling to invest the School Committee with this extraordinary power to which no limit is proposed." Minority report, *House Journal* (1868-1869), p. 561; see also *Sentinel,* April 8, 1869; *Standard,* March 3, April 3, 5, 9, 1869.
[85] February 27, 1869.

Ashley's recommendation that the state levy an *ad valorem* tax, not to exceed twenty cents on each hundred dollars' valuation, was unacceptable to the legislature.[86] Neither was the section which authorized the county commissioners to furnish free textbooks, slates, pencils, and writing materials under rules and regulations of the state board of education, nor the one which would have established a permissive compulsory attendance system, seriously debated.[87] On the other hand, his recommendation, one of the most vital to the school system, that no township be allowed to share in state or county revenue unless during the previous year schools therein were maintained for four months was hotly debated and only narrowly defeated.[88] A correspondent of the *Standard*, urging the Senate to stand firm on this and the local taxation sections, wrote: "The bill passed the Senate by a large majority, but has been rendered almost a nullity in the House, and by whom? By the solid vote of the Democrats, aided by others who do not see or feel the necessity of educating the masses."[89]

The school law of 1869, wrote into legislation the general principles and provisions set forth in Article IX of the Constitution of 1868.[90] It provided that the state board of education should manage and control all public school funds, prescribe courses of study, adopt textbooks and other materials. It was the duty of the state superintendent of public instruction to keep records, make reports, sign all vouchers for money paid out of the state treasury for schools, make general recommendations for school improvement, and apportion to the counties funds to which each was entitled.

In conformity with the constitution that authorized the division of the counties into townships, the law now made the township the unit for control. Three school committeemen, chosen by popular vote, were empowered to establish and maintain, for at least four months in each year, a sufficient number of schools at convenient localities within the township. They were to hire and dismiss teachers, fix their salaries, select textbooks from the adopted lists, and, with permission from county commissioners, repair or build schoolhouses and supervise the schools generally. A county examiner, chosen for a term of two years by the county commissioners, had control over teacher certificates. He gave examinations under rules prescribed by the superintendent, and no person could teach without a certificate, good for that county only.[91] The course of study included reading, writing, arithmetic, English grammar, geography, and other subjects deemed necessary by the state board of education. And, as has al-

[86] Legislative Papers, 1869; *Ashley's Printed Bill*, Section 106, p. 31.
[87] *Ashley's Printed Bill*, Sections 64, 100.
[88] *Ibid.*, Section 62; *Sentinel*, April 3, 1869; *Standard*, April 3, 1869.
[89] *Standard*, April 5, 1869.
[90] *Public Laws of North Carolina* (1868-1869), Chapter 184, pp. 458-477.
[91] *Ibid.*, Sections 33-38, p. 467.

ready been pointed out, separate schools were established for the children of the two races, but these schools were to be similar and equal.

On the crucial subject of school revenue and taxation, the law was an unfortunate compromise. Four sources of revenue, three state and one county, were contemplated. It authorized the use of all interest from the school fund, of three-fourths of a poll tax of $1.25 levied on men between the ages of twenty-one and fifty, and of an appropriation of $100,000 "out of any moneys in the Treasury not appropriated otherwise."[92] The poll taxes collected in each county were paid into the state treasury. The allotments from this fund were then to be made on the basis of the school census within each county.[93] This money was to pay the salaries of teachers for a four-month school term, the term commanded by the constitution. Expenses for building a schoolhouse, for repairs, and for furniture and furnishings were to be paid by the county commissioners out of ordinary county revenue. But the law did not end with state revenue; it included a provision for local taxes.

It required the school committee to make an estimate of teachers' salaries, of repairing, furnishing or building the schoolhouse, and of other expenses needed to run the school four months and to report, ten days before the time of the holding of the annual township meeting, to the township trustees and to the county commissioners. If the township trustees failed to provide the money for the school, the school committee was authorized to forward immediately to the county commissioner an estimate of the necessary money, "and a tax equal to the amount of such estimate shall be levied on the township by the county commissioners at the same time the county taxes are levied."[94] Presumably if the commissioners failed to levy the tax, they were liable to indictment under the constitution. Events proved later that this power of the commissioners was unconstitutional and that the schools were without any local revenue.

Despite the jokers in the revenue part of the school law of 1869, it was superior in many respects to any previous legislation. Clearly it contemplated a "general and uniform system of state schools." For the first time in the history of the state, taxes were to be levied and distributed on the basis of the school census. For the first time the state assumed the duty of providing educational privileges to all children, both black and white. For the first time the state had a definitely prescribed school term. In general organization the system was improved. Recognizing that the district set up before the war was too small, the township was made the unit. The state superintendent was now elected, not chosen by the legislature. These and other provisions in the school law of 1869 make it the

[92] *Ibid.*, Section 53, p. 471.
[93] *Ibid.*, Section 7, p. 459 and Section 54, p. 472.
[94] *Ibid.*, Section 25, p. 464. The township board of trustees, consisting of a clerk and two justices of the peace, had power to supervise highways and bridges, to assess property for taxation, and to levy and collect all taxes that were required to defray the *necessary expenses* of the township. *Ibid.*, Chapter 185, pp. 578-582.

foundation statute upon which the school system during three quarters of a century has been built.

Schools Under Ashley

The history of the public schools during their first year under the new system was filled with epoch making events, some of which were encouraging, others disappointing. Not the least of the hopeful developments was the work of Ashley, who promptly launched plans to open again the doors of the public schools. In a burst of energy he was active in assembling educational statistics, working out details of organization, promoting county education associations, and corresponding voluminously with county school officials and the agent of the Peabody Education Fund.[95] By November he reported that all counties except Edgecombe and Onslow had sent to his office the information requested. The number of white children in the state was 223,815, the colored was 106,766, a total of 330,581. Of the 1,906 schoolhouses reported, 176 were described as good and 685 as bad.[96] On the assumption that the schools would get an appropriation of $100,000 from the state treasury, Ashley estimated that $165,290.50 would be available for the school year, 1869-1870.[97]

Another happy development of this period was a law that authorized a state property tax for schools. When the legislature of 1869-1870 met, the opinion was pretty generally held that the appropriation of $100,000 made for the schools from any surplus in the state treasury would or could not be paid because there was no surplus.[98] Thereupon a movement in the legislature was begun to levy an additional tax for schools. Finally, the General Assembly took reluctantly a significant step in the history of public-school revenue by levying a small state-wide property tax of one-twelfth of one per cent.[99]

The reception of the new school system by the people of North Carolina varied widely. It was enthusiastically embraced by the people in some of the counties; only half-heartedly accepted by others; and by others stubbornly ignored or ignorantly opposed.[100] Nevertheless, at the end of

[95] MSS in Letter Books, 1868-1870, Superintendent of Public Instruction; *Reports of the Superintendent of Public Instruction*, November 1, 1869; *Standard*, October 23, 1869; *North Carolinian*, July 22, 1869; *Morning Star*, December 8, 1869; *Proceedings of the Peabody Education Fund*, I, 197.
[96] *Report of the State Superintendent of Public Instruction*, November 1, 1869, p. 2.
[97] *Daily Standard*, February 3, 1870.
[98] MSS in Letter Books, 1869-1871.
[99] *Public Laws of North Carolina* (1869-1870), Ch. 229, Section 2, p. 209; *Senate Journal* (1869-1870), p. 535; *House Journal* (1869-1870), p. 557; *Sentinel*, March 23, 1870.
[100] A reading of the reports from the county examiner will show the circumstances under which public schools were started during this violent era. A few typical comments taken from the *Reports of Superintendent of Schools* (November, 1870), will suffice. Stokes County (p. 70): "Citizens of Stokes take very little interest in the schools of late." Washington County (p. 74): "Many of the citizens of this county are deeply interested in this matter, and are anxious to aid in the establishment of schools." Randolph County (p. 66): "I have been holding educational meetings . . . have . . .

the year Ashley reported that 1,415 public schools were actually taught.[101] He estimated that 49,000 children, of whom between one-third and one-fourth were Negroes, attended these schools, taught by about 1,400 teachers who were paid an average monthly salary of $20.21. More than one-half of the 709 schoolhouses reported were built of logs.[102] The lack of money seems to have been a primary reason for the little progress made. Although $152,281.82 had been authorized, only $42,862.40 was actually paid for wages of teachers.[103] These and other accomplishments, admitted Ashley, were "not quite satisfactory." When thirty of the ninety counties made no reports, and the sixty that did report showed schools taught in only two hundred and seventy of the about eight hundred townships, the conclusion must be that he had ground for disappointment. The carelessness in making reports, the failure to build or repair schoolhouses, the misappropriation of school revenue, the lack of and the poor quality of teachers, and the aversion to public taxes all retarded the progress of education.[104] Yet despite the unsettled political conditions and the wide-spread distrust and hostility, the doors of the public schools were open.[105]

For the next year Ashley recommended the enactment of laws to compel a better collection and accounting of county school taxes, to increase the supervisory power of the examiner, to establish normal schools for training teachers, to organize a teacher institute within each county, and to increase the school revenue by a larger legislative appropriation and by giving to the township power to levy special taxes. No teacher, said he, should be paid less than $30 per month.[106]

---

good effect. . . . We urged everybody to rise above party strife and prejudice and make common war against . . . ignorance." Richmond County (p. 67): "Can't get qualified men on committee, an unaccountable indifference, white men refused to serve with negro." Carteret County (p. 30): "The wealthier classes have unwisely preferred to educate their children abroad . . . others not much interested."

[101] *Legislative Documents* (1870-1871), Doc. 6, p. 18.

[102] *Ibid.* Charles Lee Coon estimated that 27,942 white and 13,970 colored children were taught, making a total of 41,912; see Charles Lee Coon, *A Statistical Record of the Progress of Public Education in North Carolina, 1870-1906* (Raleigh, 1907).

[103] *Reports of the Superintendent of Public Instruction* (November 1, 1870), p. 17.

Auditor's report, year commencing October 1, 1869, and ending September 30, 1870:

From state tax on polls, 1869	$ 57,958.61
From county tax on polls, 1869	6,488.62
From special tax 1-12 of 1%	63,011.29
From tax on retailers of spirituous liquors	24,823.30
Total	$152,281.82

See *Public Documents* (1870-1871), Doc. 6, p. 7.

[104] *Ibid.*, pp. 1-15.

[105] In some of the counties schools were actually flourishing. "Some weeks since we stated that Catawba was probably the banner Public School County in the State, having 43 in active operation, but gallant old Wilkes enters her claim with, we must say, a good prospect of success. Since October last there have been opened in Wilkes 80 public schools.—Sixty-three of these were for white and seventeen for colored children."

"In the town of Washington 102 white and 313 colored pupils are attending the public schools." *Daily Standard*, May 21, 1870.

[106] *Report of the Superintendent of Schools* (1869-1870), p. 11; see also pp. 6, 7, 13.

Before the first year closed still another major development rendered inoperative and ineffective the school law of 1869, a development that for many years left its blighting effect on public education. In that law, it will be recalled that county commissioners were authorized to levy a township tax to guarantee the constitutional term of four months. Soon the purpose of the joker or contradiction in the law became clear from a controversy which started in Craven County. Here the district committee had made its estimates, had submitted the information to the trustees of township number three, and they, in turn, had ordered an election on the issue of additional taxes.[107] When the voters refused to approve the tax, the county commissioners, as the law required, proceeded to levy the tax on township number three, despite the defeat of the proposition in the previous election. Thereupon James S. Lane and other citizens of the township endeavored, by a court injunction to prevent the collection of the tax, alleging that it was levied in violation of the Article VII, Section 7, of the Constitution, which said that no county, city, town, or other municipal corporation could levy a tax without a favorable vote unless it was for a *necessary expense*. When the controversy went to the state Supreme Court, upon appeal, the Court ruled in the notorious case of Lane *v.* Stanly that this tax which was to supplement the school income was not a *necessary expense* and therefore, unconstitutional. Henceforth, according to this decision, the commissioners were not subject to indictment under the constitution and the law if the schools did not run for four months.[108] With one blow the provisions for both the term and the revenue of the public schools were nullified. Those who fought taxation in the legislature had won, with the aid of reactionary judges, an almost complete victory. More than any other factor, this decision retarded the growth of public schools and undermined the school system established by the Republican party.

In the fall election of 1870 the Conservatives gained a majority in both houses of the General Assembly.[109] As might be expected, this legislature did little to help the schools; indeed, several backward steps were taken. Under the guise of economy the salary of the state superintendent was reduced from $2,500 to $1,500.[110] To keep the Republicans from controlling the school fund its management was taken from the school board and placed in the legislature.[111]

[107] *North Carolina Supreme Court Records* (1870), 65 North Carolina 153; see also Charles Lee Coon, "School Support and Our North Carolina Courts, 1868-1926," *North Carolina Historical Review*, III (July, 1926), 399-438.

[108] In the same decision the court ruled that the limitation in the constitution on the power to tax above 66⅔ cents applied to schools.

[109] It was this legislature that impeached, tried, convicted, and removed Governor Holden from office. While that matter had no direct connection with the topic of this paper, suffice it to say that Holden was a staunch friend of public education. In his last message he looked forward to federal aid for public schools.

[110] In 1868, the Board of Education had employed the Reverend J. W. Hood, Negro, Assistant Superintendent of Public Instruction. His work during the next few years among the Negroes of the state was constructive.

[111] *Public Laws of North Carolina* (1870-1871), Ch. 279, Section 1, p. 444.

The act, however, that did the most mischief, if not direct injury, to the public schools was a law to repeal one of the cardinal features of the legislation of 1869. By it county and state taxes were collected and turned over to the state treasury. Then upon the basis of the school population the money was distributed among the counties, a long step toward the "general and uniform" system authorized by the Constitution of 1868. In 1871 a law was enacted repealing that excellent provision and requiring that the taxes levied by the General Assembly should be collected and spent in the respective counties.[112] In effect, the state tax for schools was now nothing more than a county tax.

Faced with the destruction of his handiwork, Ashley resigned in September, 1871.[113] Since his election he had been severely criticized by the Conservative press, as the symbol of bayonet rule, Negro equality, and all the mistakes and malpractices of the Republican leaders.[114] Notwithstanding his limitations, Ashley made lasting contributions to the history of education. Serving during the most critical era for schools, he did about as well as any other man might have done, possibly much better than most. Under him the schools were reopened, and they showed substantial progress the second year. The expenditures increased more than three times and the enrollment more than one-third over the first year.[115]

School Legislation 1872-1876

Governor Tod R. Caldwell appointed Alexander McIver to fill the vacancy left by Ashley's resignation. James Reid, a retired Methodist minister, having been nominated by the Republican party, was elected to the full term, but died before he qualified. Thereupon the governor appointed Kemp P. Battle. McIver, contending that he had been appointed to serve until his successor was elected and qualified, refused to surrender the office.[116] When the matter was appealed to the Supreme Court, McIver was sustained, and he served until December, 1874. A native of Moore County, he was at the time of his appointment a professor of mathematics at the University of North Carolina, having been graduated by that institution in 1853. Prior to his appointment by the Republican regime to the chair of mathematics at the University, he was a popular instructor at Davidson College.[117] Although he was a Republican and, of course, de-

[112] *Ibid.*, Ch. 237, Section 5, pp. 387-388.
[113] *Sentinel,* September 4, 6, 1871; *House Journal* (1871-1872), p. 33.
[114] Ashley, it should be added, never answered his critics publicly, except in dignified language. Though he was accused of fostering mixed schools, no one proved he violated his oath of office for that purpose.
[115] *Legislative Documents* (1871-1872), No. 6, p. 16.
[116] Greensboro *Patriot,* January 22, 1873; *Daily Era,* January 6, 13, 14, 1873.
[117] *Sentinel,* April 10, 1869. When McIver left Davidson, the students assembled in chapel adopted a resolution extending to him "heartfelt thanks for that faithful and conscientious discharge of the duties of his office which has won for him so high a place in our confidence and esteem." Although they were Democrats and he a Republican, he had not forced his political views upon them. He was characterized as "a gentleman and a scholar, and we are not ashamed nor afraid to say, before the world, that we admire him."

nounced by the Conservatives, now again generally called Democrats, McIver, for at least two reasons, was better qualified to fill this office to the satisfaction of the whites than his predecessor: (1) he was a native; and, (2) if not opposed to, he was largely uninterested in the education of the Negroes.[118]

McIver's chief legislative contribution to public education was the "astonishing" school law of 1872. Unsuccessful attempts during the first part of the session of 1871-1872 to increase the school appropriation caused J. A. Gilmer, chairman of the Senate committee on education, to ask McIver to submit a bill,[119] which, with some modifications, was eventually enacted into law.[120] It specified that any district that would run its school for four months should receive from the public school fund the sum of $2 for each student, counting the number by the average attendance for four months; and for a two-month term a school should receive $1 for each student. No school of less than two months could receive public school funds.[121] The cost of new school houses or the repair of old ones was to be shared equally by subscription or gifts and by the public school fund.[122] McIver justified this virtual reestablishment of tuition charges, specifically prohibited by the Constitution of 1868, on the ground that it was based on the principle of self-help. He contended that such a scheme would discourage private schools, and that, after a school was once started, it would become a public school.[123] Unlike Ashley, McIver seemed not to have had the slightest conception of a "general and uniform system of public schools." One year later, as a result of the confusion caused by the law, it was repealed.[124]

Fortunately, other laws passed at this same session were progressive. The state property tax was raised to six and two-thirds cents on the hundred dollar valuation, and a special school poll tax of twenty cents was added.[125] To give more centralized control in the county, the board of commissioners was made a county board of education.[126] Another progressive step was a law authorizing the organization of teachers' institutes, to each of which $50 would be paid out of the public school fund; but this law, unfortunately, was repealed in 1873.

In 1873, the state property tax was increased to eight and one-third

[118] "As to the African race, the results are doubtful, but in this age of the world, the experiment must be tried *in good faith*. While I think no system of instruction will ever lift the African to high spheres of educated mind, *yet let the role be played fairly*." *Legislative Documents* (1871-1872), No. 6, p. 9.
[119] *Legislative Documents* (1872-1873), No. 5, pp. 6-7.
[120] *Senate Journal* (1871-1872), January 26, 1872; *House Journal* (1871-1872), February 7, 1872.
[121] *Public Laws of North Carolina* (1871-1872), Ch. 189, Sec. 25, p. 314.
[122] *Ibid.*, Sec. 23, p. 314.
[123] *Legislative Documents* (1872-1873), No. 5, pp. 2-7. McIver's 2nd Report, November 1, 1872.
[124] *Public Laws of North Carolina* (1872-1873), Ch. 90, Sec. 30, p. 128.
[125] *Ibid.* (1871-1872), Ch. 189, Sec. 38, p. 318.
[126] *Ibid.*, Sec. 6, p. 309. They were empowered to "supervise free schools, settle disputes between districts, see that all school laws are enforced." *Ibid.*, Section 7.

cents and the special poll to twenty-five cents.[127] Here for almost a decade the amount remained. Three examiners were authorized and teachers' certificates were graded.[128]

Stephen D. Pool, a Democrat, was elected State Superintendent in 1874. After serving for about eighteen months without making any legislative contribution to the school system, he resigned, June 30, 1876, because of a charge of malfeasance in office.[129] Governor Curtis H. Brogden then appointed John Pool, a prominent Republican attorney, and former United States senator, to fill the vacancy. As the latter was without any training or more than passing interest in public education, he made during his six months' incumbency no contributions.[130]

Although no important legislation was added during the term, a Constitutional Convention, held in 1875, changed Article IX in two instances. A clause was added which specifically established separate schools.[131] During the previous year the debates on the Civil Rights Bill in Congress had aroused considerable apprehension even among the members of the Republican party.[132] Thus there was little or no opposition from either party to this constitutional amendment.[133] The second amendment destroyed another part of the state system, advocated by Ashley, when Section 5 was added, providing that "All moneys, stocks, bonds, . . . also the clear proceeds of all penalties and forfeitures and all fines collected in the several counties . . . shall remain in the several counties" and be used for school purposes.[134] Hitherto all such moneys were paid to the state treasury and preserved as an irreducible fund, with only the interest distributed to counties on the basis of school population.

Summary and Conclusion

The history of public education from 1870 to 1876 was characterized by slow, slow progress. Having wrecked the revenue safeguards so painstakingly written into the Constitution of 1868, the Conservatives and enemies of taxation controlled, with an iron hand, during the remainder of the period, appropriations for schools. With the local tax provision of the school law of 1869 destroyed, they had only to keep the lid on legislative appropriations. Although the agitation, in and out of the General Assembly, for local taxation continued unabated, it was successfully resisted;

[127] *Ibid.* (1872-1873), Ch. 90, Sec. 37, p. 131.
[128] *Ibid.*, Sec. 25, p. 126; Sec. 13, p. 122.
[129] *Legislative Documents* (1876-1877), No. 6, p. 17; *Peabody Proceedings*, II, 65.
[130] *Legislative Documents* (1876-1877), No. 6, p. 1.
[131] *Journal of the Convention of 1875*, p. 130; *The Constitution of the State of North Carolina*, Article IX, Sec. 2.
[132] Governor Curtis H. Brogden, Republican, in his message to the General Assembly, November 16, 1874, said: "A law passed by Congress requiring the two races to be mixed in the public schools of this State would, in all probability result in closing these schools . . . the mere pendency of such a law . . . would go very far to depress, if not destroy the . . . schools." *House Journal* (1874-1875), p. 35; see also *Peabody Proceedings*, I, 405; *Legislative Documents* (1874-1875), No. 5, p. 64.
[133] *Carolina Watchman*, February 17, 1876.
[134] *The Constitution of the State of North Carolina*, Article IX, Sec. 5.

Greensboro in 1875 cajoled the legislature into allowing this privilege under an amended charter.[135]

In 1867, George Peabody had established a trust fund, the interest of which was to be used locally to promite public education in the South.[136] During the next decade the Peabody Board spent in North Carolina about $87,600. But this amount does not indicate the good accomplished, because the money was distributed only to those towns and communities that would raise, by gifts, taxation, or otherwise, additional funds, usually two or three times the amount donated from the Peabody Fund.[137] Although somewhat general in its influence, this movement was primarily local in its activities.

The trend of state revenue for schools was gradually upward. Beginning in 1870 with only $31,397.15, the expenditure rose steadily, until, in 1876, it was $319,277.95.[138] During the latter year, the state spent for teachers' salaries, for each white child enrolled, the penurious sum of $1.87, and for each Negro child, $1.89. Calculated on the basis of the school census, the amount spent for each white child was only seventy-two cents. Significantly enough, the appropriations for Negro schools increased, during the period, at about the same ratio as did appropriations for white schools; a practice that shows the Negroes received their proportional share of the tax money, pitiably small though it was.

Salaries of teachers were variable, being dependent upon the ability of the teacher to drive a bargain with school committeemen. Although reliable information is generally unavailable, average salaries must have been little more than a dollar per day. In 1870, Governor Holden said (though his estimate was probably too high) the average monthly salary was $24.[139] Ashley advocated a minimum salary of $30 per month; McIver injudiciously opposed fixing any standards, adding that the amount from five dollars to fifty cents a day should remain for each committee and teacher to determine.[140]

Likewise, the school term varied. By decision of the state Supreme Court, the four-month term was destroyed. In 1874, McIver commented, "The average length of the term has not given generally enough to give a reliable estimate." Then he added, "It is perhaps ten weeks."[141]

Another dramatic story is told by the figures for children enrolled in

[135] *Private Laws of North Carolina* (1874-1875), Ch. 13, p. 428.
[136] An excellent evaluation of the work accomplished may be found in Edgar Wallace Knight, *Public Education in North Carolina,* pp. 271-293.
[137] Dr. E. W. Knight estimates that the amount raised during the decade by local communities was from $175,000 to $262,000. E. W. Knight, "Peabody Education Fund and Its Early Operation in North Carolina," *South Atlantic Quarterly,* XIV (1915), 178.
[138] C. L. Coon, *A Statistical Record of the Progress of Public Education in North Carolina, 1870-1906;* see also E. W. Knight, *The Influence of Reconstruction on Education in the South* (New York, 1913), p. 47.
[139] *House Journal* (1870-1871), p. 18.
[140] *Legislative Documents* (1873-1874), No. 5, p. 22.
[141] *Legislative Documents* (1874-1875), No. 5, p. 6.

the public schools.[142] In 1870, with a white school population of 243,463, and a Negro school population of 141,155, the schools enrolled only about one out of ten. Seven years later, 1876, about one child of two and one-half was enrolled.[143] As in expenditures, the enrollment for both races increased at about the same ratio; and the annual percentage of increase was an average of about four per cent, a little more at first and a little less toward the end of the period. If the enrollment was distressingly low, the average daily attendance must have been less satisfactory. The lack of statistics here is a benevolent silence.

In conclusion, it may be said that the government of North Carolina, after an epic struggle, had, by 1876, reestablished the public schools upon what proved to be a firm foundation. When one recalls that fifty per cent of the adult population were illiterate,[144] that one-third of the people was hostile to the very principle of public education, and that another third was indifferent,[145] the achievements of this era seem substantial enough. Considering the fact that many of the county school officials were tragically careless and some shockingly dishonest, the crusaders against ignorance had many problems besides legislative appropriations.[146] The most important problem that faced the schools, however, was that of obtaining adequate revenue. To supply this urgent need, Dr. Barnas Sears impatiently exclaimed, "Our great want is *statesmen* in our legislative halls."[147]

In one sense, the Reconstruction era ended in North Carolina in 1876 with the election of Governor Zebulon Baird Vance. Now both the legislative and executive departments were controlled by the Democrats. But the statement sometimes loosely made that, educationally speaking, North Carolina entered a new era in 1876 is not based upon substantial facts. Indeed, the ills that beset the public schools were far deeper than political party names.

[142] C. L. Coon, *A Statistical Record of the Progress of Public Education in North Carolina, 1870-1906.*
[143] *Ibid.*, p. 10.
[144] *Legislative Documents* (1872-1873), No. 5, p. 92. According to the census of 1870, 397,690 people in North Carolina above ten years of age could not read and write.
[145] Statement by Dr. Barnas Sears, agent for Peabody Fund, *Proceedings of the Trustees of the Peabody Education Fund from their Original Organization on the 8th of February, 1867,* 2 volumes (Boston, n.d.), I, 408.
[146] In almost every report from the superintendent of schools and from the agent of the Peabody Fund were recorded the charges of waste, dishonesty, carelessness, and indifference against school officials.
[147] *Peabody Proceedings,* I, 416.

VI

THE REPUBLICAN PARTY IN SOUTH CAROLINA, 1876-1895

James Welch Patton

In 1876 the Republican party polled over 90,000 votes in South Carolina, thereby electing three of the state's five representatives in Congress, apparently giving the South Carolina electoral vote to Rutherford B. Hayes, and failing by less than 1,200 votes to carry the state for Daniel H. Chamberlain, the Republican candidate for governor.[1] Twenty years later this party, long since virtually banished from state and local elections, had been reduced to a purely nominal status in congressional and presidential contests, and the state was well on its way toward the creation of one of the most reactionary political complexes known to American history: a state of mind in which dissent from accepted Democratic standards would be penalized by both political and social ostracism, and the elimination of the Republican party from participation in South Carolina politics would be so thoroughly accomplished as to be regarded by the average South Carolinian as a fixed political principle.

The culminating achievement in the struggle for Democratic supremacy in South Carolina was of course the Constitution of 1895, a document so craftily worded by Benjamin Ryan Tillman and his allies that for fifty years it effectively prevented voting by the Negroes, who constitute the bulk of potential Republican strength in the state, without disfranchising any significant number of white men, and at the same time successfully avoided conflict with the post-war amendments to the federal constitution.[2]

---

[1] *House Reports*, No. 175, Pt. 2, 44th Cong., 2nd Sess., p. 62. These figures are in dispute. That fraud was committed by both parties in the election of 1876 cannot be denied, but the fact remains that in voting strength the Republicans were practically equal, if not superior, to the Democrats. See also Francis Butler Simkins and Robert Hilliard Woody, *South Carolina during Reconstruction* (Chapel Hill, 1932), pp. 514-515, and Paul Leland Haworth, *The Hayes-Tilden Election* (revised edition, Indianapolis, 1927), pp. 122-156.

[2] *Constitution of 1895*, Art. II. Under this provision every male citizen of South Carolina was given the right to vote provided he had lived in the state for two years and in the county for one year, had paid his poll tax six months before the election, and had not been guilty of such crimes as bigamy, adultery, wife-beating, larceny, and receiving stolen goods. Up to January 1, 1898, any person who fulfilled these qualifications, and who could both read and write any section of the constitution, or could understand it when read by a registration official, was to be a lifetime voter. After that date any person who had fulfilled the aforementioned qualifications and who could both read and write any section of the constitution to the satisfaction of the registration officials, or, if unable to read and write, could show that he owned and had paid taxes on property in the state assessed at $300 or over, could vote. The purpose was of course to eliminate the Negro by strict enforcement of the poll tax and literacy provisions, and to enfranchise the poor or illiterate white by a loose interpretation of the "understanding clause." See *Journal of the Constitutional Convention of 1895* (Columbia, 1895), and for a shorter account, Francis Butler Simkins, *The Tillman Movement in South Carolina* (Durham, 1926), pp. 203-228.

In last analysis, however, the suffrage provisions of the Constitution of 1895 were something in the nature of a *tour de force,* merely a recognition in the state's fundamental law of a condition already existent; for the real forces which brought about the disintegration of South Carolina Republicanism took fashion in the years between 1876 and 1895.

To a superficial observer it might seem that the events of this period were nothing more than the South Carolina phase of a general movement that was in progress throughout the various southern states during these years, an attempt to eliminate the Negro from politics and by so doing insure the permanent success of white supremacy in a Democratic Solid South. But there are facets to the movement for white supremacy in South Carolina which call for special examination. The Democratic forces operating in this state were on the whole more violent than those in other states. Since there was little industry in the state to be benefitted by national Republican legislation and no significant hill-country element to find its way into the Republican fold as in Tennessee and North Carolina, the struggle tended to resolve itself into little more than a phase of the ever-present race problem.[3] And, as illustrated by the fact that third-party movements such as Populism were of slight consequence in South Carolina,[4] the aims of the Democrats would seem to have been completely achieved.

It follows, therefore, that the story of this struggle is not without significance. Such a story must inevitably convert itself into an account of inhibition through violence, threats of violence, and subtle psychological restraints, as well as legal and constitutional enactments, whereby a once numerous political element was degraded to a position of impotence and all but entirely excluded from the ballot boxes of the state. It is true that the so-called leaders of this party were usually obscure and uninfluential, their number was small, and their following was largely composed of poor and ignorant blacks; but if we look upon what happened to South Carolina Republicanism between 1876 and 1895 as the record of a great frustration, then a chronicle of the defeat of little men may be heightened into a worthy tragedy—that of the loss of Republican prestige in South Carolina through the machinations of an aggressive white terror, which, continuing to intensify itself with the passing of the years, reduced the Republicans and their black allies to a species of political serfdom in one of the most vigorously Democratic of all the American states.

Among the various factors which combined to effect the virtual anni-

[3] In the lengthy political discussions which filled the columns of the state's Democratic newspapers during the 1880's and 1890's, the terms Negro and Republican were usually regarded as synonymous, an attitude which still prevails among many South Carolinians.

[4] So far as state politics were concerned the Populist movement was captured by Tillman and incorporated into the Democratic party. See F. B. Simkins, *The Tillman Movement,* pp. 180-181. Populist electors for James Baird Weaver received 1,587 votes in 1892, about one-thirtieth of the vote of the state. Columbia *Register,* November 20, 1892.

hilation of the Republican party in South Carolina, especial importance must be attached to the nature and composition of the party itself. After 1876 the Republicans did not again offer a candidate for governor.[5] Some efforts were made to fuse the party strength with that of the Greenback party which nominated L. W. R. Blair in 1880 and J. Hendrix McLane in 1882, but without notable success.[6] Blair, a physically powerful and personally desperate planter from Kershaw County, was a man of some local importance but too bitter and abusive to attract much support. The fact that he met a violent death two years later in a quarrel provoked by his angry denial that he had been attending political meetings with Negroes, shows how little chance of success he might have in appealing to black voters.[7] McLane, a somewhat elusive figure from Fairfield County, apparently had hopes of becoming the Mahone of South Carolina, but he lacked the qualities necessary for a successful imitation of the Virginia leader's tactics. Assailed by the *News and Courier* as "an inconvertible greenback, an unredeemed pledge," suspected of being in the pay of northern interests, and embarrassed by his former connections with the Red Shirts, he made little headway in attempting to arouse the Republican voters. After various abortive efforts to instigate an independent movement, he left the state to enter the divinity school of Tufts College in Massachusetts and died of tuberculosis a short time later.[8]

In addition to the shortcomings of Blair and McLane, the other Greenback nominees for state offices in 1880 and 1882 were almost wholly unknown to the public and therefore without important strength to count upon in any locality.[9] Likewise the character of the Greenback platform was scarcely calculated to elicit more than lip service from the members of

[5] A Republican state ticket headed by Dr. John Winsmith of Spartanburg was apparently nominated in 1880, but no attempt was made to carry on a campaign. Columbia *Register,* September 3 and 5, 1880. A similar ticket to be headed by D. T. Corbin, a former carpetbagger living in New York, was nominated in 1884. All of the nominees declined to run, however, with the exception of D. A. Straker, the colored candidate for lieutenant-governor, and he received no votes. Charleston *News and Courier,* September 26 and November 6, 1884.

[6] Blair received 4,277 votes as against 117, 432 for Johnson Hagood in 1880. McLane, with more Republican support, polled 17,719 as compared with Hugh S. Thompson's 67,158 in 1882. *News and Courier,* November 22, 1880, and November 26, 1882.

[7] A strain of desperation ran through the entire Blair family. L. W. R. Blair's grandfather was hanged and his father, James Blair, the anti-nullifier congressman who gave Duff Green such a terrible beating in 1832, committed suicide. Blair himself had been tried, along with a Negro, for the murder of a white woman, and shortly after his death one of his daughters committed suicide, and a natural son was sent to the penitentiary for murder. An eye-witness testifying at the trial of Blair's assassin stated that Blair's face when he was shot was "as savage as a meat-axe." Columbia *Register,* October 7, 1880, and July 6, August 25, and September 12, 1882.

[8] While publishing the *Reform Signal,* an obscure Greenback paper, McLane, whose only visible means of support was a small farm near Feasterville, was said to be "riding about the state in a buggy and sporting kid gloves," thus leading to the change that he was subsidized by the Republican National Committee. *News and Courier,* September 7, 1882, and Columbia *Register,* September 6, 1882, September 6, 1884, March 13, 1888, and August 15, 1894.

[9] *News and Courier,* September 9, 1880, and September 7 and 8, 1882.

a party whose allegiance was pledged to the policies of Conkling, Garfield, Blaine, and Harrison.[10] Of similar ineptitude was the Haskellite movement of 1890, in which Democratic bolters sought Republican support against Tillman. A certain element of the Republican party endorsed the movement, but it was doomed to failure from the beginning.[11] It should also be kept in mind that none of these movements represented a real fusion, since genuine Republicans were in no instance given places on the state ticket.[12]

In local politics the Republicans were little more successful. The legislature elected in 1876 had sixty Republicans and sixty-four Democrats in the lower house and, including hold-overs, eighteen Republicans and fifteen Democrats in the Senate. As a result of resignations, expulsions, and special elections held after the general election of 1876, the Republican contingent in the lower house was reduced to thirty-five and that in the Senate to seven.[13] In 1878 these numbers were further diminished to three in the House of Representatives and five in the Senate,[14] figures which, except for continued reduction and final elimination of the Republicans from the Senate in 1888, remained fairly constant until 1895. Of the aggregate of about thirty-two Republicans who served in one or the other of the legislative houses between 1878 and 1895, thirty were Negroes, all from the heavily black counties of Beaufort, Berkeley, and Georgetown. Including such figures as Robert S. Anderson, Thomas E. Miller, and James Wigg, who were to sit later in the constitutional convention of 1895, they do not seem to have been molested in the performance of their legislative duties, but their influence was negligible.[15]

Information regarding the real nature of South Carolina Republicanism

[10] The state Greenback platform of 1882 contained the usual monetary planks to which the national party was committed, and also attacks upon the "no-fence law," the lien law, rings and monopolies, the legislative mileage grab, railroad rates, and prohibition except by popular vote. A sop was thrown to the Republicans in the form of a denunciation of the state registration and election laws, but in general the platform had nothing to interest a South Carolina Negro. *News and Courier*, September 6, 1882.

[11] F. B. Simkins, *The Tillman Movement*, pp. 128-134. It appears that efforts were also made in certain localities to secure Republican and Negro support for Sampson Pope, who ran as an independent against John Gary Evans in 1894, a gesture that met with no more success than the Haskellite movement. Columbia *Register*, October 31 and November 1, 1894.

[12] At the Greenback convention of 1882 the Negroes were promised that in return for their not demanding places on the state ticket, they should have full swing in the county nominations. Columbia *Register*, September 8, 1882.

[13] *News and Courier*, November 7, 1878.

[14] *Ibid.*, November 28, 1878.

[15] *Ibid.*, November 17, 1880, November 11, 1882, November 25, 1884, November 23, 1886, November 27, 1888, November 25, 1890, and November 27, 1892. The *News and Courier's* practice of printing short biographical sketches of the members of the legislature after each election is more helpful in identifying the Republican and Negro members than are the legislative journals, which make no clear distinction between black and white members. Small groups of Negro Democrats, elected on compromise tickets in low-country counties, were also to be found in nearly every legislative session between 1876 and 1895. At one session their number rose to six, but usually was much smaller.

during these years must therefore be sought in the activities of the party in presidential and congressional elections. Here the scene is a repetition of some of the more lurid phases of the Reconstruction era. Torn by internal dissensions, handicapped by poverty, and never able to deliver the electoral vote to nominees whom its delegates were instrumental in choosing, the party sank to little more than a political fiction, an aggregation of federal office holders and placemen, held together by a desire to catch such crumbs as might fall from the national Republican table when that party was in power. Hostility to reform elements which occasionally sought to improve the party policy, and failure to adopt a positive program based upon pertinent local issues and in the interest of a more wholesome state government, were damaging weaknesses which the student of South Carolina Republicanism cannot ignore.

With all due allowance for the critical attitude of the Democratic press in reporting such events, the state conventions held by the party during this period must have been models of tediousness and longevity. With their wild Gullah oratory, "the ceaseless wrangling and exhibition of inherent Republican jealousies," and "the ferocious fighting for the privilege of taking seats and doing nothing," such meetings often consumed from twelve to eighteen hours in effecting permanent organization, which under other circumstances might have required only a fraction of this time.[16] "The Simon-pure Afro-American," wrote a correspondent of the *News and Courier*, "has a chronic capacity for practicing dilatory measures. The delegates speak until they are exhausted, then take a rest and try it again. They store up eloquence for months and go to the convention with a sufficient supply to last a week. There is no mistake that some of the coal black negroes are good speakers, but they know it and never tire of showing it off." The sole desideratum, added this commentator, "seems to be to make the state house a temporary hotel, and by keeping up the wrangling until time for the outgoing trains the delegates save the expense of a night's lodging and by munching peanuts economize a breakfast."[17]

Two state conventions were ordinarily held each election year. The first, meeting in April or May, was for the purpose of reaffirming the party policy, strengthening the state organization, and in presidential election years, choosing delegates to the national convention. The second convention, in August or September, was ostensibly designed to name a state ticket; but, as previously explained, this formality was usually dispensed with, and the delegates spent the time in general wrangling, denouncing the Democrats, appealing to Congress for aid in combatting

[16] *News and Courier*, September 24, 1884, and April 20 and 21, 1892. At the convention of 1878 a long harangue over the choice of a state chairman prolonged the session into the night. No lights were available, not even a candle, and "it was so dark that the chair could not recognize the dusky members in the gloom, though they crowded up to the reporters' desk and shouted the names of their respective candidates within arm's length of the presiding officer." *Ibid.*, August 9, 1878.
[17] *Ibid.*, October 1, 1892.

the state registration and election laws, and occasionally taking the national party to task for its methods of distributing the patronage. "Every species of colored man," wrote a newspaper correspondent, "is to be found in such a meeting. A face which glistens in its blackness is seen next to that of a mulatto which can scarcely be distinguished from that of its next neighbor, a white man. It is an exhaustive collection of the curiosities of South Carolina in race and color."[18]

If the racial texture of these assemblages was mottled, the same must be said in too many instances of their moral complexion. The conclusion is inescapable that a large proportion of those who took part in such deliberations were local party hacks and holders of custom house, post office, and revenue service positions, whose interest was not in undertaking the arduous task that would have been necessary to galvanize the party into a career of usefulness and efficiency "on the scene of its grossest corruption and most stupendous infamies,"[19] when more immediate profits were to be gained from keeping solid with the national party and sending the right delegates to the national convention. Of the eighty-two Negroes and thirty-six whites in attendance at the April meeting in 1880, nearly one-third of the Negroes had previously appeared in fraud committee reports as bribe-takers, and the white delegates "with scarcely an exception, either are, or have been (and hope to be) 'federal office holders."[20] Many of these delegates were unable to pay railroad fares, and it was predicted that "whoever furnishes the transportation and supplies the indispensable bread and meat and whisky, will naturally dispose of the votes."[21]

That the existence of the above mentioned conditions was recognized and not approved by certain members of the party is amply demonstrated. The Reverend June Mobley, a colored delegate from Union, charged the white leaders in the April convention of 1880 with being interested only in choosing a delegation to the national convention; this, he alleged, they would use for their own advantage, but when the time came to run a state ticket they would declare such an attempt "inexpedient."[22] At the September meeting of the same year Thomas E. Miller accused the whites of affiliating with the Negroes only for the purpose of securing government patronage, and shrinking from the danger, or work, or social ostracism attendant upon a vigorous role in state politics.[23] Again in 1884 Miller

[18] *News and Courier*, April 21, 1892.
[19] Columbia *Register*, February 24, 1877.
[20] In the convention were nineteen office holders in the revenue, customs, and postal services alone, in addition to "several United States officials dodging around the lobbies and through the aisles of the hall looking after their interests." *News and Courier*, April 29, 1880. Of the seventeen delegates elected to this convention by the Charleston County convention six were office holders and five were former office holders, while the other six were characterized by the *News and Courier* as "chronic aspirants for office." *Ibid.*, April 23, 1880.
[21] *Ibid.*, April 28, 1880. [22] *Ibid.*, April 29, 1880.
[23] *Ibid.*, September 3, 1880. Thomas Ezekiel Miller (1849-1938), a colored lawyer, was one of the gifted members of his race. Born of free parents in Beaufort County, he was a graduate of Lincoln University in Pennsylvania, a member of the

asserted that the party was being kept alive solely for the benefit of a few federal office holders, and ridiculed "the farce of sending delegates to Chicago to nominate a President we can't vote for."[24] D. A. Straker, a prominent colored Republican, issued a public letter in 1884 denouncing "the baneful influence of money and whisky as used by another race seeking control," and lamenting that "our party is rushing headlong into ruin under the control of men whose greed is for office only and who tolerate none but those who do their bidding—political parasites who stick to us for power and office only."[25] But such protests were usually of little avail; the rank and file of the party could not be aroused to an appreciation of intelligent citizenship. As the New York *Times* aptly commented, "Their willingness to sell their certificates of registration, the value of which is not clear to them, for admissions to the circus, the value of which they thoroughly understand, is a natural result of their social and political condition."[26]

Bitter factional fights also combined to disrupt the party unity and prevent an energetic grappling with real issues. The antagonism between the Bowen and Mackey groups in Charleston was a heritage of Reconstruction days and continued for several years thereafter.[27] Later the situ-

---

state legislature both during and after Reconstruction, twice elected to Congress, a member of the constitutional convention of 1895, and for fifteen years president of the state Negro college at Orangeburg. See *Biographical Directory of the American Congress* (Washington, 1928), p. 1315, and Samuel Denny Smith, *The Negro in Congress, 1870-1901* (Chapel Hill, 1940), pp. 101-106.

[24] *News and Courier*, April 16, 1884.

[25] Columbia *Register*, August 31, 1884. Straker, once described by the *News and Courier* as looking "like a picture of Chadband done in lampblack," was a colored lawyer, said to be from Bermuda. He was active for a time in Orangeburg politics, was later principal of the law department of Allen University in Columbia, and finally left the state in 1887 to practice law in Detroit. See *News and Courier*, October 19, 1880, September 26, 1884, and Columbia *Register*, July 24, 1887.

[26] Quoted in Columbia *Register*, February 15, 1889.

[27] Christopher C. Bowen (1832-1880) was one of the most accomplished rascals of the Reconstruction period in South Carolina. Born in Providence, Rhode Island, he came South about 1850 as a mechanic and gambler. He served for a time in the Confederate army but was dismissed from the service and was under arrest for instigating the murder of his former colonel when the Union army entered Charleston in 1865. Released from custody, he secured a position in the Freedmen's Bureau, where he was arrested but never punished for selling government cotton. Later he was one of the organizers of the Republican party in South Carolina. His instrumentality in securing the dismissal of Dr. A. G. Mackey as collector of the port of Charleston alienated the latter's supporters and led to a bolt headed by E. W. M. Mackey. Bowen was a member of Congress, 1868-1871, but was defeated for reelection by Robert C. De Large, a Negro sponsored by the Mackey faction. He was elected sheriff of Charleston County in 1872, and despite the Mackey opposition remained in this office until his death. While in Washington contesting the election of De Large in 1871, he married Mrs. Susan Petigru King, a daughter of James L. Petigru; being at that time married to two other women, he was promptly indicted in two cases for bigamy. One of these resulted in a mistrial; the other in conviction, but he was soon pardoned by President Grant. After the death of Mrs. King he married a daughter of Franklin J. Moses, the scalawag governor; she survived him to marry W. N. Taft. See *News and Courier*, June 24, 1880, and *Biographical Directory of the American Congress*, p. 720. Edmund W. M. Mackey (1846-1884), the son of Dr. A. G. Mackey, was a native Charlestonian. He held various offices during the

ation was complicated by the appearance of the Taft faction,[28] the Smalls faction, and various others, all serving to keep alive the perpetual quarreling among the low-country Republicans and to cast dark shadows over the party's deliberations. In the late eighties the entire state organization was rocked to its foundations and temporarily dismembered by a dispute arising out of the conflicting ambitions of the Brayton and Webster factions, each claiming to be the genuine party and vigorously denouncing the other as spurious.[29] A meeting of the respective factions in the state convention usually led to much confusion and violent recrimination. In 1890 Fred Nix, a colored member of the Brayton element whose candidate for temporary chairman had been defeated by Robert Smalls, assailed Smalls as a pardoned felon and generally dishonest character. "You come here with your Tom Reed's rulings, but we won't stand them," cried Nix. "We know you were a Penitentiary convict, but here you come with your damned fooling. . . . You and E. A. Webster have got your slate fixed, but you can't get our votes for your ticket. I'm as good a Republican as any man in South Carolina, but I'd go home and vote for Ben Tillman before I'll support your slate."[30] At the April convention of 1892 Thomas E. Miller attacked R. W. Memminger, who belonged to an incipient reform element, for denying "the universality of baptism," and secured the adoption of resolutions characterizing the reform movement as "a small, weak, and inconsequential band of men . . . drawn together by selfish greed, while, Cataline-like, it styles itself Republican . . . pretentious and imposing, unworthy of the attention of honest and good men anywhere."[31] It

---

Reconstruction period, including the speakership of the famous Mackey House. He was twice a member of Congress and was chairman of the Republican state executive committee at the time of his death. His wife, a Charleston girl whom he caused to be educated at Oberlin College, was alleged to be of Negro descent. See *News and Courier,* April 29, 1884, and *Biographical Directory of the American Congress,* p. 1268.

[28] W. N. Taft, who died in 1889, came to Charleston as a sutler in 1865, after having supposedly served during the war in a Negro regiment from Rhode Island. He entered Charleston politics as a lieutenant of police and later held the offices of coroner, member of the lower house, state senator, and postmaster. Although a white man, he was one of the most important leaders of the Negro Republicans. See *News and Courier,* June 22, 1889.

[29] Ellery M. Brayton (1843-1907) was born in Augusta, Georgia, and came to South Carolina about 1880 as a collector of internal revenue. He was a graduate of Brown University and of the Harvard Law School, and apparently had hopes of building up a white Republican party in the state. See Columbia *State,* March 7, 1907. E. Alonzo Webster (1849-1901), the son of a northern Methodist minister who was the first president of Claflin College, was born in Vermont and came to Orangeburg with his parents about 1866. A graduate of Wesleyan University, a lawyer, and for a time professor in Claflin College, he was active in politics from 1876 to his death, and for a considerable portion of this time was the ruling spirit among the regular Republicans in South Carolina. See *ibid.,* September 18, 1901.

[30] *News and Courier,* September 18, 1890.

[31] *Ibid.,* April 20, 1892. Memminger, a white man, was an aspirant for the Charleston postmastership, and was alleged to have stated in 1888 that "the baptism of Christ can never regenerate a black baby." Just what this cryptic remark may have implied is not clear, but the incident is illustrative of the triviatities used by the South Carolina Republicans in besmirching each other.

is small wonder that a Democratic editor, contemplating such exhibitions, was moved to write: "The Republicans in South Carolina have a queer way, whilst denouncing the Democratic men and measures as oppressive and unjust to them, to go on diligently and ardently to declare to the world that they themselves are the most unwashed villains on the face of the earth, if what one side of the pow-wow says of the other be at all true. They certainly do not give each other good characters."[32]

We may discount the unfriendly comment of the *News and Courier* to the effect that the Republicans' candidates, "when they have any, are notoriously unfit for the offices they seek,"[33] and also that of a disgruntled colored delegate to the September convention of 1880, who exclaimed that "if the Republican party waits to find enough men to put on the ticket who haven't been 'cused of stealing, they'll never get up a ticket";[34] but the fact remains that a large number of the candidates offered by the party were by no means the best choices under the existing circumstances. While there were some notable exceptions, the congressional contests between 1876 and 1895 reveal the presence of too many Republican aspirants of the type of Robert Smalls, Samuel Lee, George W. Murray, and Absalom Blythe, who if not downright dishonest were certainly believed to be.[35]

[32] Columbia *Register*, September 20, 1890.

[33] *News and Courier*, April 17, 1884. The unfavorable attitude of the South Carolina Democratic press must always be taken into account in any study of the Republican party in this state. Upon his return to Georgia after serving as special counsel for the United States government in the election cases of 1883, Emory Speer asserted, "Liberty of the press in South Carolina! There is none. The metropolitan Thunderer, the *News and Courier*, issues its Jovian mandate, and the country newspapers croak, 'Me, too; Me, too; Me, too,' like the little slender frogs in the pond when some huge amphibian makes general proclamation. . . . Since I have been in your state, every little fellow who could muster 'a blacking box full of printing ink and a shirt tail of type' has been bellowing his small anathemas at me." Atlanta *Constitution*, quoted in Columbia *Register*, December 20, 1883.

[34] *News and Courier*, September 3, 1880.

[35] Robert Smalls (1839-1915) was born a slave in Beaufort. He rose to the rank of captain in the United States navy during the Civil War, entered politics as a Republican in 1866, and except for a few brief intervals was in office until 1913. In 1877 he was convicted of accepting a bribe of $5,000 while state senator and sentenced to three years in prison, but was pardoned by the Democratic Governor William D. Simpson while the case was on appeal. Although the bank check which he received was produced at the trial, Smalls always claimed that this was a political persecution and that he had not asked for pardon. See Allen Johnson and Dumas Malone, eds., *The Dictionary of American Biography*, 21 volumes (New York, 1928-1936), XVII, 224-225, and S. D. Smith, *The Negro in Congress*, pp. 95-101. Samuel Lee, a Sumter Negro, "notorious as an outrage grinder before the Teller committee," was supported by about 8,000 Democrats in preference to Rainey in 1874, but in 1880 his reputation had apparently changed and he was being charged with malfeasance as a probate judge. *Carolina Spartan*, May 5, 1880, and S. D. Smith, *The Negro in Congress*, pp. 133-134. George W. Murray (1853-1926), often referred to as "the black Bald Eagle of the Gamecock county," was elected to Congress and served, 1893-1895, but was later convicted of fraud in connection with real estate dealings in Sumter, and fled to Chicago while under bond. S. D. Smith, *The Negro in Congress*, pp. 106-109. Absalom Blythe, a white man, became a federal marshal after being defeated for Congress in 1880, and along with several other southern marshals investigated by the Springer committee, was charged with a shortage in his accounts and tried but not convicted. Columbia *Register*, February 13, February 22, and April 20, 1884.

Of equally bad policy was the nomination of James H. Rainey, a bitter and vindictive Negro who spent the greater portion of his time in Connecticut where he owned a costly home;[36] of Carlos J. Stolbrand, a Swedish born immigrant who had come to the state with Sherman's army, and whose difficulty with the English idiom caused his speeches to bristle with such expressions as "Aitchfield" (Edgefield), "der rade-shuts" (the red-shirts), and "der tarrf" (the tariff);[37] and of S. E. Smith, an Aiken Negro of limited education, who in attempting to expound to his dusky hearers the party's views on such matters as the tariff and the Blair bill usually "got into a tangle on these knotty subjects."[38] Except in the one overwhelmingly "black district," candidates of this sort apparently had no hopes of winning and were in the race merely as a proof of loyalty to the national organization, in expectation of a post office, marshalship, collectorship, or some other political plum which might fall to one making a sacrifice for the party in a remote province. Also there was the possibility that a neat sum might be secured from Congress to be used as "expenses" in contesting the election.[39]

Further evidence of the party's artificial character may be observed in the platforms adopted by the state and district conventions. Often copied from those of northern states, or lifted bodily from the national Republican platform, these documents abounded in irrelevancies and inconsistencies. Attacks upon the state registration laws, denunciations of racial discrimination, and pleas for the enactment of the Lodge election bill, though perhaps lacking in expediency, may have been in accord with the interests of South Carolina Republicanism; but continued insistence upon the tariff and financial policies of the Reed-Harrison wing of the national party by "a constituency which has not a dollar invested in manufactures of any description, and a race which is excluded from employment in most, if not all, of the protected industries in the Republican states,"[40] can only be regarded as an example of self-deluding rhetoric. Yet scarcely a convention was allowed to adjourn without the framing of platform planks affirming a belief in "the protection of American labor and industries and that the best interest and future prosperity of the State are identified with the principles of the National Republican party as set forth in its protective policy";[41] approving "the declared intention of the Republican party, by steadfastly maintaining the policy of protection of American labor, to elevate the masses of the people, and by a wise extension of the doctrine of reciprocity to enlarge our markets for the pro-

[36] *News and Courier,* November 15, 1878.
[37] *Ibid.,* November 2, 1880, and February 4, 1894.
[38] Columbia *Register,* October 14, 1888.
[39] Both Rainey and Lee were allowed $1,200 each for their expenses in contesting the election of 1874; and in the Bowen-De Large contest, although De Large received the certificate of election and was allowed to sit from March 4, 1871 to January 24, 1873, the seat was declared vacant, and both were paid their salaries. *Congressional Record,* 44th Cong., 2nd Sess., p. 1560, and *News and Courier,* June 24, 1880.
[40] *News and Courier,* April 14, 1892.   [41] *Ibid.,* May 2, 1888.

tection of our farms and workshops";[42] or endorsing "the financial policy of the [Harrison] administration as wise, economical, and safe, and must inspire the confidence of capital and labor alike and insure encouraging growth and prosperity throughout the vast domain of this country."[43]

That the real economic status of the South Carolina Republicans was in glaring contrast to their capitalistic utterances is clearly revealed by an examination of the usual condition of the party's exchequer. On the eve of the convention of 1878 it was reported that, "So much stress was laid in the different counties on the importance of raising money to defray the expenses of the delegates, that it is safe to assume that 'the party,' cut off from public stealing is in dire distress, pecuniarily as well as morally, and that numbers of palpatating patriots will be prevented, by want of the greasy greenback, from putting in an appearance this morning." The substantial accuracy of this prediction was appropriately confirmed by the financial committee's report, which showed the entire cost of holding the convention to have been only $13.54.[44] There were objections to the party's entering the state contest in 1880, on the ground that the expense of running a ticket would fall exclusively on a few white members.[45] At the April convention of 1884 Robert Smalls, the chairman, announced that some arrangement would have to be made with regard to a matter of $30.00 to pay for gas and the hire of two laborers who had fixed up the hall. He suggested a contribution, but the passing of the hat brought no sufficient response.[46]

Even more important than the inherent weaknesses of the party in accounting for its dissolution were the vigorous measures adopted by the Democrats to discourage and prevent Republican voting. A complete list of all the schemes, tricks, and legal devices utilized by the whites in keeping Negroes away from the ballot box between 1876 and 1895 would extend this treatment far beyond the space here allotted, but no explanation of the decline of South Carolina Republicanism would be adequate without reference to some of these expedients.

That violence was often resorted to cannot be denied. There were Red-Shirt parades in the campaign of 1878,[47] and perhaps later; and extensive evidence was adduced by the federal government to show the prevalence of threats and intimidation on the part of Democrats in 1882.[48] In the

[42] Columbia *Register*, September 19, 1890.
[43] *News and Courier*, October 1, 1892.
[44] *Ibid.*, August 7 and 12, 1878.   [45] *Ibid.*, September 3, 1880.
[46] *Ibid.*, April 16, 1884. For further illustration of the scanty character of the party's resources, see the account of a Garfield-Arthur ratification meeting attended by about 1,500, mostly Negroes, in Sidney Park, Columbia, on July 31, 1880. "The stand was a rotten, rickety structure of pine boards, and was adorned with one or two United States flags, one or two prints of Garfield and Arthur, and a table with a green cover, on which sat a glass vase with a forlorn looking bunch of crepe flowers and ribbon grass in it." Columbia *Register*, August 1, 1880.
[47] *News and Courier*, various dates for September and October, 1878.
[48] See, for example, the Fairfield election cases, *ibid.*, March 8, *et. seq.*, 1883, and the Charleston cases, prosecuted by Emory Speer and Samuel M. Melton, *ibid.*, various dates for December, 1883.

congressional election of 1880 the Edgefield poll "was held upstairs in the court room, and one of the double doors was securely closed, whilst the other, 18 inches wide, was kept by a Democratic guard, so that those Republicans who succeeded in running the gauntlet of the one hundred Democrats who thronged and crowded the staircase, were held here and subjected to further insult and violence until they could struggle out, with their clothes cut, and whilst the gallery or porch over the outside entrance was filled with Democrats armed with brickbats, and the Masonic Hall opposite was occupied by a military company, the Edgefield Rifles."[49] With regard to another precinct in the same county, a United States supervisor testified that he was prevented from performing his duties by Democrats "who struck me with a stick and asked me what was my business there. I told them I was a United States supervisor. One said . . . 'God damn you; you will smell Hell here before night.' . . . A Democrat snatched my hat off and hung it up. I put it on; he snatched it off again, saying, 'I hung it up; let it stay or the first thing you know your head will be hanging there.' "[50]

Such desperate measures were not long necessary, for the Negroes realized the futility of attempting to enjoy the franchise, and except in the "black district" soon ceased to offer a serious threat to white supremacy. But there is little doubt that the whites would have continued their resort to violence should it have been deemed essential. "The spirit of resistance is not dead in our people," said the Columbia *Register* in 1892; "The yeomanry of the Palmetto State would again raise the banner of revolt and shed their blood like water before submitting to be robbed by capitalists and ruled by Negroes."[51] Three years later this same editor was writing: "It may as well be understood right now by all parties concerned that the Anglo-Saxon citizens of South Carolina will continue doing business at the same old stand and in very much the same old way"; and that the government of the state "will remain in their hands, every Federal judge in the United States to the contrary notwithstanding."[52] When

[49] *Digest of Election Cases, 1880-1882, House Misc. Docs.*, No. 35, 47th Cong., 2nd Sess., p. 434. The numerous reports of contested congressional elections in South Carolina provide a vast store of information regarding political conditions and electoral practices in the state. Usually partisan in character, these documents must be used with caution, but their thousands of pages reveal a volume of evidence that is always suggestive and often naïvely confessional.

[50] *Ibid.*, p. 446. See also the testimony of Paris Simkins of Edgefield and George Knight of Aiken, *ibid.*, pp. 437, 454. Violence and intimidation were also used by Negro Republicans in heavily black areas to prevent members of their own race from voting Democratic. In the seventh district congressional campaign of 1886 the adherents of Robert Smalls were charged with interrupting Negro Democratic meetings with sticks, stones, cursing, and shouting, of turning Negro Democrats out of their churches, having them beaten by Negro women, and inducing their wives to leave them; but such measures were, for obvious reasons, less effective in determining election results than were those used by the whites. See *Digest of Election Cases, 1882-1888, House Misc. Docs.*, No. 63, 50th Cong., 2nd Sess., pp. 681-699.

[51] Columbia *Register*, April 20, 1892.

[52] *Ibid.*, April 20 and May 9, 1895. This was in reply to the decision in Mills *v.* Green (68 *Federal Reporter*, 818), in which United States Circuit Judge Nathan Goff declared the state registration law unconstitutional. Goff's decision was later overruled.

Colonel J. J. Dargan, a native South Carolinian, attempted to speak against the registration law at Edgefield in June, 1895, he was told that there was "no debate on the Negro question in Edgefield county. That's a settled question here. We have got the Negro down, and, by God, we are going to keep him down. . . . Resent it if you dare, and I will cut your damned heart out."[53] The determined attitude of the whites in this respect is perhaps best summarized in Ben Tillman's angry retort to the decision of "a dirty Republican judge" invalidating the state registration law. "The devil forgot," said Tillman, "that while the registration law may go out, and the Eight Box Law amount to nothing, that the shotgun has gone nowhere."[54]

Space permits the discussion of only a few of the various legal devices adopted for keeping Negroes away from the polls after 1876. Among these was the act of March 22, 1878, abolishing voting precincts in areas with heavy Republican majorities, thereby compelling large numbers of Negroes to walk twenty miles or more, and to cross wide low-country rivers where the ferries had a way of getting out of order on election day, in order to vote.[55] Of similar effect was the refusal, in most instances, of Governor Hampton and his successors to accord the Republicans representation on the boards of election.[56] Still another device was a system of gerrymandering adopted after the redistricting of the state in 1882, by which it was possible for the Democrats to control all except one of the seven congressional districts.[57] This arrangement provided for white majorities in two districts, slight colored majorities in four others, and a colored majority of over 25,000 in the seventh or "black district."[58]

The formation of the Seventh District, with its numerous eccentric lines and anomalous angles, was one of the most complete and curious pieces of gerrymandering known to American history. "Its curves, its in-shoots, its out-shoots, and its crafty drops," said the Washington *Post,* "would be worth a fortune to a modern baseball pitcher."[59] Created in defiance of all laws of harmony and proportion, its boundaries extended from the capital of the state to Savannah, Georgia, a distance of 150 miles, and embraced the Republican portions of five earlier districts. Only three entire counties, each located in widely separated areas, were included, to-

[53] *News and Courier,* June 28, 1895. Dargan was accorded respectful hearings when he spoke on the same subject in Sumter, Darlington, and Florence. Columbia *Register,* February 17, 1895, and Columbia *State,* July 11 and 17, 1895.
[54] *News and Courier,* May 11, 1895.
[55] *Statues at Large of South Carolina,* XVI, 565-570.
[56] In reply to a committee of Republicans in 1888, Governor John P. Richardson recalled "the disgraceful scenes and unscrupulous manipulations" of Reconstruction days, and stated that "the comatose condition of the remnant of the Republicans in this state for many years would surely justify" their exclusion from the election boards. Columbia *Register,* October 2, 1888.
[57] *Statutes at Large of South Carolina,* XVII, 1169-1171.
[58] Population figures based on the Census of 1880 and printed in *News and Courier,* July 4, 1882.
[59] Quoted in Columbia *Register,* December 2, 1892.

gether with an irregular patchwork comprising sections of six others.[60] To secure the appearance of contiguity it was necessary to regard a part of the ocean as dry land, since at one place the district was run into the Atlantic for the purpose of excluding the Democratic precincts of McClellanville and Mount Pleasant in Berkeley County and Sullivan's Island in Charleston County. The population of the district was 20,000 greater than that of the next highest district, and 52,000 more than the average for the other six districts in the state.[61] At the time of its creation the assumption seems to have been that the Negroes would be allowed to remain secure in their control of this district,[62] but the Democrats were soon making plans for the capture of the "black district."

The legislature of 1882 also adopted a stringent registration law, and a complicated voting device known as the Eight Box Law. The first of these made registration a prerequisite for voting and required that all prospective electors must be registered during May and June, 1882. After the completion of this period the books were to be closed and not reopened again except, at the county seat on the first Monday of each month from December to July inclusive, for such persons "as shall thereafter become entitled to register." In this latter category were persons coming of age after June, 1882, those whose certificates had "become defaced by time or accident," and those who had removed from one residence to another in the same precinct, from one precinct to another in the same county, or from one county to another.[63] Although a subsequent amendment allowed the renewal of lost certificates provided it could be proven that they had not been "sold, bartered, or parted with for any pecuniary consideration,"[64] there was no arrangement whereby a person entitled to register and failing to do so before July 1, 1882, might escape perpetual disfranchisement.

The machinery of registration was especially designed to hinder a compliance with the law on the part of Negroes. Sufficient time and facilities for registration were not allowed in many instances. During the original registration period a supervisor of registration, appointed by the gov-

[60] The whole counties were Georgetown, Sumter, and Beaufort, with portions of Richland, Williamsburg, Orangeburg, Charleston, Berkeley, and Colleton.

[61] Like other legislation of this type the gerrymander was justified by South Carolinians as being dictated by "the bidding of supreme necessity." See, for example, John H. Evins' reply to Roswell G. Horr, a Michigan Republican, who had attacked the redistricting law in Congress: "But if there ever was an excuse for gerrymandering, we in South Carolina have a better one than can be offered by the people of any other state. . . . Why, my friend, we did not do it for the purpose of pleasing you. We had no idea of consulting you as to what we should do. We did it because we wanted to do it, and because we thought it was right to do it. We . . . hold ourselves responsible, not to the Republican party, but to the government of the country." *Congressional Record,* 47th Cong., 1st Sess., p. 6221.

[62] Congressman Samuel Dibble of Orangeburg denied this in 1888, and said that the Seventh was regarded from the beginning as "fighting ground." Columbia *Register,* September 29, 1888.

[63] *Statutes at Large of South Carolina,* XVII, 1110-1115.

[64] *Ibid.,* XVIII, 489.

ernor for each county, was required to open the books for not less than one nor more than three days in each precinct; and at the county seat, on such days as remained before July 1, for corrections and the registration of those who had failed to enroll in the precincts. The supervisor and two assistants were given full discretion, both during the original period and thereafter, as to who were entitled to register; anyone denied a certificate might appeal, but must give notice to this effect in writing within five days and commence proceedings in court within ten days—"a special remedy with a fifteen-day statute of limitations." All applications for transfer of certificates had to be made at the county seat of the county in which the original was issued. A supervisor was given arbitrary power, whenever he had reason to believe that persons had died or had removed from the county, to strike the names of such persons from the registry list without posting the names or giving notice to anyone concerned. The requirement that a voter must secure a new certificate upon changing residence, which was interpreted to mean a new registration every time he moved from one house to another even on the same farm, was a particular hardship on Negro tenants and laborers, many of whom were of necessity compelled to make frequent changes in their dwelling places.[65]

Added to these legal hindrances were numerous obstacles which a registration officer might interpose on his own volition. Although the law specified that the supervisor should keep the books at the county seat and open them on the first Monday of certain months, there was no requirement that he should give notice of where he kept his office or books. There was also no limitation regarding the amount of time he might consume in registering an applicant, or any regulation that applicants should be registered in the order in which they appeared. "In many counties," it was reported, "a diligent search on the part of Republicans fails to discover the supervisor's office, or, when it is found, so many hindrances and obstructions are interposed that the voters fail to get transfers or registry, although they apply at every opportunity during every month of registration in the year of a general election."[66] Another subterfuge was the issuance of certificates which failed to give the name of the voter's precinct, the correct number of the ward in which he lived, or the proper street number of his residence, thereby invalidating the certificate when presented at the ballot box.[67] Nor can the partisan character of the registration officials be overlooked. Testifying before a congressional investigating committee in 1890, E. Alonzo Webster stated that,

Just before the closing of the office [of a supervisor who lived ten miles from town and did not open his office regularly] I presented to the supervisor of

[65] This provision often operated in such a way as to violate the state constitution, which provided that any male citizen otherwise qualified might vote if he had resided in the precinct for sixty days prior to the general election, whereas this law denied him the right to vote unless he had been in the precinct in June.
[66] *Digest of Election Cases, 1889-1891, House Misc. Docs.,* No. 137, 51st Cong., 2nd Sess., p. 513.
[67] *Ibid.,* p. 515.

registration a large number of affidavits of lost certificates collected from voters present from the seventh district . . . requesting that he should issue certificates thereon, which he refused to do. . . . Certificates were issued to Democrats without personal application. I protested this, as Republican county chairman, as being unfair. The supervisor, who is a Democrat, stated to me that he was not compelled under the law to make these changes and issue certificates except on personal application, but *that if he chose to favor his political friends he should do so.*[68]

A careful review of the evidence leaves little reason for doubting that "by delay in the issuing of certificates, by seeming investigations, by excuses, by favoritism, and by discrimination against the colored voters, unquestionably many hundreds were prevented from registering."[69]

Passed as a complementary phase of the registration act, the so-called Eight Box Law was calculated to procure disfranchisement through indirection. The distinctive features of this arrangement were: (1) at each polling place there should be as many boxes as there were offices to be filled, and each elector, being given a corresponding number of ballots, must, unassisted, deposit the appropriate ballot in each box, or suffer the penalty of having any ballot found in the wrong box thrown out and not counted; (2) all ballots must be printed on "plain white paper of two and a half inches wide by five inches long, clear and even cut, without ornament, designation, mutilation, symbol, or mark of any kind whatever, except the name or names of the person or persons voted for, and the office to which each person or persons are intended to be chosen"; and (3) that "if more ballots shall be found, on opening the box, than there are names on the poll list, all the ballots shall be returned to the box and thoroughly mixed, and one of the managers, or the clerk, shall, without seeing the ballots, draw therefrom and immediately destroy as many ballots as there are in excess of the number of names on the poll list."[70] This act, said its author, "was the result of an earnest and honest effort to secure the control of the government to the intelligence, education, and property of the state, as against the ignorance and robbery of Negro rule, without resort either to fraud or violence."[71] The requirements for a separate box for each office and plain white ballots without symbol or ornament virtually amounted to an educational test for voting,[72] and together with the registration law so chastened the Negroes that, as previously explained, they made no further effort to regain control of the state.

[68] *Ibid.*, p. 514.
[69] *Digest of Election Cases, 1789-1901, House Docs.,* No. 510, 56th Cong., 2nd Sess., p. 544.
[70] *Statutes at Large of South Carolina,* XVII, 1116-1121.
[71] Statement of Edward McCrady, in Columbia *Register,* November 29, 1888.
[72] There was a provision that "the managers, on demand of the voter, shall be required to read to him the names on the boxes," but there was no stipulation that they should designate the respective boxes while pronouncing the names, or read the names in any particular order; and by frequent shifts in the positions of the boxes throughout election day, the managers could prevent watchers from memorizing and communicating to an illiterate voter the order in which his various ballots should be deposited.

The most notorious uses of the Eight Box Law were naturally made in low-country congressional elections. Here the enormous Negro majorities could be overcome only by resort to systematic trickery, to which the more sinister phases of the election law could be readily adapted, and against which "the unterrified Democracy" of South Carolina seems to have entertained few scruples.[73] The law made no provision for challengers, yet it was alleged that on numerous occasions "a Democratic challenger was on duty, and in nearly every instance a privileged character within the polling place, while at each precinct the officers of election were all Democrats . . . and in no case where the challenge was exercised was the voter allowed a hearing or permitted to vote."[74] One provision of the act calling for a separate space or enclosure for federal elections, "at such distance from the polling place for state offices as the commissioners of election for each county shall determine," was in at least one case interpreted to allow the placing of the state and congressional boxes six miles apart, with the registry list kept at the state poll and the Republicans denied the right to vote at the congressional poll on the ground that this was a new precinct requiring a separate registration.[75] Endless technicalities were interposed against the size, shape, color, and wording of Republican ballots, and the practice of ballot-box stuffing was reduced to a fine art.

Since the law made no provision for the actual preparation of ballots, and each candidate was therefore under obligation to arrange for his own, it was easy for the Democrats to pick out slight variations which might occur under such circumstances, and use these in attempts to void an election. In 1890 it was charged that the ballots cast for Thomas E. Miller, Republican candidate for Congress in the Seventh District, were illegal in that: (1) the ballots were one-sixteenth of an inch shorter than required by law; (2) the word "For" appeared on each ballot just preceding "Congress"; and (3) they were not printed on "plain white paper." Although a printer testified that the variation of one-sixteenth of an inch, apparently caused by an accidental slip in the cutting machine used in trimming the ballots, was not regarded by the printing trade as a real variation, and there was evidence that some of the ballots used by the Democratic candidate were one-sixteenth of an inch too wide, the statute was nevertheless construed literally as to the Republican candidate. The prepo-

---

[73] An exception to this attitude was that of A. B. Williams, a Greenville editor, who vigorously denounced the Democrats for attempting to carry the Seventh District in 1886. "It is useless to preach honesty and integrity while the leading and most trusted men of the state publicly use and sanction such methods as have been used to count out Smalls. We condemn . . . the use of flagrant unfairness to defeat the choice of the colored Republicans in the one congressional district allotted to them [as] contrary to the principles of our people and party, a miserable political blunder, and a moral wrong." Greenville *Daily News*, November 20, 1886.

[74] *Digest of Election Cases, 1789-1901, House Docs.*, No. 510, 56th Cong., 2nd Sess., p. 544.

[75] *Digest of Election Cases, 1883-1889, House Misc. Docs.*, No. 63, 50th Cong., 2nd Sess., pp. 719-720.

sition "For" on Miller's ballots was held to be in violation of the rule forbidding any symbol or ornament, and here again the law was given a literal interpretation, although the canvassing boards in certain counties which also contained precincts included in other congressional districts, while rejecting Miller's ballots, counted those cast for Crum in the first and Smith in the second, which likewise had the word "For" on them, and despite the fact that Miller's ballots had contained this designation in 1888 and were not then claimed to be illegal on such grounds. Printers also testified that "plain white paper" was a vague term subject to wide variation in the trade, and that Miller's ballots, though alleged to be of "dirty white paper," came well within the former category, yet 7,026 Miller votes were thrown out in Beaufort County alone, thus giving the election to the Democrats by a majority of 478.[76]

The custom of ballot-box stuffing was in no sense new to South Carolina politics. In the election of 1880 more votes were returned in Edgefield and Aiken counties than there were males over twenty-one years of age in these counties as shown by the census of that year, although large numbers of electors were known to have been prevented, by intimidation and other causes, from voting. Notwithstanding the evidence that nearly all the colored voters were Republicans, the returns showed that if Tillman, the Democratic candidate, had received all the white votes, he must also have received more colored votes than white votes.[77] In the Mackey-O'Connor contest of the same year, it was found that the ballot boxes were stuffed in forty-five precincts, or two-thirds of those in the entire district. "The average excess [over the poll list] in these 45 precincts was 139 ballots, and in one box 1,071 extra ballots were found. The total excess in all the precincts was 6,247 votes." In one case 23 tissue ballots were found inside one Democratic ballot box, and in one precinct there were 465 more Democratic ballots than there were voters of both parties.[78]

Under the law each ballot box was required to have an opening only large enough to admit the entry of one ballot at a time, but this could be evaded by the use of Democratic tissue ballots which could be folded inside a regular ballot and thereby deposited in the box, or by depositing large

[76] Miller's ballots were also rejected in Berkeley, Colleton, and Orangeburg. *Digest of Election Cases, 1891-1893, House Misc. Docs.*, No. 77, 53rd Cong., 3rd Sess., pp. 180-187. A similar attempt was made to void the election of George W. Murray in the same district in 1892, but the state canvassing board refused to recognize the validity of the Democratic contentions—the real reason being, it was alleged, that Moise, the Democratic candidate, was a Cleveland Democrat and therefore obnoxious to the Tillmanites who were in control. *News and Courier*, November 9 and 27, 1892, and Columbia *Register*, December 13, 1892. This episode was for many years an issue in South Carolina politics, and the fact that Coleman Livingston Blease was a member of the board which voted to seat Murray often exposed Blease to the charge of having once voted against white supremacy.

[77] *Digest of Election Cases, 1789-1901, House Doc.*, No. 510, 56th Cong., 2nd Sess., p. 383.

[78] *Ibid.*, p. 389. See also *Digest of Election Cases, 1880-1882, House Misc. Docs.*, No. 35, 47th Cong., 2nd Sess., pp. 526-560, and *Digest of Election Cases, 1882-1888, House Misc. Docs.*, No. 63, 50th Cong., 2nd Sess., pp. 729-732.

numbers of tissue ballots in the box, with the connivance of the managers, before the polling began. When the box was purged, as provided in the law explained above, the official performing this task could distinguish the tissue ballots with his fingers, and draw out and destroy only genuine ballots in reducing the excess over the number of names on the poll list. Every Republican ballot so drawn out and destroyed diminished the Republican count by that much, while any Democratic ballot removed still had another Democratic tissue ballot remaining in the box to take its place.

An illuminating account of such procedure is given in the testimony of E. M. Chisolm, a colored supervisor at Gloverville precinct, Colleton County, in the election of 1888. This official was on the scene very early in the morning, and while standing with several voters around a fire in front of the usual polling place, was informed by one of the managers that the poll would be held in a nearby store. Shortly afterward, the proprietor of the store, who was one of the managers of the election, unlocked the doors from the inside, and the electors entered to vote, along with the supervisor who asked that the box be opened for inspection before the election commenced. He was told that the voting had already begun, and that five persons had cast their ballots. All but one of these had slept in the store during the night, and had been allowed to vote before it was possible for the supervisor to enter the polling place. After the close of the poll, asserted Chisolm:

Then Joe Dodd, one of the managers, said, "Every one of you leave the room, and all of the white men come in." "Chisolm," he said, "you can stay; I did not mean you, and Abrahm Smalls can stay with you." Before they commenced counting they seemed somewhat confused as to how they should count. That is, Joe Dodd, who seemed to be the chief, and Caesar Chisolm, they stepped off a space holding a secret talk. They came back and suggested how they should count, which was they should throw all the ballots out of the small box into a larger one, which they did. Then Caesar Chisolm commenced to count right off; then Joe Dodd, pointing his finger, said, "Hold on, you must stir the votes up first; stir them up; keep your eyes out." Then they went on; they then counted without giving candidates any credit at all, after which they had a considerable lot of votes over the names on the poll list—229 in all the box. They then found that the total number of names on the poll list was 134. . . . The question came up as to the excessive votes—what was to be done with them. One of the managers then turned his back, but not his eyes. I then observed that the general Republican votes were folded, and a portion of the Democratic votes were folded and the rest were twisted. Then they would draw one of the folded votes—the twisted ones were never drawn—destroying as they drew. The managers then suggested that we go into a general drunk, which was done.[79]

These measures had their desired effect in removing the Republican party from congressional campaigns except in the one "black district," and even there its candidates, when successful, were often subjected to long

[79] *Digest of Election Cases, 1889-1891, House Misc. Docs.,* No. 137, 51st Cong., 2nd Sess., p. 522.

election contests before being allowed to take their seats. In the three elections, 1876-1880, two Republicans were admittedly elected to Congress, and three others were seated as the result of successfully contested elections.[80] From 1882 through 1894 only two Republicans were elected without protest, one of these over another member of the same party, and three secured seats by contest.[81]

There is no doubt that the Democrats of South Carolina regarded themselves as thoroughly justified in executing the measures that have just been described. To them the Republican party was a black horror, bent upon "keeping alive the impending menace of Negro domination";[82] a party "under the lead of the most unprincipled, brutal leaders ever known . . . a monstrous wrong to human society";[83] an odious organization "for the promotion of partisan ends," whose systematic efforts "to obstruct reform in South Carolina" had resulted in turning the federal offices in the state into "political infirmaries and training schools for the defeat of honest government."[84] The Negro, it was held by white South Carolinians, had been "puffed up as a political factor of the Republican party into a self-importance sure to meet with a downfall";[85] he was "unfit for office and yet a chronic office-seeker";[86] a prey to "the sinister influences of evil and designing demagogues";[87] an adder which "the Anglo-Saxon who must depend on his daily toil for support will find, when he makes the Negro his political equal, that he has warmed to life... to sting to death his own liberties."[88]

[80] Richard H. Cain and Robert Smalls, both colored, were elected without protest in 1876. Joseph H. Rainey successfully contested the election of John S. Richardson in 1876, and Robert Smalls and E. W. M. Mackey were successful in their contests against George Tillman and M. P. O'Connor, respectively, in 1880. Samuel Lee contested the seat of John S. Richardson, and Carlos J. Stolbrand that of D. Wyatt Aiken, both unsuccessfully in 1880.

[81] E. W. M. Mackey. a white Republican, was elected over Samuel Lee, a colored Republican, in 1882, and Smalls over William Elliott in 1884. Thomas E. Miller successfully contested the seat of Elliott in 1888; and George W. Murray won over E. W. Moise before the state canvassing board in 1892, and over Elliott before a congressional committee in 1894. Smalls and Miller respectively contested the election of Elliott in 1886 and 1890, but without success in either case.

[82] M. C. Butler in Philadelphia *American*, quoted in Columbia *Register*, March 3, 1881.

[83] Columbia *Register*, July 22, 1882.

[84] State Democratic Platform, 1884, *ibid.*, June 27, 1884.

[85] Columbia *Register*, January 17, 1882.

[86] John S. Richardson in Philadelphia *American*, quoted in *ibid.*, March 4, 1881.

[87] M. P. O'Connor in Philadelphia *American*, quoted in *ibid.*, March 5, 1881. The political incompetence of the Negro was abundantly illustrated in the various reports of contested elections, where much of the evidence, though designed to discredit the Democrats, artlessly tended to justify their action. *Cf.* testimony of Cuffy Manigault in Smalls *v.* Elliott: "Q. Can you read and write? A. No. Q. Who told you you voted for Smalls? A. April Singleton. Q. Do you know the solemnity of an oath? A. No, sir, I don't. Q. If you were to tell a lie would you stick to it? A. No, I'm not going to try to tell any." In the same case Jack Mitchell was asked: "Q. Did anyone read your ticket for you before you voted? A. No, sir, I read it myself." Counsel then handed him the name of Smalls in print, and witness said it was Elliott. *Digest of Election Cases, 1882-1888, House Misc. Docs.*, No. 63, 50th Cong., 2nd Sess., pp. 667-668.

[88] Columbia *Register*, September 6, 1892.

As a consequence, it was believed to be the first duty of every Democrat "to maintain the power of white society, so as to have any state at all."[89] All white men were expected "to stand in a solid column with a common touch of the elbow, where anything will be done, anything endured, before one jot or one tittle of the claims of white civilization will be surrendered."[90] There should be toleration within party lines, "but those who abandon the party or oppose it . . . make themselves the enemies of good government, whether they choose to masquerade as Independents or boldly flaunt the black flag of the Republican party."[91] According to the editor of the Greenville *News,*

There is no liberty of political action for white men in this state and never can be while the colored vote remains solid. We may fret and fume and kick about it all we like, but that is the fact. We must take care of our homes first. No financial reform or tariff reform or anything else would help us if we had a state government like those from 1870 to 1876. That is why we must swallow bitter doses as our turns come and submit to many things against which reason, conscience, and instincts revolt.[92]

It therefore came to be accepted as a cardinal tenet of South Carolina politics, that,

One of the greatest misfortunes that could occur would be an oblivious disregard of a former experience that, upon the least cessation of vigilance, might, and would almost surely, again become a terrible possibility. The same elements of evil are here, the same forces present, though latent; but . . . I do not think there can ever come any deluge of Lethean waters so overwhelming as to sink into oblivion the bitter memories of the past. Sad, indeed, would be the sure results of criminal forgetfulness of a lesson so roughly taught, so heroically learned. No, this can never be. We are again in the house of our fathers, as masters and rulers, and we are here to stay as such for all time.[93]

In such a political climate the future of South Carolina Republicanism was obvious.

[89] *Ibid.,* July 22, 1882.
[90] *Ibid.,* January 15, 1882.
[91] Address of the State Democratic Committee, 1882, Spartanburg *Herald,* August 30, 1882.
[92] Quoted in Columbia *Register,* October 17, 1893.
[93] Inaugural Address of Governor John P. Richardson, 1886, *ibid.,* December 1, 1886.

VII

SOME ASPECTS OF THE CONVICT LEASE SYSTEM IN THE SOUTHERN STATES

FLETCHER MELVIN GREEN

The problem of the control of convicts in such manner as to render them least troublesome and expensive to the government and at the same time to insure them humane and proper treatment has always been a perplexing one. It has involved not only protecting and safeguarding the rights of others but also the attempted reformation of the criminal so that he may once again take a proper place in the life of his community. Prison practices of the United States, inherited from England, have gone through several stages of development, each adding some reformatory principles and practices to its predecessor; not yet has the ideal solution of the problem been found.

During the last quarter of the eighteenth century the American states began to substitute imprisonment for the death penalty for all except the more heinous crimes. This was done because of the gradual acceptance of the philosophy that the chief end of punishment was to prevent the criminal from doing further injury to society, and to "prevent others from committing the like offence," not "to torment a sensible being, nor to undo a crime already committed"; and in the belief that punishment could be reformative only "when compassion and humanity shall penetrate the iron gates of dungeons."[1] At that time the local jail, the chief prison at hand, was found entirely unsuited to reformatory functions and the states began to establish new and more up to date prisons where the prisoners were doomed to solitary confinement or else set to work at various productive tasks. Overcrowding, disruption of industry, difficulty of discipline, and other evils led reformers to condemn bitterly the common jails and prisons. Consequently during the second quarter of the nineteenth century two new and rival penitentiary systems were developed. These were the Pennsylvania or solitary confinement and the Auburn, a practical compromise between separate confinement and congregate labor under a silent system.

The latter system was largely shaped by Louis Dwight of the Boston Prison Discipline Society. Dwight was more concerned with the redemption of unfortunate sinners than the punishment of criminals. In order to reclaim the sinner Dwight and his followers organized Sabbath schools and introduced Bibles and religious services into the penitentiaries. But another and more significant feature of Dwight's program was the de-

[1] Cesare Beccaria, *An Essay on Crimes and Punishments with a Commentary by M. de Voltaire* (English translation, Edinburgh, 1788), p. 51; see also Blake McKelvey, *American Prisons: A Study in American Social History Prior to 1915* (Chicago, 1936), p. 2.

velopment of prison industries. Shortly after the Auburn prison was established an enterprising citizen applied for and was given a contract to operate a factory within the prison walls using convict labor. Soon this and other penitentiaries were realizing a net profit from the labor of convicts over and above all expenses.[2] Here then was one answer to the problem of maintaining a state prison without taxing the people for its support. While the penitentiary system was concerned with the reformation of the convicts as well as punishment—it was designed to give the prisoner time to meditate upon his sins and to teach him a trade—profits from the convict's labor soon became the central idea in the operation of the penitentiary. The American distaste for taxation was proverbial and the burden of supporting an ever increasing number of idle convicts had been a major cause for popular dissatisfaction with early prisons.

Three major systems of employing convict labor had developed prior to the American Civil War.[3] These were the Public Account, the Contract, and the Lease. Under the Public Account system the state itself managed and supervised the work of convicts who were generally engaged in manufacturing enterprises within the prison walls but sometimes in internal improvement projects for the state outside the prison. The convicts labored for the state, not for the pecuniary benefit of any individual or corporation. The state had entire control over the convict, and guards, foremen, wardens, and supervisors were state officials. This was generally regarded as the ideal convict labor system.[4]

The Contract system, however, was the more prevalent one. Under it the prison officers advertised for bids for the employment of the prisoners of their respective institutions, the highest bidder generally securing the contract. The contractor engaged to employ a certain number of convicts at a fixed sum, the prison or state furnishing power, sometimes machinery, and on rare occasions even tools for the convicts. The prisoners were generally employed within the walls, and the state did not surrender its control over the convict; it hired only his labor to the contractor who in turn expected to make a profit on convict labor.[5]

In 1883 Zebulon Brockway introduced the Piece-Price modification of the Contract system whereby the contractor had nothing whatever to do with the prisoners or their work. The contractor merely furnished the warden with material ready for manufacturing and the prison officers returned the finished article, made by convict labor, to the contractor and received a fixed price per piece.[6] This method was quite similar to the old domestic manufacturing system.

Under the Lease system the state would lease to the highest bidder all or part of the convicts for a fixed sum; the lessee would meet all ex-

[2] Blake McKelvey, *American Prisons*, pp. 6-12.
[3] *Second Annual Report of the Commissioner of Labor, 1886. Convict Labor* (Washington, 1887), p. 4.
[4] *Ibid.*, pp. 379-380.   [5] *Ibid.*, pp. 311, 372-373.
[6] *Ibid.*, p. 379; see also Blake McKelvey, *American Prisons*, p. 95.

penses of management, including housing, protection, food, clothing, and guarding, connected with the employment of the prisoners. He was also given complete authority over the control and punishment of the prisoners, subject of course to the terms of the lease, and might sublease them at will. The state was relieved of all obligation and responsibility, and the payments by the lessee were clear profits to the state.[7]

In degree of more or less excellence the operations of penitentiaries under Public Account, Contract, and Piece-Price

whether under official directors or contractors were harmonized with those features of the prison management that looked to the secure detention, the health, the discipline, and the moral reformation of the prisoners, the execution of the law's sentence upon him in its closest and furthest intent, and, if possible his return to the outer world, when he must be returned, a more valuable and less dangerous man. . . .[8]

It was the absence of many of these features, and often of all, that made the difference between these systems and that known as the Lease.

Prior to the Civil War the southern states had developed their penitentiary systems along the same general line as those of the northern states. Since Negro slaves, constituting a large element of the population, were largely disciplined and punished for their crimes either on their respective plantations or in special courts, the prison population of the South was relatively smaller than that of the North. Nevertheless all the southern states, except the two Carolinas and Florida in which convicts were imprisoned in county jails, had established state penitentiaries by 1860. Most of these were of the modified Auburn system, and were managed under the Public Account or the Contract system. Some of the southern penitentiaries had inaugurated what, for that day, were progressive reforms. The Baltimore prison early established special women's quarters and employed a chaplain to conduct Sunday classes. The Richmond prison was the first in the United States to use honor badges and the grading system as rewards for good behavior.[9] The Baltimore and Frankfort prisons were among the first to provide dining room accommodations. The Louisiana penitentiary conducted model cotton and shoe factories and gave its inmates training in the skills. Tennessee in 1836 was the first state to grant a reduction of sentence for good behavior over a period of years.[10] Edward Livingston of Louisiana formulated a prison plan for model reform schools for juveniles, houses of correction for minor offenders, and two grades of imprisonment. The prisoner was to be given a certificate of good behavior and promoted to better quarters and given the privilege of associating with like good conduct prisoners as a reward for good be-

[7] *Second Annual Report of the Commissioner of Labor*, p. 381.
[8] George Washington Cable, "The Convict Lease System in the Southern States," *Century Magazine*, V (February, 1884), 584.
[9] Blake McKelvey, *American Prisons*, pp. 19, 26.
[10] *Ibid.*, p. 43.

havior.[11] Unfortunately no state adopted Livingston's program in its entirety.

On the other hand Kentucky in 1825 gave Joel Scott a five year contract for its penitentiary at $1,000 per year, and thus inaugurated the Lease system, although Massachusetts had in 1798 permitted wardens to hire the labor of prisoners to anyone who worked them near enough to the prison to permit the warden to exercise general supervision. Scott built cell blocks modeled on the Auburn system, a dining room, a chapel, model and profitable factories, and maintained excellent discipline. [12] He was in good repute with Dwight and the Boston Prison Discipline Society, and his management of the penitentiary was considered exemplary. Alabama followed Kentucky in 1845 by leasing her penitentiary. While imprisonment in these two state institutions was degrading, it was not more so than that in most state prisons, North as well as South. Enoch Cobb Wines and Theodore William Dwight, two distinguished penologists, concluded in 1867 that there was "not a state prison in America, in which the reformation of the convict is the supreme object of the discipline."[13] In fact the development of prosperous prison industries was the most earnest concern of the wardens in all state prisons, and the penitentiary that was least expensive was considered most successful.

The Civil War greatly affected the prison policies of the southern states. It halted the development of the penitentiary system; and the social, economic, and political unrest of the Reconstruction period fixed the Lease system upon the South almost to the exclusion of other forms of labor. The cruelty and brutality which followed has rarely been equaled in modern times. One student of American prison history has concluded that "since the Civil War the southern states from a penalogical point of view never really belonged to the Union."[14]

Specific factors influencing the shift to the Lease system are obvious. The penitentiaries of several of the states had been burned or otherwise destroyed during the war, and others had been so damaged as to be unusable.[15] The state governments were bankrupt and there was little property upon which to levy taxes to secure the funds necessary for rebuilding. The poverty and unrest of the post-war years caused a great increase in the number of white criminals, and the abolition of slavery brought the problem of Negro criminals to the fore. Prior to 1865 the Negro had been

[11] Edward Livingston, *Code of Reform and Prison Discipline* (Washington, 1828).
[12] William C. Sneed, *A Report on the History and Mode of Management of the Kentucky Penitentiary* (Frankfort, 1860).
[13] Enoch Cobb Wines and Theodore William Dwight, *Report on the Prisons and Reformatories of the United States and Canada, Made to the Legislature of New York, January, 1867* (New York, 1867) quoted by Blake McKelvey, *American Prisons*, p. 39.
[14] Blake McKelvey, *American Prisons*, p. 172.
[15] The Georgia and South Carolina penitentiaries were burned by federal troops; those of Alabama, Arkansas, Louisiana, Mississippi, Tennessee, and Texas were badly damaged and misused during the war; and that of Virginia was burned when Richmond was evacuated.

controlled and punished by his owner and only rarely came before the courts. As a freeman he became subject to the civil and criminal law in like manner with the white man. Since the federal government did little to give the new freedmen economic security, and since the freedmen were possessed of no property, the Negroes were dependent upon the fruit of their labor for the necessities of life. Few white landlords had money with which to pay wages; moreover they distrusted the free Negro as a worker, and many were guilty of acts of aggression against him. Hence, facing starvation, the Negro turned to thievery and robbery and was caught up in the toils of the law.

The large criminal population, white and black, entailed greatly increased expenditures for food, clothing, and guards and for penitentiaries in which to house the convicts. The impoverished states did not have and found it impossible to secure the additional funds. On the other hand railroad companies, lumbering, mining, and other business interests were anxious to secure cheap labor that they could easily control. What more natural then than that the states should lease their convicts to private industry, escape the heavy costs of building penitentiaries and caring for large numbers of criminals, and, at the same time, secure much needed revenue for their depleted treasuries. Under these circumstances the southern states ignored the trend in the North where model prisons were being built and where programs of reformation were being instituted. They chose instead to follow the path of least resistance and to lease their convicts for ready money.

The first of the new leases were instituted by the provisional and military governments on a temporary, short-term basis. The Republican Reconstruction governments accepted the Lease as the solution of the convict labor problem and the "home rule," or Bourbon, Democratic governments greatly expanded the system and instituted long-term leases. The Georgia legislature, one of the first to turn to the Lease, considered the possibility of rebuilding its penitentiary, burned by federal troops in 1865, but, anticipating a great increase in Negro convicts, decided to look for a new solution.[16] In December, 1866, it authorized the governor to farm out the penitentiary to the highest bidder provided the state should be relieved of all expenses connected with the upkeep of convicts.[17] Governor Charles Jones Jenkins did not see fit to act but General Thomas Howard Ruger, the military governor, in May of 1868 leased one hundred convicts to the Georgia and Alabama Railroad for one year. The railroad was to bear all expenses of housing, guarding, feeding, and clothing the convicts and pay the state $2,500 for their labor. The lessee was given full power to discipline and control the convicts.[18] Rufus Brown Bullock, Republican

[16] Judson Clements Ward, Jr., "Georgia Under the Bourbons, 1870-1890" (Unpublished doctoral dissertation, University of North Carolina, 1947), p. 379.
[17] Georgia *Acts* (1866), pp. 155-156.
[18] Antoinette Elizabeth Taylor, "The Convict Lease System in Georgia, 1866-1908" (Unpublished master's thesis, University of North Carolina, 1940), pp. 7-8.

governor of the state, followed Ruger's lead and leased all the state convicts. Under the Bullock leases the state was not paid for its convicts but was relieved of all expenses.[19] The short-term leases required the lessees to "treat convicts humanely" and "to feed them well," but forbade them "to inflict . . . corporal punishment upon the convicts unless absolutely necessary to secure discipline."[20] The law of 1874 required the lessee to provide "humane and kind treatment" for the convicts and to segregate "those convicted of crimes involving great moral turpitude" from others.[21]

When the Democrats regained control of the state they accepted the Lease system and in 1876 the legislature passed an act authorizing the governor to lease all the state's convicts to the highest bidder for a period of twenty years. Under this act three companies were formed and agreed to pay the state $500,000 for the convicts for the period. The state was relieved of all expenses except the salary of a penitentiary physician and that of a chaplain whose duty was "to aid in reforming the moral character of the convicts."[22]

Shortly after its erection in 1841 the Alabama penitentiary was leased to private individuals but the state warden retained full responsibility over the convicts who were to be worked within the prison walls. This system, really a Contract, was continued until 1862 when the state resumed full management. Federal troops released the convicts in 1865 but returned the badly damaged penitentiary to the state; the next year the prison and its inmates were leased to private contractors, and in 1867 the lessees were permitted to work the prisoners outside the walls. The lessees fed, clothed, and housed the convicts but paid the state nothing and even failed to repay a state loan of $15,000 negotiated for the repair of the penitentiary.[23] One student of the problem declared that "During the entire Reconstruction period Alabama convicts were poorly, if not actually corruptly managed," and entailed a financial burden on the state.[24]

When the Democrats gained control of the Alabama legislature in 1874 they determined to revise the leases so as to realize revenue for the state. Short term leases, from one to five years, were negotiated with railroads, iron and coal mining companies, and planters at from $2.50 to $5.00 per month per convict and the state began to reap considerable profits.[25] Nevertheless criticism of the system led by Doctor Jerome Cochran, state health officer, caused Warden John Hollis Bankhead to recommend changes. He proposed to concentrate all convicts at one place near the mines where the larger portion of them were working so that they might be supervised directly by himself and the prison physician. Following

[19] *Report of the Principle Keeper* (1872-1873), p. 22.
[20] A. E. Taylor, "Convict Lease System in Georgia," p. 23.
[21] Georgia *Acts* (1874), p. 28.
[22] Georgia *Acts* (1876), pp. 42-43.
[23] Allen Johnston Going, "Bourbon Democracy in Alabama, 1870-1890" (Unpublished doctoral dissertation, University of North Carolina, 1947), p. 387.
[24] A. J. Going, "Bourbon Democracy in Alabama," p. 390.
[25] *First Biennial Report of the Inspectors of Convicts to the Governor*, pp. 3-6.

Bankhead's suggestion the legislature made some modifications in the system. Heretofore the counties had been permitted to lease their convicts direct rather than to sentence them to the state penitentiary, and the lessees had secretly agreed to divide their bids among the counties and thus prevent competitive bidding. The state in 1883 assumed control over county convicts and put a stop to county leasing;[26] and in 1887 all convicts were concentrated at the Pratt Mines and on two Black Belt plantations. The next year the Tennessee Coal Iron and Railroad Company acquired the Pratt Mines convicts and secured a ten year lease from the state.[27]

The Mississippi Penitentiary was partly destroyed during the war and General Alvin C. Gillem, the military governor, farmed out all the state convicts to Edmund Richardson, a planter, paying him $18,000 per year for maintenance and $12,000 for transportation.[28] His Republican successor, Governor James Lusk Alcorn, opposed this system. He was unable to abolish it, but did obtain some revenue for the state from the leases.[29] When the Democrats came to power in 1876 they leased all convicts to Jones S. Hamilton, a counterpart of the "Robber Barons" of the North and West, who in turn subleased to various planters, railroad companies, and levee contractors. Later the state leased all convicts to the Gulf and Ship Island Railroad and in 1887 forbade subleasing.[30] So corrupt was the Railroad that its lease was later cancelled and the state returned to individual leases.

The story of convict leasing in Arkansas, Louisiana, Tennessee, and Florida parallels that of Georgia, Alabama, and Mississippi. Arkansas, after experimenting with short leases under which the state paid a small fee for the support of each convict, under Democratic control turned to a single fifteen year lease whereby the state received $25,000 annually. Louisiana entered into a twenty year lease at $20,000 for the first year but with increasing returns with the increase in the number of convicts. Tennessee leased all her convicts to the Tennessee Coal Iron and Railway Company for $101,000 annually. Florida had no state prison prior to the Civil War but in 1866 secured the federal arsenal at Chattahoochee where "during the eight years of reconstruction the boodlers in charge housed an average of eighty-two convicts at a total cost of $234,473."[31] The Democrats changed the system and leased the convicts from year to year trying to improve the state's bargain. So cruel and barbarous were conditions in the Florida lease camps that one of the guards characterized the penitentiary as "the American Siberia."[32]

[26] A. J. Going, "Bourbon Democracy in Alabama," p. 391.
[27] *Inspectors Report* (1888), pp. 1-2.
[28] Mississippi *House Journal* (1870), Appendix, p. 58.
[29] Vernon Lane Wharton, *The Negro in Mississippi, 1865-1890* (Chapel Hill, 1947), p. 238.
[30] V. L. Wharton, *The Negro in Mississippi*, p. 242.
[31] Blake McKelvey, *American Prisons*, pp. 175-176.
[32] J. C. Powell, *The American Siberia; or, Fourteen Years' Experience in a Southern Convict Camp* (Chicago, 1891).

The remainder of the former slaveholding states fall into a somewhat different category; they followed wholly neither the practices of the states of the Lower South nor those of the North. Texas at first employed her convicts on state owned railroads, and after the roads were sold to private interests confined the convicts in the penitentiary where they were worked under the Public Account system. The convict population of the state grew so rapidly that a second prison was built. The two soon became inadequate and the convicts were scattered over the state at railroad and bridge construction, mining, iron blasting, and farming. Under these private contracts or leases the penitentiary superintendent maintained efficient inspection, regulation, and control of the convicts.[33] Kentucky, North Carolina, and South Carolina like Texas followed a combination of Public Account-Contract-Lease system and escaped some of the worst evils of leasing as practiced in the Lower South. The North Carolina Constitution of 1876 prohibited the state from surrendering the control of state convicts to the lessee. Missouri combined Contract, Public Account, and Piece-Price. Maryland, Virginia, and West Virginia followed the Contract system where the penitentiary was the center of convict labor.[34] Outside of the South only Nebraska, New Mexico, and Washington leased convicts to private industry after the Civil War.

The evils of the Lease system were self evident. In the first place the system was based primarily on the economic motive, revenue for the state and profit for the lessee. If there was no collusion of government and businessmen at first it soon developed and high ranking public officials lined their pockets with the sweat, blood, and tears of convict laborers. Governors Joseph Emerson Brown and John Brown Gordon were members of the Three Penitentiary Companies which leased Georgia's convicts for a twenty year period. Edmund Richardson utilized convict labor in Mississippi to become the biggest cotton planter in the world. Jones S. Hamilton, who dabbled in both Republican and Democratic party politics in Mississippi was another who made a fortune from convict lease labor. And John Hollis Bankhead, warden of the Alabama penitentiary, founded a long and powerful line of politicians in that state. Efficient lobbies were maintained and newspaper support was bought up by the lessees, and there is evidence that the Prison, or Convict, gang was closely tied up with the Bourbon Democratic machines;[35] the tie up was also close between the local court house rings and the lessees. Pressure was brought to bear on officials to arrest, and the courts to convict, all offenders so that the lessees might secure more convict laborers for their fixed payments.[36]

[33] Blake McKelvey, *American Prisons*, p. 177.
[34] See tables in *Second Annual Report of the Commissioner of Labor, 1886. Convict Labor*, pp. 82-87.
[35] Mrs. William Harrell Felton, *My Memoirs of Georgia Politics* (Atlanta, 1911), pp. 438-439, 463-466; "Report on Prison Rings," *Tennessee House Journal* (1879).
[36] Governor James M. Smith of Georgia said the Lease system increased the number of convicts by securing "a more rigid and proper enforcement of the laws." Georgia *Senate Journal* (1872), p. 139.

The Lease system had a distinct color tinge. In most states Negroes made up an overwhelming majority of the convicts; in all their number was considerably higher than their population percentage. The infamous "Pig Law" of Mississippi seems to have been especially designed to ensnare Negroes. Certainly under it the number of Negro convicts increased by leaps and bounds and convict leasing became a big business in that state.[37] Of the 1,239 convicts in Georgia in 1878 1,124 were Negroes. Of this number 36 were women while only 2 of the 115 whites were women.

The incarceration of young boys and girls, first offenders, with old and hardened criminals under the Lease system was a flagrant disregard of the reclamation ideal. Among the convicts leased in Georgia in 1883 were 137 boys between eleven and seventeen years of age. In 1886 there were 30 boys under fifteen; in 1897, 34 boys and 2 girls under fifteen, and in 1904 there was one boy only eight years old.[38] In 1874 Tennessee leased 123 convicts under eighteen years of age; 54 of these were under sixteen, 3 were twelve, and one only ten years of age.[39] Of 981 Arkansas convicts in 1895, 105 were between 12 and 15 years of age. And in 1882 Texas had 509 convicts under twenty years or age, one of whom was only seven years old.[40] Manifestly what these states should have done was to build reformatories for their juvenile offenders.

The chief evil of the Lease system was its cruelty and barbarity, its disregard for human life. Despite the fact that most leases contained such phrases as, "care should be taken to preserve the punitive and reformative character of the Penitentiary," reform was ignored and southern "penal institutions instead of tending to reform, . . . [became] veritable nurseries of crime, anarchism and degradation." One Tennessee critic maintained that of the nearly five thousand convicts released from the penitentiary of that state over a thirty year period "none practically are reformed, but most all are cultivated in crime, contaminated, debased, degraded and embittered."[41] Jesse De Vancey, a Georgia guard who whipped Aaron Byron a Negro convict to death declared: "I whipped him for impudence and for refusing to work; . . . I whipped him on the bare skin . . . shirt turned up and pants [turned] down." Despite such practices one legislative report praised the state lessees because they had "reduced the present system of farming out convicts to a complete success to the state, as well as to themselves,"[42] and this evaluation was generally accepted by state officials and a majority of the citizens.

But from the very beginning there was severe criticism of the condi-

[37] V. L. Wharton, *The Negro in Mississippi*, p. 237.
[38] A. E. Taylor, "Convict Lease System in Georgia," p. 78.
[39] John Berrien Lindsley, *Our Prison Discipline and Penal Legislation, with Special Reference to State of Tennessee* (Nashville, 1874), p. 38.
[40] George Washington Cable, *The Silent South—Together with the Freedman's Case in Equity and the Convict Lease System* (New York, 1885), p. 176.
[41] Knoxville *Journal*, March 10, 1893.
[42] John T. Brown of Georgia. *Inspectors Report* (1872-1873), p. 4.

tions of convicts under the Lease. Some newspapers pointed out the evil conditions in all the states. The Mobile *Register* of February 15, 1875, declared that Alabama convicts "Laboring with manacled limbs in swamps and sleeping in the unwholesome atmosphere . . . died like cattle in slaughter pens."[43] The Huntsville, Alabama, *Gazette,* a Negro Republican newspaper, dedicated itself "to the abrogation of the inhuman, barbarous and vicious convict labor system."[44]

Liberal and progressive leaders, business men, ministers, and teachers condemned a system that advertised to the outside world that they were a barbarous people. Organized labor attacked the system especially in Tennessee. Women like Mrs. Rebecca Latimer Felton of Georgia and Miss Julia Tutwiler of Alabama organized crusades against the Lease which they described as "not only a disgrace" to the state "but a disgrace to civilization." Physicians attacked the practices of the lease camps that impaired the health and contributed to the moral degeneracy of the inmates. The mortality rate was so high in Tennessee that a physician's report declared: "Before these figures humanity stands agast, and our boasted civilization must hide her face in shame." In both Georgia and Florida there were lease camps containing at one time twenty-five or more illegitimate children born of convict mothers. Finally political leaders were aroused and legislative reports exposed the evil conditions: Men and women, stripped naked and beaten in the presence of others with leather straps studded with wooden shoe pegs; Negroes beaten with heavy whips until the blood oozed from the open wounds, and these beatings repeated day after day, opening old wounds and making new ones, until death finally released the unfortunate victim. These and many other whippings, "the most brutal ever inflicted by one human being upon another,"[45] forced the state governments to abandon the Lease.

Mississippi led off in 1890 when a provision was incorporated in the constitution that forbade the lease of any convict "to any person or persons or corporation, private or public . . . after December 31, A. D., 1894." Tennessee acted in 1895 after several years of strikes and disorders involving convicts and free labor in the mines. Troops had been called out to suppress the disorders and even these joined the strikers. Governor Hoke Smith called a special session of the Georgia legislature that abolished the Lease in that state in 1908. Florida acted in 1924, only after the brutal whipping to death of a young North Dakota convict by a penitentiary guard (because the convict refused to shine the guard's shoes) had inflamed public opinion throughout the nation. North Carolina retained her modified Lease system longer than any other state. That state finally abolished it in 1933 when control of the state convicts was transferred to the Public Works Commission.[46] Unfortunately the county chain gang

[43] Quoted by A. J. Going, "Bourbon Democracy in Alabama," p. 394.
[44] A. J. Going, "Bourbon Democracy in Alabama," p. 425.
[45] Georgia *House Journal* (1895), p. 829.
[46] Hilda Jane Zimmerman, "Penal Systems and Penal Reforms in the South Since the Civil War" (Unpublished doctoral dissertation, University of North Carolina, 1947), pp. 387-390. This work is by far the best account of the abolition of the Lease.

system for working public roads that was substituted for the Lease in several states was almost if not altogether as bad. This was notably true of Georgia. And southern penal practices still contain vestigial evidence of a system that left a trail of dishonor and death that could find a parallel only in the persecutions of the Middle Ages or in the prison camps of Nazi Germany.

One finds it difficult to explain why a civilized people would have for so long tolerated the barbaric Lease system. Why did not the people smash the evil thing? How could anyone, even a guard in a convict camp, treat his fellow man with such fiendish cruelty as thousands and thousands of men, women, and children were treated in prison camps scattered throughout the South? Economic conditions which prevailed during the last quarter of the nineteenth century are a partial answer. The southern states, devastated by war, needed rebuilding, and the political leaders, both northern and southern, seized avidly upon industrialization as the one sure road to economic recovery. The industrialists were not averse to exploiting human labor as the long hours and low wages of the country testify. Neither did the governments hesitate to aid the employer as he exploited the laborer. Congress enacted a Contract Labor Law and the state legislatures gladly leased convicts to private industry. As a consequence contractors in the North and West used immigrant contract laborers and those of the South used convicts to build railroads, to mine coal, iron, and phosphates, to cut timber, and to manufacture brick. They were even used to construct government buildings. Were not all of these beneficial to the economic well-being of society? Why then should anyone condemn the labor system by which they were brought about? So reasoned Southerners, and the southern Bourbon Democrats saw no incongruity in taking convict blood money and earmarking it for public education.

The prevailing race feeling also helps to explain why the southern states retained the Lease system until well into the twentieth century. There was practically no sympathy for the criminal and little more for the Negro. Since a large part of the convicts were Negroes the state governments, controlled by the whites, could easily ignore reforms that would so largely redound to the benefit of the blacks. Of less importance but of some significance was the fact that the number of women prisoners was proportionately far less in the South than was the case in the North. Had the number of white women convicts been large an appeal to the sense of chivalry and protection of women might have been effective in overthrowing the Lease system.

Another factor in the apathy of the people was the fact that the Lease camps were generally located in isolated areas where the evils of leasing were hidden from public view. The convicts were scattered in the swamps and forests at lumber camps, in the hill and mountain sections at coal and iron mines, in the rural areas on large cotton plantations; others were located at railroad and construction camps where one who had no economic interest at stake seldom saw them. Hence the masses of people were actually unaware of the evil conditions that obtained.

Significant too was the fact that there were few trained prison workers in the South. Prison wardens and supervisers in the North in increasing numbers began to look upon their work as an honorable profession, and took pride in developing standards and techniques of prison discipline and reformation. Not so in the South where wardens, guards, and other penitentiary employees were either political appointees or men selected by the lessee for the purpose of driving the convict laborer to secure a maximum output. Consequently the majority of prison employees in the South had no interest in their profession and little interest in the well being and reclamation of the convicts under their control.

Those people who did see the degradation and feel shame for the evils of the Lease were able to force piecemeal reforms that ameliorated the worst features of the system. Miss Julia Tutwiler of Alabama organized an Anti-Convict League, composed of teachers, preachers, miners, workingmen, and merchants, and memorialized the legislature for reform. Similar groups in other states followed suit. The attacks upon the citadel of intrenched interests gradually brought results. First offenders were segregated from hardened criminals; reformatories were established; separate women's prisons were provided for and women prisoners removed from the Lease camps; laws were passed to shorten the hours of labor and to lighten the tasks of convicts; religious services were made available in the camps; books and schools were provided; the state boards of health began to take an interest in the health of convicts; and some attention was paid to recreation and the general social and spiritual welfare of the convicts. Baseball teams were organized; and the convicts were furnished musical instruments with which they gave band concerts. Paroles were granted and long term sentences were shortened for good behavior.

In the twentieth century the better penological trends of the North and West have had their counterparts in the South but the decentralization which came with county chain gangs retarded the advance of reform. Hence much remains to be done in the field of prison reform before the southern states can claim a modern, reformative penal system.

VIII

THE IDEOLOGY OF WHITE SUPREMACY, 1876-1910

GUION GRIFFIS JOHNSON

The American Civil War, as is the case in most wars, had been a conflict of ideologies[1] as well as a trial at arms. The ideological conflict had revolved chiefly around the function of government, the nature of the union, the innate capacities of mankind, the structure of society, and the economic laws which control it. The triumph of the federal government automatically established the *de facto* status of that cluster of ideologies which shall be referred to loosely as representing the point of view of the North and the *de facto* destruction of those ideologies typical of the South.

The history of Reconstruction amply bears out the fact that neither the North nor the South was consolidated in a united front on any of the great questions which had been the subject of controversy. The passage of the Fourteenth Amendment, for example, made it necessary for a number of northern states hastily to change their laws in order to permit an equality of civil rights to Negroes, and it was not until the passage of the Fifteenth Amendment that Negroes won the ballot throughout the North.[2] The act of writing into the Constitution the Fourteenth and Fifteenth Amendments was in itself an ideological revolution. This revolution established the *de jure* status of the position which the North had assumed in the pursuit of the Civil War, and the Amendments were in themselves a logical consequence of this position.

Although the dialectics[3] of the pro- and anti-slavery advocates often led into other fields of inquiry, the major assumptions around which these systems of thought revolved had to do with the status and capacities of the

[1] Ideology, as used in this essay, signifies a system of thinking, however vaguely expressed, which attempts to define and to justify personal and group relations of whatever nature. The ideology is usually a set of value-loaded premises from which a platform of social dynamics may be formulated either through orderly political action or through extra-legal means. It is the content of thinking with which this essay is concerned and not the end results of these patterns of thought.

[2] Gilbert Thomas Stephenson, *Race Distinctions in American Law* (New York, 1910), Ch. XI.

[3] For a discussion of the pro-slavery position see William Sumner Jenkins, *Pro-Slavery Thought in the Old South* (Chapel Hill, 1935); Vernon Louis Parrington, *Main Currents in American Thought, An Interpretation of American Literature From the Beginnings to 1920* (New York, 1930), II, 3-125; and for a discussion of the anti-slavery position see *ibid.*, pp. 137-473; Dwight Lowell Dumond, *Antislavery Origins of the Civil War in the United States* (Ann Arbor, 1939); Mary S. Locke, *Anti-Slavery in America from the Introduction of African Slaves to the Prohibition of the Slave Trade, 1619-1808* (Boston, 1901. Radcliffe College Monographs, No. 11); Alice Dana Adams, *The Neglected Period of Anti-Slavery in America, 1808-1831* (Boston, 1908. Radcliffe College Monographs, No. 14); William Frederick Poole, *Anti-Slavery Opinions Before the Year 1800* (Cincinnati, 1873); *Anti-Slavery Tracts* (New York, 1855-1856. Nos. 1-20. 1860, ten nos. variously listed).

Negro. The major assumptions of the anti-slavery school were that (1) the Negro is one of the great races of mankind; and (2) it is morally wrong to deny the Negro the basic rights of mankind. The pro-slavery school, on the other hand, held that (1) the Negro is a "peculiar" type of mankind; and (2) the basic rights of mankind do not apply to "peculiar" types.

This is not to say that fundamental economic differences did not exist between the two sections and the various regions of these sections. It is conceivable that differences over the tariff, for example, were more antagonistic than differences over the capacities of the Negro. But the Negro was declared to be the point at issue, and the agitation over this question came to partake of the nature of the basic issues. In other words, while North and South may actually at one time have been very close ideologically on the question of the status and capacities of the Negro, this very status was capable of being used as an excuse to achieve the triumph of more fundamental objectives.

The discussion in this essay will be confined to an analysis of the value premises with respect to the Negro as set forth by southern whites in their efforts to negate the assumption of equality implied in the Fourteenth and Fifteenth Amendments. This is not to ignore the economic realities of the period, but to emphasize the fact that the status of the Negro rapidly became after 1865 as it was before that time the *raison d'etre* of any controversy which arose involving the general welfare of the South or the relation of the South to the federal government.

It would be desirable to attempt some correlation between class structure and racial ideologies in the post-war South, but the limits of this essay preclude such a discussion. It may be said as a generalization, bearing in mind that all generalizations have notable exceptions, that the old aristocracy, or planter class, was tolerant of the Negro and kindly disposed toward him, although quick enough to exploit his services. The white "mechanic" class, the "tradespeople," and small farmers who during ante-bellum days often had to compete with the slave, protected by his upperclass owner, were anti-Negro during slavery days and remained the black man's implacable foe thereafter. The poor whites—the landless, unskilled laborers—reacted toward the Negro in a variety of ways. Some apparently had little, if any, antagonism toward the black man while others bitterly resented his presence in American society, "eating the white man's bread in a white man's country."

The anti-slavery leaders had based their claims for the Negro upon the theory that the laws of nature and of nature's God endow every man at birth with the rights of life, liberty, and the pursuit of happiness. Man in the pre-social state of nature had possessed these rights, but tyrannical power, in the form of kings or even in the form of a representative government such as the United States, had deprived him of his fundamental rights. Of all groups in America, the Negro suffered most at the hands of tyranny, and it was the duty of the friends of liberty to restore to him the equal rights of which he had been unjustly deprived. The argument in behalf of the American Revolution had run in much the same vein, and this frame of reference was used again in the anti-slavery crusade with telling effect. The natural rights theory had also idealized the man of nature. The Negro thus became to anti-slavery advocates "a simple child of nature" to be admired as such because of his qualities of honesty, virtue, and manly strength which are always characteristics of simple peoples who live close to nature. The Negro, then, had only to be free and to exercise the rights of a free man to become a useful citizen. The undesirable traits of the Negro, which were often over-emphasized by the pragmatists, were the result, so the anti-slavery leaders thought, of the stultification of the native personality of the Negro, for slavery was an evil which corrupted both the slave and the master. These undesirable traits, it was argued, would soon disappear once the Negro was liberated.

Southern leaders who had accepted the natural rights theory of the American Revolution but who had clung to slavery on the plea of necessity were convinced that slavery soon must disappear.[4] The debates over the Missouri Compromise, however, indicate that the South was rapidly changing its position with respect to the nature of the slave institution. It was now being argued that all were not equally capable of exercising liberty and, therefore, were not entitled to an equal share of it. Society is served best, it was argued, when those less capable of exercising liberty are restricted in their use of it. From this position it was now necessary to show that the Negro was less capable than the white man of exercising liberty. As proof, the pro-slavery advocates pointed to the physical traits of the Negro, his undesirable social traits, and to his variability as a laborer. Late in the ante-bellum period, Dr. Josiah Clark Nott[5] came forward with the pluralistic theory of the origin of man which sought to clinch the pro-slavery argument by establishing the assumption that the Negro had a separate origin from the Caucasian and was, therefore, in reality a separate and distinct type of man.

If the Negro was a different type of man than the Caucasian, it might be established that slavery was a positive good. The pro-slavery school thus argued that slavery actually protected the Negro's best interests. It was his duty, therefore, to conform to slavery and thereby serve the general welfare. Negroes constituted a class, so John Caldwell Calhoun had argued, which was the very basis of good government, the only means by which equality among equals might be obtained. The argument was but another phrasing of absolutism which had been a dominant concept at the time of the framing of the federal constitution. It had been held

[4] W. S. Jenkins, *Pro-Slavery Thought*, pp. 22-47.
[5] Josiah Clark Nott and George R. Gliddon, *Types of Mankind: or, Ethnological Researches, based upon the ancient monuments, paintings, sculptures, and crania of races, and upon their natural, geographical, philological and Biblical history* (Philadelphia, 1854).

then by such a person as John Adams[6] that government existed for the best people—the intelligent, educated, and, incidentally, the wealthy. Pro-slavery advocates held that in a society where all are equally free and share alike in political privileges there were some more fit for the exercise of good government than others. The more fit constituted the upper classes who had time for leisure and study. Wherever there was any large proportion of the uneducated, laboring element present, the possibilities of republicanism were hampered; but in a community, such as the South, where the menial labor was performed by a particular class, such as the Negroes, devoted to that purpose and excluded from political participation, the tendency was toward the elevation of the remainder of society. The bestowal of suffrage was the means by which a democratic state could recognize and reward those deserving equality. From this position southern political leaders argued during Reconstruction that conferring suffrage upon the freedmen was tantamount to conferring social equality.

Between the anti-slavery and pro-slavery dichotomy there was obviously little hope for a logical solution acceptable to both sides. The South, with a ballot purged of the old slaveholding regime, had ratified the Fourteenth and Fifteenth Amendments which declared the Negro to be entitled to equal citizenship, but it was not until 1876 that the South at last made its peace with Congress. By the terms of the compromise following the Hayes-Tilden election, the election of Hayes was to be accepted in return for the withdrawal of federal troops. After eleven years of attempting to bring the South into conformity with the national idea of equal rights, the federal government had retired from active participation in the experiment of the social revolution, leaving behind a Negro political machine protected by a legal equality and rewarded with federal patronage.

The period of conflict had produced a temporary consolidation of interests among southern whites. The old controversies between upper classes and lower classes, low country and up country, commercial and agrarian interests were to reappear time and time again only to be whipped into line by the cry of Negro domination until at last the Negro had been removed as an important factor in southern politics.[7] There were still southern men who could lift their voices in behalf of the Negro, but the number was steadily growing fewer as the composition of the upper classes

[6] See his *Discources on Davila, a Series of Papers on Political History Written in the Year 1790* (Boston, 1805), and his *A Defence of the Constitutions of Government of the United States of America* (3rd ed., Philadelphia, 1797).

[7] See Paul Lewinson, *Race, Class, and Party; a History of Negro Suffrage and White Politics in the South* (London and New York, 1932); Alex Mathews Arnett, *The Populist Movement in Georgia; a View of the Agrarian Crusade in the Light of Solid-South Politics* (New York, 1922); Benjamin Bangs Kendrick, "Agrarian Discontent in the South, 1880-1890," American Historical Association *Report,* 1920, pp. 267-272; Charles Chilton Pearson, *The Readjuster Movement in Virginia* (New Haven, 1917); Francis Butler Simkins, *The Tillman Movement in South Carolina* (Durham, N. C., 1926); Comer Vann Woodward, *Tom Watson, Agrarian Rebel* (New York, 1938); Hilary A. Herbert (ed.), *Why the Solid South? or, Reconstruction and Its Results* (Baltimore, 1890).

was steadily changing from the old planter aristocracy with its strong paternalistic motivation, to the new-rich, recruited from "tradespeople" and "mechanics," with their anti-Negro neurosis.

In the North the reaction had set in soon after the passage of the Fourteenth Amendment. The strong equalitarian sentiment of the negrophiles and the general feeling that the southern freedmen had become the wards of the nation had given rise to a profound sympathy for the Negro in the abstract, but the actual status of the northern Negro was little changed for the better. As the rumor of misgovernment and fraud under Negro domination circulated in the North, the doctrine of the immediate fitness of the Negro for all the rights of citizenship came more and more to be questioned, and the way was rapidly being prepared for *laissez faire* in the South. It came to be said in the North that the equality of man could be achieved only through the slow processes of time and that the Negro offered a flat denial to the American assumption that all who came to this country's shores would first be assimilated and then absorbed.[8]

The philosophy of the anti-slavery school bore in itself the seeds of *laissez faire*. If the Negro had only to exercise liberty in order to know how to use it wisely, federal intervention in his behalf was obviously unnecessary. Having been guaranteed the rights of citizenship, the Negro was now upon an equal footing with every other citizen of the United States and must not expect special favors. "It is not well for these people to be protected at every turn," wrote a federal agent in 1865 after his experience in dealing with the freedmen in Louisiana; "it is only by being cheated a while that they will learn to take care of their own interests."[9] In 1908 Charles Francis Adams expressed the same idea from a political platform in Richmond, Virginia. The third generation of freedmen was now rising. ". . . from this time on," said Adams, "it is but reasonable to demand of those composing it that they work out their own destiny. It is for the Afro-Americans, as for the American descendant of the Celt, the Slav, or the Let, to shape his own future, accepting the common lot of mankind."[10]

Even before the passage of the Fourteenth and Fifteenth Amendments, many political, financial, and religious leaders in the North had accepted the theory of rugged individualism as applied to the Negro. Now that he was no longer a slave, Pompey in the cotton field, it was argued, had as much a chance of making his own way as an Andrew Carnegie just off an immigrant ship. Both stood penniless in the land of opportunity.

[8] Charles Francis Adams, *"The Solid South" and the Afro-American Race Problem* (Boston, 1908). James Bryce had stated a similar position in his Oxford lecture *The Relations of the Advanced and Backward Races of Mankind* . . . (Oxford, 1902). He thought that it was not desirable for advanced and backward races to mix, that "the Teutonic races, as well as the French, seem likely to keep their blood quite distinct from all the coloured races," that "the general opinion of dispassionate men has come to deem the action taken in A. D. 1870 a mistake."
[9] *The Christian Examiner* (Boston, Mass.), LXXVIII (1865), 389.
[10] *The "Solid South" and the Afro-American Race Problem*, p. 18.

A northern man who had watched the experiment of free labor in Louisiana before the close of the war summarized in 1865 the dominant economic theory of the time as applied to the Negro. "The prevailing superficiality of thought" with respect to "the necessary antagonism of labor and capital" in the South would not, he declared, be assumed by "democratic thinkers in this country in any other relation of society than this; but as soon as it comes to considering the freed slave, in his new relation as a hired laborer, the liveliest suspicions are aroused." He then analyzed the "facts" which were rapidly being accepted in the North.

The fact is,—and this must be the foundation of all philosophy upon the subject,—the negroes are just what we should expect them to be after generations of slavery. If they were not, as a rule, lazy, dishonest and licentious, the chief argument against slavery would lose its weight.[11]

Impractical theorists in the North "have done their best to excite discontent among the laborers" at the South and "spoil them with absurdly unreasonable expectations; so that the wages they have demanded would alone, in some cases, have more than covered the whole value of the crop."[12] The situation was obvious enough, he thought.

This great mass of needy freedmen must either be supported by charity, or work must be found for them. Their necessities, as well as the general interests of the community, demand the regular cultivation of the great staples,—cotton and sugar. But this cannot be had without capital, and capital will not come from its safe Northern investments, unless under the temptation of very high profits. It is all very well to say, that this is grasping and illiberal. The fact remains,—Northern capitalists will not assume the enormous risks from brigandage, overflow, and the uncertainties attendant upon a new branch of business, unless the chance of profit is made commensurate with the risk. The question simply is, whether to allow them these rates of profit, or to leave the negroes to struggle on by themselves, without assistance, to produce such crops as we ourselves saw, last year, disgracing the fields of Port Royal and the Mississippi Valley. We feel sure, that it is much better for these people to be employed by humane white persons, than by those of their own color; for, in the first place, there are almost none of them who would not for a while be benefitted by the watchful supervision of a skilful agriculturist; and, in the next place, they are notoriously harsh and unreasonable in their exactions as regards one another. . . .[13]

The talk of dividing the confiscated and abandoned lands or the public land in the South among the freedmen he thought to be equally absurd.

Another subject, upon which there has been great confusion of mind and endless debate, is the tenure of land. We pass over the absurd assumption, often put forth, that the freed people are by right the owners of the land upon which they have toiled. It is the practical question, whether it is wise to divide lands among them as a free gift, that we wish to consider. We believe that no possession will benefit them which they have not themselves earned . . . they must

[11] "Free Labor in Louisiana," *Christian Examiner,* LXXVIII (1865), 395.
[12] *Ibid.,* 396.
[13] *Ibid.*

earn the right to possess land, by steady, thrifty industry . . . why should a worthless vagrant, because he is a negro, receive the gift of a farm, the value of which a hard-working farmer's son in New England would think himself fortunate to acquire in ten years? Let the thing settle itself. We shall find out soon who are fit to own land; for these will buy it themselves, in an open market, with money that they earned by their own toil.[14]

Here was a clear statement of policy outlined according to the accepted theory of classical economics. The assumptions of this theory had been the basic philosophy which had guided the government since the time of Alexander Hamilton. The widespread acceptance of the theory, despite the agitation of extremists, spelled the ultimate defeat of equalitarianism as embodied in the Reconstruction Amendments, for it was obvious to these extremists at the time (hence the advocacy of subsidies to the freedmen and active government intervention in their behalf) that it was only by a firm policy of support from the outside that the *status quo* in the South would be overthrown, the organic law of the nation to the contrary notwithstanding. In a society such as the South where economic interests were based upon a system of labor, where profits of labor were in part dependent upon cheap labor, the changing of the status of labor which demanded a diminution of these interests necessarily involved a conflict between the new status and the old interests. The old interests, of course, were in a much better position to bargain and obtain their ends than was labor once federal intervention had been removed. *Laissez faire* now became the federal policy in the South despite frequent waving of the bloody shirt for political purposes;[15] or, in the words of the time, "the South was left to work out its own problems."

The basic economic philosophy of the South was this same philosophy of rugged individualism. Of the classical economists, perhaps Malthus, whose theories were widely accepted in the ante-bellum South,[16] continued most to influence southern thinking after the war. Upon the basis of the Malthusian doctrine, supported by the writings of Thomas Carlyle,[17] southern whites erected their economic philosophy concerning Negro labor. The basic assumption was that the Negro would not work without compulsion.[18] From this premise, southern whites derived three impor-

[14] *Ibid.*, pp. 397, 398.
[15] In a letter to President Hayes in 1888, Atticus Greene Haygood, later a bishop in the Methodist Episcopal Church, South, pointed to the influence of northern economic interests in the South. When his pessimistic friends spoke of federal intervention and a return to Reconstruction days, "I tell them no," he wrote; "if there were no other reason, there is too much money invested by Northern people in the South." See Curtis W. Garrison (ed.), "Slater Fund Beginnings: Letters from General Agent Atticus G. Haygood to Rutherford B. Hayes," *The Journal of Southern History*, V (1939), 243.
[16] See Joseph John Spengler, "Malthusianism and the Debate on Slavery," *The South Atlantic Quarterly*, XXXIV (1935), 170-189.
[17] See especially his "The Nigger Question," in *Latter-Day Pamphlets* (London, 1858), pp. 1-28.
[18] On this point compare Carl Schurz's analysis of southern white attitudes toward Negro labor in *Speeches, Correspondence and Political Papers of Carl Schurz* (ed. by Frederic Bancroft. New York, 1913), I, 318, 320, 326, 341.

tant corollaries: (1) the Negro needs the direction of the white man in order to be industrious and actually prefers it to the supervision of another Negro; (2) without this supervision and compulsion the Negro degenerates; (3) the Negro is inherently "lazy, shiftless, and licentious."

Southern whites held with the North that Negro labor should compete in the open market with white labor without the advantage of favoritism which federal intervention had given. Men who, like Edmund Ruffin, had contended before 1860 that slave labor was as efficient as free white labor now tended to argue that free Negro labor was as efficient as free white labor only when directed by whites.[19] It was this latter contention which southern whites used in defense of the Black Codes passed immediately after the close of hostilities. Those, however, who like Hinton Rowan Helper[20] of North Carolina had thought that Negro labor was inferior to white labor, came now to complain bitterly of the inefficiency of free Negro labor and to throw out inducements for immigrant labor to come South. When no such flow of white labor followed these overtures, it came to be said that "bad labor drives good labor out."[21]

For example, Philip Alexander Bruce, a Virginia historian, thought in 1889 that an easy solution of the southern race problem would be the inducement southward of white foreign immigration. The inefficient Negro laborer could not compete on equal terms with the white laborer, and economic competition alone would solve the Negro problem. But fewer white immigrants were coming South than before the war; cheap Negro labor made the region unattractive to them.[22] The shiftless, self-indulgent Negro laborers were breeding more rapidly than the more frugal, self-denying whites and might "by the irresistible pressure that will result from an enormous numerical disproportion between the two races" eventually drive the whites out or produce an open contest for possession of the land. From these assumptions, Bruce arrived at a position similar to that which Lincoln had applied to the nation as a whole. "The South," declared Bruce, "cannot remain permanently half black and half white."[23] Through-

---

[19] Thomas Nelson Page wrote of Negro labor in 1904: "In 1865, when the Negro was set free, he held without a rival the entire field of industrial labor throughout the South. . . . And he was fully competent to do it. Every adult was either a skilled laborer or a trained mechanic. It was the fallacious teaching of equality which deluded him" into exchanging his skill as a craftsman for "book learning." *The Negro: The Southerner's Problem* (New York, 1904), p. 127. But in 1866 Dr. Josiah C. Nott wrote a pamphlet "to prove that the Negro is instinctively opposed to agricultural labor." *Instincts of Races* (New Orleans, 1866), p. 17.

[20] His *Noonday Exigencies in America* (New York, 1871) was an open letter to white laboring classes North and South to organize against Negro labor. Helper addressed the book to William J. Jessup, president of the New York Workingmen's Association with the request that the matter be taken up at the National Labor Convention in 1869.

[21] Compare Carlyle E. McKinley, *An Appeal to Pharaoh: The Negro Problem and Its Radical Solution* (New York, 1889) and Albion Winegar Tourgee, *An Appeal to Caesar* (New York, 1884).

[22] *The Plantation Negro as a Freeman, Observations on His Character, Condition, and Prospects in Virginia* (New York, 1889), p. 256.

[23] *Ibid.*, p. 256. Bruce modified his views when later census returns showed that the Negro population was increasing less rapidly than the 1880 census seemed to predict. See his, *The Rise of the New South* (Philadelphia, 1905), pp. 468-472.

out the period the question of the relative efficiency of Negro labor was to be raised until at last Negro migration into the war industries of the North and West began after 1917 to drain off the surplus.[24]

If it was necessary, as the southern ideology contended, for the whites to have constant and immediate supervision of the blacks in order to force Negro labor to be efficient, it was also necessary that the whites be able to maintain this supervision without being confronted with the embarrassing assumption that the Negro was politically equal.[25] The elimination of the Negro voter was worked out slowly and with it the curtailment of his civil rights. It was not until 1890, the year which marked the peak of agrarianism in the South, that the first serious attempt arose to disqualify the Negro. A Mississippi constitutional convention led the way in devising means of depriving the Negro of the vote without seeming to contravene the Fifteenth Amendment and at the same time without wholly eliminating illiterate white voters. The Mississippi Constitution included a variety of alternative qualifications including a poll tax receipt, property ownership, and an educational or understanding test of reading or reasonably interpreting any clause of the federal constitution to the satisfaction of the registering officer. Seven states followed the example of Mississippi between 1895 and 1910.[26] The literacy and property tests automatically disfranchised large numbers of Negroes and the discretionary power of the registering officer might complete the work. The so-called grandfather clauses adopted by some of the states were designed to protect illiterate whites. By this means persons who had the vote in 1867 and their descendants or persons who had served in the United States or Confederate armies or in the state militias and their descendants might obtain permanent registration within a given time limit without further qualifications.[27]

In the year that Mississippi initiated the constitutional restrictions, Henry W. Grady felt justified in writing, "The Negro as a political force has dropped out of serious consideration."[28] The year 1890 also saw the close of the period of Negro lawmakers in South Carolina, and the newly elected governor, Ben Tillman, paid his respects to white supremacy in his inaugural address.

The whites have absolute control of the government, and we intend at any hazard to retain it. The intelligent exercise of the right of suffrage is as yet beyond the capacity of the vast majority of the colored men. We deny, without

[24] For a summary of attempts made to keep Negro labor in the South see U. S. Department of Labor, *Negro Migration in 1916-17* (Washington, 1919).
[25] On this point see the argument of George Washington Cable, *The Negro Question* (New York, 1890).
[26] For provisions of the various states see G. T. Stephenson, *Race Distinctions*, pp. 296-322; Charles Staples Mangum, Jr., *The Legal Status of the Negro* (Chapel Hill, 1940), pp. 371-424.
[27] The Supreme Court held the grandfather clauses to be unconstitutional in 1914 in the case of Guinn *vs.* U. S. 347. The clauses also expired by their own terms.
[28] Joel Chandler Harris, *Life of Henry W. Grady, including his writings and speeches* (New York, 1890), p. 244.

regard to color, that all men are created equal; it is not true now and was not true when Jefferson wrote it.[29]

The South defended disfranchisement by an elaboration of the Calhoun doctrine that the Negro is unsuited to a participation in the equality on which the union rests. Suffrage, then, became a privilege and not a right. It should be enjoyed by those—the educated, tax-paying, property-owning, and virtuous citizenry—most capable of exercising it judiciously for the good of the whole. This position marked a return to the theory of the federal period which had with few exceptions based suffrage upon a property qualification. After a controversy marked in some states—North Carolina, for example—by almost seventy years of contention, the South had come by 1860 to accept the theory of manhood suffrage as applied to the whites and the theory of limited citizenship as applied to the free Negroes.[30] While retaining the ante-bellum theory of "civil slavery" with respect to Negroes, the South was now forced theoretically to reverse its position as to manhood suffrage for the whites in order to avoid the appearance of discrimination which would do violence to the federal constitution. Thus in its determination to maintain a biracial social structure, the South was forced constantly to penalize the whites who rested at the lowest end of the economic scale and to load with an additional weight the already important factor of wealth.

This aristocratic conception of race was usually explained in the terms which had been employed for many years to defend absolutism. The group of Virginia citizens who extended a platform to Charles Francis Adams in 1908 stated the formula of biracialism much as John Adams[31] had defended the property qualifications of the suffrage: "The race question has been solved in Virginia in a manner which assures the supremacy of intelligence; gives to people of all races a fair opportunity to work out their destiny upon their merits, and offers a just reward to good citizenship."[32]

[29] Cited in F. B. Simkins, *The Tillman Movement*, p. 137. But Tillman also declared that there "never was any just reason why the white man and the black man of Carolina should not live together in peace," and he asked for a law giving the governor power to remove from office a sheriff who failed to protect a Negro against mob violence. The bill, however, was defeated on the ground that it would "gratify the Chief Executive's lust for more power" (*ibid.*, p. 140).
[30] Fletcher Melvin Green, *Constitutional Development in the South Atlantic States, 1776-1860: A Study in the Evolution of Democracy* (Chapel Hill, 1930).
[31] *A Defence of the Constitutions of Government of the United States of America* (1787-1788); also in *Works* (ed. by Charles Francis Adams. Boston, 1850-1856), VI. "We may appeal," Adams said, "to every page of history . . . for proofs irrefragable, that the people, when they have been unchecked, have been as unjust, tyrannical, brutal, barbarous and cruel as any king or senate possessed of uncontrollable power. . . . All projects of government, formed upon a supposition of continual vigilance, sagacity, virtue, and firmness of the people, when possessed of the exercise of supreme power, are cheats and delusions." *Works*, VI, 10, 95. The real test for capacity to govern was wealth, birth, and education. The people in general might be divided into two groups, the gentlemen and the simplemen. The gentlemen, as a rule, were the "well-born and wealthy"; the simplemen, the "laborers, husbandmen, mechanics. . . ." *Ibid.*, 185.
[32] Charles Francis Adams, *"The Solid South" and the Afro-American Race Problem*, p. 18.

In 1889 James Bryce approved the southern position in his *The American Commonwealth* by declaring, ". . . in the hands of the Negroes at the South, or the newly enfranchised immigrants of the larger cities, a vote is a weapon of mischief."[33] He thought the great American assumption that citizenship automatically fitted one for intelligent participation in government to be absurd and illogical. "It is an afterthought to argue that they will sooner become good citizens by being immediately made full citizens. A stranger must not presume to say that the Americans have been prudent, but he may doubt whether the possible ultimate good compensates the direct and unquestionable mischief."[34]

The process of limiting the civil equality of the Negro in the South began earlier than did the attempt to seek constitutional means of depriving him of the ballot. The Federal Civil Rights Act of 1866 had been general in its terms as were also the provisions of the Fourteenth Amendment, but the Civil Rights Act of 1875 enumerated specific rights. All persons within the jurisdiction of the United States should be entitled to the full and equal enjoyment of the accommodations, advantages, facilities, and privileges of inns, public conveyances on land or water, theaters, and other places of public amusement, subject only to the conditions established by law and applicable alike to citizens of every race and color regardless of any previous condition of servitude. The law carried provisions for specific punishments and specific modes of redress.

In five different cases having to do with the civil rights of Negroes which reached the Supreme Court in 1883, the Court took the position that individual discrimination against Negroes was not prohibited by the Thirteenth and Fourteenth Amendments. Indeed, that seems to have been the prevailing opinion of Congress at the time of the passage of the Amendments, for Thaddeus Stevens, Radical Republican leader, had said in explaining his doctrine of civil equality that it did not mean a Negro "should sit on the same seat or eat at the same table with a white man"; that was a matter of taste which every man had to decide for himself and over which the law had no jurisdiction.[35] The effect of the test cases in the eighties was to declare that the federal government cannot prevent the curtailment of the civil rights of Negroes by individuals unless such individuals are acting under the sanction of a particular kind, and the federal court could declare state statutes in such instances unconstitutional. Within these limits the states might proceed to define and to secure civil rights for Negroes.[36]

[33] Volume II (2d ed. London and New York, 1891), 698.
[34] *Ibid.*, 100.
[35] *Congressional Globe*, January 3, 1867; cited in Thomas Frederick Woodley, *Great Leveler; The Life of Thaddeus Stevens* (New York, 1937), p. 8.
[36] Civil Rights Cases, 190 U. S. 3, 3 Sup. Ct. 18 (1883). For an able prediction as to the ultimate consequences of this decision, written anonymously by a white lawyer of Baltimore for the (Negro) Brotherhood of Liberty see, *Justice and Jurisprudence: an Inquiry Concerning the Constitutional Limitations of the Thirteenth, Fourteenth, and Fifteenth Amendments* (Philadelphia, 1889).

The definitions which the South employed looked steadily toward favoritism in behalf of the whites. After 1883 few of the southern states passed civil rights acts as such but depended upon the courts to determine the rights of citizens in public places. The first of the racial separation laws looked toward the continuation of the old ante-bellum laws against interracial marriage. The so-called Jim Crow laws, calling for racial separation in railroads and streetcars, began with a sweeping statute in 1875 in Tennessee abrogating the rule of the common law giving a right of action to any person excluded from any hotel, or public means of transportation, or place of amusement, and it even gave public conveyances the privilege of refusing to carry Negroes.[37] This law was set aside, and legislatures thereafter were more careful in wording their statutes. All of the southern states fell in line in the passage of Jim Crow laws in the eighties and nineties, and the concept of racial separation also found expression in legal action to prevent the eligibility of Negroes to be served in white hotels, barber shops, restaurants, and in any but restricted areas of public amusement.[38] Specific laws made the education of Negro and white children in separate systems mandatory. As a matter of course the poorer accommodations fell to the lot of Negroes. They lived in the worst residential districts; their amusements were such as they could provide for themselves; they were either excluded entirely or segregated in public gatherings; they were segregated on public conveyances; their schools received the lowest allotment of public funds; and they continued to fill the lowest occupations in the field of labor.

Thus when the old social and economic structure fell with the Civil War, the South immediately began the erection of a new structure upon the basis of the old philosophy. By the turn of the twentieth century that adjustment had become fixed in a biracial social and economic order. As stated by Bishop Charles Betts Galloway at the seventh annual meeting of the Conference for Education in the South held in Birmingham in 1904, the position of the southern whites was as follows:

First.—In the South there will never be any social mingling of the races. Whether it be prejudice or pride of race, there is a middle wall of partition which will not be broken down.

Second.—They will worship in separate churches and be educated in separate schools. This is desired alike by both races, and is for the good of each.

Third.—The political power of this section will remain in present hands. Here, as elsewhere, intelligence and wealth will and should control the administration of government affairs.

Fourth.—The great body of the Negroes are here to stay. Their coerced colonization would be a crime, and their deportation a physical impossibility. And the white people are less anxious for them to go than the Negroes are to leave. They are natives and not intruders.[39]

[37] C. S. Mangum, *Legal Status of the Negro*, p. 31. Delaware passed a Civil Rights Act similar to that of Tennessee.
[38] *Ibid.*, pp. 26-77; G. T. Stephenson, *Race Distinctions*, pp. 116-118.
[39] *The South and the Negro* (New York, 1904), p. 8.

This solution of the race problem scarcely deviated in philosophy from the major assumptions of the slavery regime. The Negro was presumed to be an inferior type of man, but he was wholly acceptable within a given sphere of activity; "he was all right in his place." Any relationship which brought the inferior Negro except in the capacity of a menial into association with the superior white man tended to elevate the inferior and automatically to degrade the superior. Political, religious, or educational equalities were tantamount to social equality, and social equality would inevitably lead to intermarriage and the deterioration of the white race. The extremists would conclude from these assumptions that the Negro must be removed from American civilization or be ground down so effectively that there would never be any temptation to cross the race line.

Southern whites felt that the Fourteenth and Fifteenth Amendments negated the major assumption of Negro inferiority. So long as the amendments remained a part of the federal constitution, they were sleeping thunder which might be hurled against the "domestic tranquility" of the South at any moment by a Congress or a Supreme Court favorable to the Negro.[40] The South, therefore, was driven back into the defensive position which it had occupied since 1820. Southern leaders must now rationalize the caste status of the Negro as it had once rationalized his slave status.

The caste status to which the Negro had been assigned since the colonial period but which had often been softened by the personal relationships of slavery became frozen after emancipation by the fewer and fewer contacts possible between whites and blacks except in economic relationships. Once the property status of the Negro was removed the kindliness of the white man toward the oppressed race must depend entirely upon humanitarian impulses *per se*. The white South which had declared in 1860 that slavery was the cornerstone of its social structure quickly realized that emancipation had not destroyed that cornerstone. The South before 1860 knew what the status of a free Negro was and it also knew what it meant to lose property in slaves. After 1865 a mass of white men who had lost property in slaves was left to confront a mass of free Negroes. It was only logical that the old relationships should continue as before; that the dominant white race should seek in every possible way to rule the subordinate Negro race as before. While emancipation may have lost to the planter his particular set of Negroes, it did not deprive him of dependent Negro labor.

[40] A definite movement began among Democrats toward the close of the nineteenth century to repeal the Fourteenth and Fifteenth Amendments. W. B. Cockran, a New York Democrat, in a speech in 1900 before the Southern Society for the Promotion of the Study of Race Conditions advocated a constitutional amendment "restoring control of the suffrage to the State." *In the Name of Liberty, Selected Addresses* (ed. by Robert McElroy. New York, 1925), p. 88. Senator Carmack of Tennessee gave notice in 1903 that he would bring in a bill to repeal the Amendments, but nothing came of the effort. The *Edinburgh Review*, CCI (1905), 67-71, summarized northern opinion as follows: "While a large portion of the people of the North admit that the enfranchisement of the former slave immediately after the war was a mistake, they are not prepared to repeal the Amendments and thus stultify themselves in the eyes of the civilized world."

Negro labor was as much dependent upon the white employer as before. Public subjugation came now to be substituted for the old private subjugation under slavery.

The processes of public subjugation had begun long before 1865, for no sooner had Negro slaves been imported in this country in large numbers than the theory of "the taint of Negro blood" began to be enunciated.[41] Most southern states, in an attempt to define who might be enslaved, soon found it necessary to make "the Negro" a fixed legal term. South Carolina, however, steadfastly refused to say what amount of Negro blood would bring one within the proscribed term. "We cannot say what admixture . . . will make a colored person," declared the State Supreme Court in State vs. Cantey in 1835. "The condition . . . is not to be determined solely by . . . visible mixture . . . but by reputation . . . and it may be . . . proper, that a man of worth . . . should have the rank of a white man, while a vagabond of the same degree of blood should be confined to the inferior caste."[42] In an earlier case the South Carolina court had declared that when free Negroes had lost the "mark which nature has put upon them" they tend to become elevated in society; "some who have lost that distinctive mark, hold offices, as well as lands, and even seats in the the legislature."[43] It was not in fact until the last decade of the nineteenth century that South Carolina at last put a legal penalty upon the possession of Negro blood.

The usual test applied by the southern states to decide whether persons came within the legal term was to declare a person of color to be one who was descended from a Negro to the third generation inclusive though one ancestor in each generation may have been white.[44] In 1770 Thomas Jefferson had argued a case in which he declared that it would be wicked to carry legal proscription "to the 'nati et qui nascentur ab illis,' "[45] and a South Carolina judge in 1835 had pronounced such a demarcation to be "very cruel and mischievous." It was left for the twentieth century to extend the legal definition to "that slight trace,"[46] a definition which popular opinion had already sanctioned.

[41] When a distinction in the case of a Negro was made with reference to perpetual or limited servitude, the assumption establishing hereditary slavery was at first dependent upon the matter of infidelity. Once Christianity was declared incapable of rescuing one from hereditary slavery, so declared by legislative act in Virginia beginning in 1667, the test of life servitude now became physical appearance. See Helen Tunnicliff Catterall, *Judicial Cases Concerning American Slavery and the Negro* (Washington, D. C., 1926), I, 53-71; James Curtis Ballagh, *A History of Slavery in Virginia* (Baltimore, 1902), Ch. II; Edward Raymond Turner, *The Negro in Pennsylvania, Slavery, Servitude, Freedom, 1639-1861* (Washington, 1911), pp. 17-21.

[42] H. T. Catterall, *Judicial Cases*, II, 359.

[43] Hardcastle ads Porcher, Harper, 495; H. T. Catterall, *Judicial Cases*, II, 534.

[44] C. S. Mangum, *Legal Status of the Negro*, Ch. I.

[45] Thomas Jefferson, *Reports of Cases Determined in the General Court of Virginia*, p. 96.

[46] Alabama *Acts* (1927), p. 219; Georgia *Laws* (1927), p. 272, and Virginia *Acts* (1930), Ch. 85 set up the assumption of permanent taint in their acts placing certain disabilities upon persons of Negro blood no matter how remote the admixture.

The literature attempting to define and analyze the caste status of the American Negro is extensive, but it was not until 1853 that a young octoroon, William B. Allen, professor in radical Central College in McGrawville, New York, analyzed the status from the point of view of the proscribed caste. Having barely escaped violence at the hands of a mob when he sought to marry a young white girl, daughter of an abolitionist, Allen wrote with feeling concerning the American caste system:

Whatever a man be in his own person,—though he should have the eloquence, talents, and character of Paul and Appollo, and the Angel Gabriel combined,— though he should be as wealthy as Croesus,—and though, in personal appearance, he should be as fair as the fairest Anglo-Saxon, yet, if he have but one drop of the African flowing in his veins, no white young lady can ally herself to him in matrimony, without bringing upon her the anathemas of the community, with scarce an exception, and rendering herself an almost total outcast, not only from the society in which she formerly moved, but from society in general.

Such is American caste, . . . notwithstanding the claims set up by the American people, that they are Heaven's Vice-regents, to teach to men and to nations as well, the legitimate ideas of Christian Democracy. . . . The laws of the Southern states, on the one hand . . . have deliberately, and in cold blood, withheld their protection from every woman within their borders, in whose veins may flow but half a drop of African blood; while the prejudice against color of the Northern States, on the other hand, is so cruel and contemptuous of the rights and feelings of colored people, that no white man would lose his caste in debauching the best educated, most accomplished, virtuous and wealthy colored woman in the community, but would be mobbed from Maine to Delaware, should he with that same woman attempt honorable marriage.[47]

In 1869 Charles Sumner sought to analyze the basis of caste in a scholarly lecture in Boston. He thought the theory of American caste to be similar to that of the divine right of kings. In America the theory had been converted into "a claim of hereditary power from color."[48] This outworn theory of absolutism should be discarded, he thought, for the more fundamental concept of the common humanity of man, a fact to which all fields of science pointed: ethnology, geology, paleography, anatomy. When the mass of mankind was considered, the importance of color and other ethnological differences disappeared; the fact that all mankind was capable of changing from a lower to a higher level of civilization was the important consideration.

During the height of the agrarian controversy in the South, a southern man, George Washington Cable of Louisiana, also spoke out against the American caste system. Like Sumner he thought the American proscription of the Negro arose from the old theory of divine rights, but he also thought that the Americans had given the theory an Oriental emphasis. "Its principle declares public safety and highest development to require the subjugation of the lower mass under the arbitrary protective supremacy

[47] *The American Prejudice Against Color* (London, 1853), pp. 7-8, 12-13.
[48] *The Question of Caste* (Boston, 1869), pp. 21-22. Charles Sumner attributed to Johannes Mueller's *Cosmos* most of his ideas on race.

of an untitled but hereditary privileged class, a civil caste." It was not an aristocracy which the South was attempting to set up, "for an aristocracy exists, presumably, at least, with the wide consent of all classes, and men in any rank of life may have some hope to attain to it by extraordinary merit and service; but a caste; not the embodiment of a modern European idea, but the resuscitation of an ancient Asiatic one."[49]

Cable declared that the Negro as a free man was never given a chance to prove his capacities. "This scheme was never allowed a fair trial in any of the once seceding States. Every effort to give it such was powerfully opposed by one great national political party throughout the whole Union, 'while . . . the greater part of the wealth and intelligence of the region directly involved held out sincerely, steadfastly, and desperately against it and for the preservation of unequal public privileges and class domination.'"[50] For this reason, one heard much of "Negro supremacy," "a black oligarchy," "the Africanization of the South," and "race antagonism" which is "natural, inborn, ineradicable," and some writers had the temerity to "stand up before the intelligent and moral world saying, 'If this instinct does not exist it is necessary to invent it.'"[51]

Cable thought that the "tap-root of the Negro question" and, therefore, of the caste system itself was fear. Although he never specifically defined the basis of this fear, the implication throughout his discussion was that this fear was twofold. It rested upon the economic fear of loss of services in the labor of the Negro and upon physical fear of the Negroes in case they should outnumber the whites and, realizing their strength, decide to take revenge for long-continued mistreatment. "It is only where a people are moved by the fear of Negro supremacy," he said, "that the simple *belief* in a divinely ordered race antagonism is used to justify the withholding of impersonal public rights which belong to every man because he is a man, and with which race and its real or imagined antagonisms have nothing whatever to do."[52] No economic theorist, but a humanitarian after the school of Heber and Ruskin, Cable saw in the Negro "a kindly race of poor men" whom progress, speeded up by conscious human direction, might develop into industrious citizens. Cable was denounced as a sentimental theorist, and public opinion finally drove him from the South.

Numerous theories, already well-worn in the ante-bellum period, were at hand to justify the caste system. Among the patterns of thought most frequently exhibited in the writings and platform oratory of the time were the ideas clustering around the concepts of (1) retrogression, (2) progress, (3) paternalism, (4) romanticism, and, for lack of a better term, (5) negrophobia.

The theory of retrogression, widely popularized by Thomas Carlyle's

[49] G. W. Cable, *The Negro Question*, p. 27.
[50] *Ibid.*, p. 97.
[51] *Ibid.*, p. 99, citing Henry Woodfin Grady, "In Plain Black and White," published in *Century Magazine* (1885), 911.
[52] *Ibid.*, p. 98.

The Nigger Question, which had been written after emancipation in the West Indies, was used in the ante-bellum period as a justification of slavery and it became now a convenient justification of white supremacy. It was argued that the Negro as a freeman could not stand up under the competition of civilized life and would retrogress to savagery and meet the fate of ultimate extinction. This assumption had been based primarily upon Malthusian arguments, but, even before Malthus, the natural scientists had outlined the concept of retrogression.[53] At the time of emancipation it was widely predicted that the Negro would rapidly die out and become as rare in American life as the Indian. The anonymous author of "The Negro and the Negrophiles," published in the *Edinburgh Review* of May 1866, declared that with Negroes "liberty and the grave speedily become one and the same blessing." Since the Negro would not work without compulsion, economic laws, "typhus and smallpox, aggravated by filth and famine, make short work of the black man, and relieve overburdened charity of a task, which charity may have the will, but not the means or power, to perform."[54] The census of 1870 still left the question open, for, having been taken in a time of general unrest among both the southern whites and blacks, it was generally conceded that the returns were inaccurate and consequently inconclusive. When, however, the census of 1880 showed a large increase of Negroes, in some areas a doubling of the population in a decade, the news aroused consternation in many quarters and produced a quick revision of concepts.

While some were unwilling to accept the count of the 1880 census as accurate, others abandoned the theory of extermination of the Negroes through natural causes but they did not cast aside the doctrine of retrogression. Indeed, the fact of a rapidly increasing Negro population made the predictions of the theory seem even more alarming, for an essential premise was the cultural deterioration of the Negro when removed from direct supervision of the dominant race. "The time has come for honest, manly effort," declared Bishop T. U. Dudley of the Protestant Episcopal Church of Kentucky. "Separated from us, their neighbors and their friends," the Negroes "must retrograde toward the barbarism whence they are sprung, and then, alas, we might be compelled to wage relentless war against them for our own preservation."[55]

Philip Alexander Bruce, with ancestry in the old planter aristocracy of Virginia, was one of the first Southerners to make a serious study of

---

[53] In this connection it is interesting to note that the theory had been used by natural scientists before 1785 to predict the ultimate decline of American civilization. It was argued for example, that the sparcity of the indigenous animal population in America at the time of its discovery was proof that animal life degenerated as a result of the combined forces of American soil and climate and that European animals, including man, when transplanted would ultimately degenerate for the same reason. De paw and Abbé Raynal accepted the full implications of this argument, and Comte de Buffon stopped only one step short of it.

[54] P. 596.

[55] "How Shall We Help the Negro," *Century Magazine,* XXX (1885), 287.

the problem from this point of view. His *The Plantation Negro as a Freeman,* written in 1889, was an exposition of the southern situation in the light of a rapidly regressing Negro population. Believing that an examination of Negro character and society "without partiality and without prejudice" would be the only approach to a solution of the problem, Bruce described Negro family life, character, education, religion, and superstitions. He appraised the Negro as a citizen, a laborer, landowner, and criminal. His conclusion was that ultimately, and at no distant date, the Negro would "revert to the African original." "The return of the race to the original physical type involves its intellectual reversion also . . . . Every circumstance surrounding the Negro in the present age seems to point directly to his future moral decadence. . . . The influences that are shaping the character of the younger generations appear to be such as must bring the blacks in time to a state of nature. . . ."[56] Such a condition was further complicated by the high fertility rate of Negroes. "The probability is that, in a few generations, formal and legal marriages will be much less frequent than they are now, and the promiscuous intercourse between the sexes will grow more open and unreserved."[57]

The Negro might be expected to increase at an alarming rate another half century, "because, during that period of time, the soil must remain comparatively cheap and abundant, and the negro be in sufficient demand as a laborer to supply him with all that is necessary to his existence."[58] The unlimited increase of the blacks was "pregnant with innumerable calamities." "It virtually means that a period will come when there will be a sharp contest between blacks and whites for the possession of a large part of the Southern States. . . ."[59] The whites might kill off the blacks, or they might in disgust migrate and leave the blacks in barbaric enjoyment of the southern region. The only real solution, he thought, was immediate and complete deportation. In the meantime, an alternative stopgap would be an attempt to elevate the race through education fostered either by the public school system or by the white evangelical denominations sponsored by northern philanthropy. But this effort would in the end prove abortive, and he predicted that "in the course of the next ten decades American institutions would be subjected to a severer strain than they have yet endured. . . ."[60]

In accordance with the Malthusian system, Bruce believed that a barbaric race might be elevated to a higher cultural level only when supervised by a civilized race under a paternal system of compulsion. Wherever he found whites to be in a considerable majority, he discovered retrogression to be going on at a slower rate. Instead of calling for deportation as the only remedy to prevent race war, Bruce might have argued as logically

[56] Pp. 243, 245, 246.
[57] *Ibid.,* p. 246.
[58] *Ibid.,* p. 255.
[59] *Ibid.,* p. 256.
[60] *Ibid.,* p. 26.

the spread theory which was used at the time of the Missouri Compromise and which was to reappear in southern thinking in the twentieth century.[61] But the possibility of reducing the ratio of blacks to whites through the processes of black migration was ruled out of his thinking by the assumption that "the negro is only useful to the Southern States, and through those States to the Union" as an agricultural laborer. Bruce also assumed that Negro personality tarits would forever prevent the black mans' becoming assimilated as a workable part of American society. He enumerated these traits as being "intellectual blindness, moral obtuseness, and a thoughtless indulgence of every appetite." If the Negro were "in full possession of all the noble qualities that adorn human nature, the white people would be as little prompted to pass him by with indifference and contempt, socially, as if he belonged to their own race," but the ignorance and licentiousness of the typical Negro "would make him highly objectionable to refined sensibilities and cultivated minds, even if his skin were that of a Caucasian."[62]

Guided by apprehensions based upon the theory of retrogression, a movement was started in the late nineteenth century to bring the whites and blacks of the South into more cordial relationships so that the pessimistic outlook which such men as Bruce foresaw might be prevented. Bishop Dudley urged such a policy in 1885. He wanted the Negro welcomed back to the polls and to the white churches. "The separation of the Negro race from the white race means for the negro continued and increasing degradation and decay. His hope, his salvation, must come from association with that people among whom he dwells, but from whose natural guidance and care he has been separated largely by the machinations of unscrupulous demagogues."[63] When the "machinations of unscrupulous demagogues" continued to drive the blacks and whites further apart, and foreign observers as well as Southerners continued to point out that "there is less chance than there ever was of their working together peacefully for good; and increasing racial antagonism, nourished by both sides, grows daily,"[64] a definite movement toward interracial cooperation

[61] See for example, R. H. Leavell, "The Negro Migration From Mississippi," in U. S. Labor Department, *Negro Migration,* p. 41. The latest recrudescence of the spread theory was the offer in the opening days of the 81st Congress of Senator Richard Brevard Russell of Georgia to exchange with the North an equal number of Negroes for whites "to lessen the evil consequences of the President's Civil Rights Program" in case it should be enacted.
[62] P. A. Bruce, *The Plantation Negro as a Freeman,* pp. 49-50. It should be borne in mind throughout this discussion that the personality traits which the whites thought desirable in the Negro were the traits which the classical economists approved. It was a set of hypothetical traits which the whites as a group also had difficulty in meeting.
[63] "How Shall We Help the Negro?" *Century Magazine,* XXX (1885), 278. Walter Hines Page relates in his novel, *The Southerner* (pp. 202-203) how a southern newspaper editor rises to a seat in the legislature through capitalizing upon white fears by playing up a case of rape committed by a drunken Negro.
[64] William Laird Clowes, *Black America: a Study of the Ex-Slave and His Late Master* (London, 1891), p. 90.

was launched through the combined efforts of southern leaders and northern philanthropists. Begun first as conferences on southern education, the movement, after the Atlanta riot of 1906, became a definite program to bring southern white and black leaders in closer touch so that they might discuss problems of mutual importance.[65] The interracial movement as an organization with regional, state, and local branches did not come into existence until the third decade of the twentieth century.

No American writer of the period who tried seriously to analyze the race problem failed to find some comfort in the hope of education. The extent of hope usually depended upon the writer's concept of the theory of progress, and the theory of progress was itself undergoing a vast change at the very time that equalitarianism was being incorporated into the federal constitution. The hypothesis of progression from a lower to a higher state was expressed first by the moral philosophers and then by the natural scientists. From this position it was but a step to the application of the theory to all plant and animal life including man. If particular races of men seemed less advanced than others, it was because they had not progressed as far on the scale of evolution. The theory of progression had already affected northern thinking before the period of Reconstruction. Such men as Charles Sumner and Carl Schurz accepted it as proof that the Negro possessed the ability to develop and lacked only the opportunity to prove it. To the theory of progress they added the immediacy concept of the extreme natural rights wing of the anti-slavery school. But the progression theory was also capable of proving the incapacity of the Negro for immediate citizenship.

It would be difficult to determine who contributed most to American thinking on progress as applied to the Negro. Comte had outlined the theory of progress in the philosophical school and Maillet and Lamarck had devised scientific theories of development. The works of Charles Darwin, *The Origin of the Species,* published in this country in 1859, and *The Descent of Man,* published in 1871, seem to have influenced most the thinking of social scientists in the period following Reconstruction. In 1908 Charles Francis Adams attributed the vast change since 1865 in American thinking on the Negro to "a different conception of the facts" which had been produced by Darwin's profound works.[66] The Negro was no longer

---

[65] Booker T. Washington, founder of Tuskegee Normal and Industrial Institute for Negroes, Tuskegee, Ala., was the southern Negro leader in this movement. Northern Negro leaders, as a rule, were skeptical of the results. Kelly Miller wrote of the interracial movement in 1908: "Several years ago I sat on the platform of a meeting in Atlanta composed of about equal numbers of the two races. . . . Local representatives on both sides of the race line vied with each other in vowing racial affection and ties of endearment. . . . But as I sat there, I divined, as I thought, a hidden spirit not revealed in the spoken words, which seemed to me to be simply verbal civilities and diplomatic platitudes. When the meeting adjourned each went to his own company with no surer knowledge of the real feeling or purpose of the other than when it convened. *Race Adjustment: Essays on the Negro in America* (New York, 1908), p. 59.

[66] Charles Francis Adams, *The Solid South,* pp. 16-18.

considered "the Hamitic man . . . God's image carved in ebony, only partially developed under unfavorable fortuitous circumstances," but a race lower on the scale of evolution, "of widely different interests, attainments and ideals. . . ."[67] The Darwinian hypothesis explained the origin and perpetuation of species of animals and plants by a process of natural selection and survival of the fittest. Man was protected in this process of selection and survival by certain inborn instincts. By implication, acquired characteristics might also be inherited.

Josiah Clark Nott, who had attempted in the ante-bellum period to establish the theory of the permanency of type, thought the Darwinian hypothesis "would not controvert the facts and deductions I have laid down," for "even this school require[s] millions of years for their theory" to operate.[68]

Southern theology had rejected Nott's theory of the permanency of type because it was based upon an anti-Biblical concept of the origin of man.[69] For many decades the South denied for the same reason the theory of evolution, but did not reject the Darwinian implication of inborn instincts. Southern theologians and, indeed, many northern ones as well employed the idea of race instincts, or "certain inborn antipathies" to explain and justify segregation in the churches.

Separate Negro congregations under the supervision of white ministers were encouraged in the South during the slavery period on the assumption that the black man was not sufficiently acquainted with American institutions to understand the intricacies of denominational creeds and the attempt was made to evangelize rather than to ritualize the Negro. Northern missionaries who flocked to the South in the closing days of the Civil War encouraged the withdrawal of the former slaves from connections with their masters' churches and the Negroes themselves showed an inclination to set up their own church organizations. The Methodist Episcopal Church, South, was one of several denominations that made some effort to retain their Negro congregations, but when this effort failed, Atticus Greene Haygood, president of Emory College and later a Methodist bishop, placed the full responsibility for withdrawal upon the Negro's race instinct.

This instinctive disposition to form Church affiliations on the color basis may be wise or unwise. But it is in them—deep in them. The tendency is strengthening all the time. This instinct will never be satisfied till it realizes itself in complete separation. Whether we of the white race approve or disapprove matters little. . . . We may, all of us, as well adjust our plans to the determined and inevitable movements of this instinct—that does not reason, but that moves steadily and resistlessly to accomplish its ends. It is a very grave question to be considered by all who have responsibility in this matter: Whether over-repression of race-instincts may not mar their normal evolu-

[67] *Ibid.*, pp. 17-18.
[68] "The Problem of the Black Races," *DeBow's Review* (New Series. New Orleans, 1866), I, 272n.
[69] W. S. Jenkins, *Pro-Slavery Thought*, pp. 281-282.

tion—may not introduce elements unfriendly to healthful growth—may not result in explosions? I have seen a heavy stone wall overturned by a root that was once a tiny white fiber. Instinct is like the life-force that expresses itself in life or death.[70]

Here was a convenient theory, based, as it was thought, solidly upon objective science which relieved churchmen of the burden of applying Christian ethics to the lower caste. It was possible actually to interpret the Golden Rule in terms of segregation. Yet, religious philosophy did not, except in the mouths of extremists, deny the concept of the Fatherhood of God and the brotherhood of man. The Negro was generally conceded to be one of God's children, but the theory of race instinct and the concept of retarded races made it possible to hold that the full implications of brotherhood could not apply to the Negro. If brotherhood *could* not be applied, it was an easy step to the conclusion that brotherhood *should* not be applied and that if it were applied, even on rare occasions by opening the doors of the white church to a visiting Negro minister or to an unsegregated audience, such application was tantamount to social equality. Southern white churches went a step further and also applied caste relationships to northern white missionaries who worked among the emancipated slaves. Southern churches, both white and Negro, thus tended to become the most militantly race conscious institutions in the post-war era.

Not all southern theologians condoned this generally accepted caste position of the white churches. Pride of race, declared Bishop T. U. Dudley of the Protestant Episcopal Church of Kentucky, "is but a pretext to excuse the conduct which, in our heart of hearts, we know to proceed from the old root of bitterness—the feeling of caste which demands that the liberated slave shall be forever a menial. I charge the Christian white men of the South to mark that the effect of this separation, on which we have insisted, has helped to drive these people into a corresponding exclusiveness, and is constantly diminishing the influence of our Christian thinkers upon their beliefs and their practice."[71]

Even Bishop Dudley would admit that the practices of Negro churches were becoming "more and more like the African original." Likewise northern missionaries who had in the beginning attributed the undesirable traits of the Negro to the evils of slavery now placed less emphasis upon slavery and more upon "barbarism." The "wild ravings" of the Negro ministers and the emotional behavior of the congregations became another proof that the Negro was an African and not a "lamp-blacked white man."[72] Percy Stickney Grant's *Socialism and Christianity* of 1910 illustrates the shift in ideologies which had taken place following the Civil War.

When, in 1866, we came to deal with a race which had no such traditions or political ancestors as the American colonists—to a race sadly near an unpoetic

[70] *Our Brothers in Black*, pp. 235-236.
[71] "How Shall We Help the Negro," *Century*, XXX (1885), 279.
[72] *Ibid.*, p. 279; see also *Proceedings of the American Missionary Association, 1867-1910*.

state of nature—"natural rights" were granted, "equality" was affirmed and "fraternity" demanded. . . . We are now (in the generation after the war) confronted by our failures, but are also, luckily, at the same time attended by a new philosophy that explains our failures and bids us not to be discouraged. The theory of evolution takes for granted human inequality and consequently knows nothing of natural and universal rights. In place of jumps it discloses steps; in place of catastrophies and sudden transformation, slow processes.[73]

The physical and cultural inferiority of the Negro should be taken for granted, he argued, and means employed to "oil the wheels of progress." The Biblical concept of brotherhood and equality now became in the light of evolution the concept of brotherhood and inequality. "It points to heights of human attainment where further development is possible only along spiritual lines, by the exercise of altruism and brotherhood, and so says, 'Be patient and helpful.'"

Once the present inferiority of the Negro was admitted, the southern position became more tenable, and once it was admitted that there was a grain of truth in the southern position the easier it was to accept the whole of it. Thus, for almost two generations after Reconstruction the attitude toward the Negro on the part of northern Christians may be described as "patient helpfulness" and on the part of southern Christians a stout defense of segregation in the sanctuary "because it is desired alike by both races, and is for the good of each."

The concept of progress resolved itself into a controversy similar to that which had existed before 1860: Was the Negro permanently inferior to the Caucasian or could he be brought up to the level of the "higher" race? Was it possible for a retarded race to skip some of the steps toward advancement and thereby ultimately catch up with the "superior" race? Or must a backward race repeat the historical experience of the superior race in order to progress to a higher level and thus be forever behind? The southern position on white supremacy seemed to imply permanent inferiority, but whenever the question was discussed in the pulpit or the press the Negro was usually given to understand that his race might eventually by hard work and self-denial, win civil and economic equality—, but never social equality. Those who believed in permanent inferiority tended to reject the Negro as a permissible component of southern population and called loudly for expulsion. This position will be discussed under the category of negrophobia.

The writings of Edgar Gardner Murphy, an Episcopal clergyman of Montgomery, Alabama, were typical of scholarly southern thinking of the period. To Murphy, the Negro was "a backward and essentially unassimilable people" whom "the consciousness of kind," a phrase which he borrowed from the Columbia University sociologist, Franklin H. Giddings, would forever set apart from the whites. Yet the Negro had it within his power to work out his own salvation and eventually to win the respect of the dominant race. By using "the positive liberties and advantages of

[73] Pp. 135-136, 138.

education and of industry, of religion and of political freedom," the Negro in America might, Murphy thought, "through the acceptance of a programme of positive progress, . . . enter into a larger heritage than is open to any like number of his race in any quarter of the world. Important are some of the advantages which he has not; but more important are the many advantages which he has."[74] The freedmen in 1865 were by no means in a state of development worthy of being brought within the democratic assumptions of the constitution. "White supremacy, at that stage in the development of the South, was necessary to the supremacy of intelligence, administrative capacity and public order, and involved even the existence of those economic and civic conditions upon which the progress of the negro was itself dependent."[75]

Murphy denied, however, that the fundamental question at issue was the capacity of the Negro race. The fundamental was the attitude of the dominant race toward the Negro. These antipathies should be explained and an attempt made to understand them in the hope of redirecting them for the good of society.[76] The state should begin a positive policy of development, and this policy should be applied to both races. The black race should be educated to the level of the white race and the white race should be educated to a better understanding and appreciation of the blacks. Murphy sought to allay the fears of the whites by assuring them that the operation of the principle of the consciousness of kind would forever prevent widespread social mingling and amalgamation.

Thomas Nelson Page, whose romantic novels of ante-bellum life did much to perpetuate the fiction of the golden age of the plantation regime, also thought that the Negro might be developed through education, but he would not admit that the race was as capable of progress as did Murphy. He would stop, in fact, only one step short of permanent inferiority, reluctantly admitting that the concept of permanent inferiority would close the door of hope forever to the Negro who was also one of God's children. Page's estimate of the history of the Negro race and its capacities to develop strongly resembled ante-bellum ideology. He thought that the history of the Negro race revealed that for four thousand years it had "exhibited the absence of the essential qualities of a progressive race." Page declared that the Negro had always been an inferior race. "In the earliest records of the human race, the monuments of Egypt and Syria, he is depicted as a slave bearing burdens; after tens of centuries he is still a menial." Page could find nothing of value which the Negro mind had contributed. "In art, in mechanical development, in literature, in mental and moral science, in all the range of mental action, no notable work has up to this time come from the Negro."[77]

[74] *The Present South* (New York, 1904), p. 183.
[75] *Ibid.*, p. 190.
[76] *The Basis of Ascendancy, a Discussion of Certain Principles of Public Policy Involved in the Development of the Southern States* (New York, 1909), p. xviii.
[77] *The Negro: the Southerner's Problem* (New York, 1904), pp. 249-250.

The white novelist could not find an instance where the Negro race had risen of its own efforts, but he would not say that "because a Negro is a Negro he is incapable of any intellectual development. On the contrary, observation has led me to think that under certain conditions of intellectual environment, of careful training, and of sympathetic encouragement from the stronger races he may individually attain a fair, and in uncommon instances a considerable degree, of mental development."[78] He did not think that the formal education which the Negroes had been receiving since emancipation was the type needed to achieve the elevation of the race, and the race, he declared, must either be elevated or deported. ". . . the earnest effort of the South to educate the Negroes, extending through a generation, at an expense of over $110,000,000, contributed out of the property of the Southern whites, has been a complete failure in that the beneficiaries of this effort are not as good workers, or as good citizens, as the generation which preceded them, and use the education so given them, where they use it at all, in ways which are not beneficial to themselves and are injurious to the whites."[79] The Negro needed, he thought, a training different from that of the whites, character training especially. ". . . the Negro must be taught the great elementary truths of morality and duty. Until he is so established in these that he claims to be on this ground the equal of the white, he can never be his equal on any other ground. . . . Until then, he is fighting not the white race, but a law of nature, universal and inexorable—that races rise or fall according to their character."[80]

It was typical of the romantic school of writers, such as Thomas Nelson Page, to compare the rising generation of Negroes with the Negroes born in slavery only to find that those born in freedom fell far short of the old ideal. Edgar Gardner Murphy complained of this nostalgic class interpretation of the Negro problem when he wrote in 1909: "It is idle to talk of the fineness of the old-time negro who was illiterate. He, and the paternalistic conditions which created him, are gone forever."[81] Nevertheless, there were both romanticists and paternalists among southern whites whose attitude on the Negro problem, while contributing nothing dynamic to the discussion, often helped to ease the friction of the times. Page referred to the practice "so commonly to be found in the South" among the upper classes of treating their Negro retainers, even "the weakest and worst of them with . . . mingled consideration and indulgence."[82] The South had been turning toward romanticism during the last two decades of the ante-bellum period. The regional fiction of the time indicated the trend. The movement was the effect of Victorianism, or sentimental humanitarianism, which may be traced in other parts of the country as well

[78] *Ibid.*, p. 250.
[79] *Ibid.*, p. 303.
[80] *Ibid.*, p. 310. This "inexorable law of nature" was the Malthusian principle of self-denial.
[81] *The Basis of Ascendancy*, p. 11.
[82] T. N. Page, *The Negro,* p. x.

as in the South. In New England, for example, Thomas Bailey Aldrich, editor of the *Atlantic* from 1881 to 1890, was fighting for the preservation of the genteel against such purveyors of realism as Walt Whitman and Mark Twain.

The movement in the post-war South was the defense of the old aristocracy against the forces which had uprooted the social structure. The romantic school turned wistful glances back to slavery, found it good, and with it "de old darkey" of plantation days. Writers of this school stressed the good conduct of the slave during the war, fondly recalled the "black mammy" of their childhood, and the "pickaninny" who entered into their youthful sports. They usually attributed the "bad conduct" of the Negro during freedom to fundamental errors taught him by northern emissaries who knew nothing whatever of the true nature of conditions. These errors were: "first, that the Southern white was inherently his enemy, and, secondly, that his race could be legislated into equality with the white."[83] Such writers as Joel Chandler Harris not only dramatized the Negro of slavery, but excused his faults since emancipation and hoped that time would eventually teach him the error of his ways. An excerpt from a speech which W. M. Cox of Mississippi made early in the twentieth century illustrates the tolerant spirit of this group of thinkers.

> When I consider all the circumstances of the case, the Negro's weakness, his utter lack of preparation for freedom and citizenship, and the multitudinous temptations to disorder and wrong doing which have assailed him, the wonder to me is, not that he has done so ill, but that he has done so well. No other race in the world would have borne itself with so much patience, docility, and submissiveness. It is true that many grave crimes have been committed by Negroes, and these have sorely taxed the patience of the white people of the South. I do not blink at their enormity, and I know that they must be sternly repressed and terribly avenged. But I insist that the entire race is not chargeable with these exceptional crimes, and that the overwhelming majority of the race are peaceable, inoffensive and submissive to whatever the superior race sees fit to put upon them. Their crimes are not the fruit of the little learning their schools afford them. They are the results of brutish instincts and propensities which they have not been taught to regulate and restrain.[84]

The recollections of slavery days to be found in the memoirs of this period were written chiefly in the romantic vein, and southern historians have also helped to perpetuate the tradition.[85] A flood of romantic novels cast a halo around the plantation with its benign master and genteel mistress and shed a beneficent glow upon the slave.[86]

Romanticists tended toward paternalism when dealing with the Negro. This spirit of kindliness, sometimes sorely grieved at the conduct of the

---

[83] *Ibid.*, p. ix.
[84] C. B. Galloway, *The South and the Negro*, pp. 14-15.
[85] Francis Pendleton Gaines, *The Southern Plantation. A Study in the Development and Accuracy of a Tradition* (New York, 1925).
[86] For a Negro writer's estimate of the effects of the romantic school upon race relations see Amory Dwight Mayo, *The Duty of the White American Toward His Colored Fellow Citizen* (Washington, c1903), p. 4.

Negro but usually explanatory and tolerant, sprang directly from the paternalistic philosophy of the patriarchal state fostered by the theologians of the ante-bellum period. The correlative rights and duties which the paternalists stressed in the post-war years were strongly reminiscent of Filmer and Burke. The whites had the right to control the government by reason of their superior intelligence and wealth, but they were also obligated to protect the Negroes and lift them up to a higher plane of civilization. In return it was the duty of the Negroes to look to the whites for guidance and to accept cheerfully the status which the whites assigned them. The role of the Negro should be implicit acceptance of the biracial social structure; he must always "keep his place." The role of the whites should be that of *noblesse oblige*. A resolution passed by the legislature of North Carolina after the state government had returned to the hands of the Democratic party with Zebulon Baird Vance as governor illustrates the philosophy of paternalism of the time.

Whereas, in the province of God, the colored people have been set free, and this is their country and their home, as well as that of the white people, and there should be nothing to prevent the two races from dwelling together in the land in harmony and peace;
Whereas, we recognize the duty of the stronger race to uphold the weaker, and that upon it rests the responsibility of an honest and faithful endeavor to raise the weaker race to the level of intelligent citizenship; and
Whereas, the colored people have been erroneously taught that legislation under Democratic auspices would be inimical to their rights and interests, thereby causing a number of them to entertain honest fears in the premises,
The General Assembly of North Carolina do resolve, That, while we regard with repugnance the absurd attempts, by means of "Civil Rights" Bills, to eradicate certain race distinctions, implanted by nature and sustained by the habits of forty centuries; and while we are sure that good government demands for both races alike that the great representation and executive offices of the country should be administered by men of the highest intelligence and best experience in public affairs we do, nevertheless, heartily accord alike to every citizen, without distinction of race or color, equality before the law.
Resolved, That we recognize the full purport and intent of that amendment to the Constitution of the United States which confers the right of suffrage and citizenship upon the people of color, and that part of the Constitution of North Carolina conferring educational privileges upon both races: that we are disposed and determined to carry out in good faith these as all other constitutional provisions.[87]

While the South was soon to reverse this statement on the matter of suffrage and civil rights, it does not admit to have altered its position with respect to the remaining propositions. If it is said, for example, that the South discriminates against the Negro in matters of appropriations for education, it is pointed out that the Negroes are given an equal share in accordance with their ratio in the general population or their ratio of the taxable wealth. The most liberal of the paternalists, however, would reply that it is the obvious duty of the white race to bear the greater proportion

[87] North Carolina *Session Laws,* 1877.

of the burden until the Negro race is able to assume its full share of the responsibility.

Arrayed against the paternalists and all those who were willing to concede that the concept of progress applied to the Negro as well as to the whites was that still larger group of white Southerners who maintained that the Negro was permanently inferior and, therefore, a menace to American society. This position led some to an unreasoning fear of the Negro which amounted to a phobia. Others were willing to tolerate the Negro so long as his services were cheap and he "kept his place." Given the fact of present degradation, most Southerners argued *a priori* that the Negro was and had always been inferior. Alfred Holt Stone, planter in the Yazoo-Mississippi delta, whose magazine articles on the status of the Negro in the South were written in the early years of the twentieth century, based his entire philosophy upon the theory of permanency of type.[88] He declared that the racial status of the Negro had been fixed several thousands of years ago ". . . the Negro is one of the oldest races of which we have any knowledge, and . . . its very failure to develop itself in its own habitat, while the Caucasian, Mongolian, and others have gone forward, is in itself sufficient proof of inferiority. . . . if we blot out the achievement of the American Negro who has passed through slavery, what has the race left to boast of? And if we go one step further, and from the achievements of the 'American Negro' obliterate all that the American mulatto has accomplished, what ground indeed would be left to those whose sentiment and sympathy have apparently rendered them so forgetful of scientific truth?"[89]

From this pseudo-scientific approach, Stone summarized and justified the prevailing public opinion. The Negro was an inferior type of man with predominantly African customs and character traits whom no amount of education or improvement of environmental conditions could ever elevate to as high a scale in the human species as the white man. Many were the complaints of "the burden" which the South had to bear from "the menace" of its black population. It was pointed out that when the world came to look upon the Negro as the African that he really was, a better understanding of the South's plight might be obtained. This was the position of E. H. Randle of Virginia, writing in 1910 *Characteristics of the Southern Negro* in reply to Andrew Carnegie's optimistic article on the Negro which appeared in the *North America Review* of June, 1908.

The first important thing to remember in judging the Negro, Randle thought, was that his mental capacity was inferior to that of the white man. The Negro mind seldom developed "beyond that of the twelve-year-old white child, although there seems to be much less difference in the mental capacity of the children of the two races. . . ."[90] He declared that

---
[88] *Studies in the American Race Problem* (New York, 1908), p. 207.
[89] *Ibid.*, pp. 428-429.
[90] P. 11. This idea was also prevalent during the ante-bellum period and was used as a justification of slavery.

education did not improve the Negro. "We have tried that for nearly a half century," he wrote, "and the contrary is the result. He has exchanged common sense for a small quantity of parrot book-learning; energy for laziness, efficiency, for shiftlessness—with a moderate number of good exceptions. The lands have declined most where there are the most negroes."[91] Given the assumption of permanent inferiority, the outlook for the South and for the white man in the South was gloomy unless the Negro could forever be "kept in his place." The Negro was an encumbrance because he drove away northern and foreign white immigration, because it was an increasingly heavy tax burden to attempt to educate and to police him, and because he was inefficient as a laborer.

Randle saw a dark future ahead. ". . . think of the black belts where there are many negroes to one white man. When most of them get a smattering of education and begin to want to hold the county offices, and to possess the lands; stirred up by one of their number or some bad white man, they may organize on a large scale and start out to kill and possess." The time, he thought, was not far off. "I am of the opinion," he warned, "that it is only a question of time when such attempts will be made, and so are many others. If the attempt should be extensive and succeed somewhat at first, it would be an end of the negro, and the solution of the problem would be crimsoned with more blood than was required to break the bonds of slavery."[92] This was the same fearful cry of a Negro insurrection which had gone up in the South since the eighteenth century.

The corollaries of the assumption of permanent inferiority which were accepted in the ante-bellum period were still held to be incontrovertible. It was argued that race mixing was harmful and that the mulatto, although he might not be the physical inferior of the Negro,[93] was certainly the trouble maker in race relations, and, therefore, an objectionable member of society. It was said that if one made a concession of equality on any ground, the Negro would accept it as unlimited equality. The lesson of Reconstruction had been: "Give the Negro a political inch and he will

[91] *Ibid.*, pp. 76-77.

[92] *Ibid.*, pp. 77-78. It was often said during slavery that the whites and blacks could not live together in peace if both were free. Abraham Lincoln was himself of that opinion and used every effort to find a place outside the limits of the United States where the freedmen might be colonized. See *Complete Works of Abraham Lincoln* (ed. by John G. Nicolay and John Hay (New York, c1905), VIII, I, 5-6, 97-98; Charles Howard Wesley, "Lincoln's Plan for Colonizing the Emancipated Negro," *Journal of Negro History,* IV (1919), 9ff; *Diary of Gideon Welles, Secretary of the Navy under Lincoln and Johnson* (Intro. by John T. Morse, Jr. Boston, 1911), III, 428 and *passim;* Carter Godwin Woodson, *The Negro in Our History* (4th ed. Washington, 1927), pp. 367-368.

[93] This point was still in dispute, although as the years passed and the mulatto did not prove sterile as such men as Dr. J. C. Nott and Dr. J. H. Van Evrie had predicted during the ante-bellum period, it came to be said less and less that the mulatto was the physical inferior of the true Negro type. No detailed scientific study has been made of Negro-white mixtures, but see Caroline Bond Day, *A Study of Some Negro-White Families in the United States . . .* (with a foreword and notes on the anthropometric data by Earnest A. Hooton. Cambridge, Mass., 1932).

take a social ell." The only solution to the race problem, therefore, was either to force the Negro always to keep his place or to rid the country of him entirely.

Southern whites who let their minds dwell long upon such a dismal picture reacted emotionally. Schizophrenic thought and behavior patterns were the result. Frenzied mobs lynched a Negro on slight evidence of guilt and there were those in the market place heard to say that "the only solution to the Negro problem was a first class lynching Monday of every week." Such extreme statements did not necessarily mean that those who uttered them were consistently cruel to Negroes. If they employed Negro labor they were likely to ameliorate their relationships with kindliness, saying that this procedure brought best results. Others were less expedient and pursued an uncompromising attitude toward the Negro at all times. Still others, the extremists, would not permit Negroes about them under any circumstances. They would not hire Negro labor and they would not eat food prepared by Negro hands. Hinton Rowan Helper, author of *Impending Crisis of the South,* seems to have been such a one.

The negrophobist had short patience with the "sickly sentimentality" of the romanticist and the paternalist who were constantly pointing out the duties which the white people of the South owed the Negro because he was the basis of their labor, and, therefore, the "mud-sill"[94] of their civilization; because he was a weaker race, and, therefore, "a ward of the white people." Nor did he have any patience with those who argued that progress through education would eventually raise the average intelligence of the Negro. The phobist had thought from the time that education was first agitated that it "would ruin the Negro for work," but the Reconstruction legislatures had passed the Negro education bills with the argument that education would make the Negro "a better man, a better citizen and a better Christian."[95] The result of education had confirmed the worst fears of the phobists. The Negroes had shown, the phobists declared, an increasing tendency to get out of place, to push the southern white man off the sidewalk, and, what was far less endurable, to despoil the white woman. Dunbar Rowland, director of the Mississippi Department of Archives and History, addressing the Alumni Association of the University of Mississippi in 1902, pointed out that "thoughtful men in the South" were beginning to lose faith in "the power of the education which had been heretofore given to uplift the negro" and to complain of the burden thus placed upon "the people of the South in their poverty."[96] He argued that the Negro did not advance because he lacked the ability to do so; for the South had given him every opportunity to rise. The

[94] The term used by Governor James H. Hammond of South Carolina in 1858 to explain the theory of the dual form of labor. See *Congressional Globe,* 35 Cong., 1st Sess., App., p. 71; W. S. Jenkins, *Pro-Slavery Thought,* p. 286, 286n.
[95] Inaugural Address of Governor Longino of Mississippi cited by Dunbar Rowland, *A Mississippi View of Race Relations in the South* (Jackson, Miss., 1903). p. 18.
[96] Dunbar Rowland, *Mississippi View of Race Relations,* pp. 17, 18.

154   THE JAMES SPRUNT STUDIES

South could not always bear the burden of an improvident population which furnished the basis of an increasingly large criminal class.[97]

The most extreme form which negrophobia took in this period was Charles Carroll's restatement of the Pre-Adamic theory of the origin of the Negro race in his two volumes, *The Negro a Beast* (1900), and *The Tempter of Eve* (1902).[98] Carroll's assumption that the Negro was created prior to Adam and, therefore, was not of the genus *homo sapiens* bore close resemblance to the outline of the theory which Buckner H. Payne, writing under the signature of "Ariel," had set forth in 1867 in *The Negro: What Is His Ethnological Status?*[99] Carroll departed from Payne, however, in his assumption that the Negro was the serpent mentioned in the Bible as the tempter of Eve. In 1860 S. A. Cartwright of Mississippi, accepting the conclusion of Adam Clark, the English Biblical scholar, that the tempter of Eve was an orangutan and not a serpent, also had declared the tempter of Eve to have been a Negro.[100]

A large part of Carroll's *Tempter of Eve* was devoted to a lengthy effort to prove from geological and ethnological sources as well as from Biblical data that the betrayer of the human race had been a Negro woman. Amalgamation, he argued, was cursed of God because it gave rise to a creature who was the offspring of *homo sapiens* and a beast. This spurious issue, like the pure Negro stock itself, was devoid of a soul and, therefore, outside the pale of redemption. Carroll thought that speculative philosophy which had developed the theory of progress had "led us to accept into the Adamic family" as "a man and a brother . . . a creature whom God made an ape; this assault upon God's plan of creation led to amalgamation with this animal; and amalgamation—that crime of crimes—has not only depopulated nations, but continents of their Adamic stock, and has damned millions upon millions of souls."[101]

Negro writers frequently pointed to such extravagant statements as these from "the crazy Carroll" as well as to the widespread publicity given

[97] The Reverend C. C. Penick, agent of the Protestant Episcopal Church for work among the Negroes, pointed out in 1897 that the Negro criminal tended to come not from the group which had been born in slavery but from the young people. (William Dwight Porter, ed., *Encyclopedia of Social Reform* (New York, 1897), p. 929). He said, "When we contrast . . . the wonderful strides of the race in education and religiousness since 1865, the revelations of its criminal record are both surprising and appaling, as the following facts, gathered from the census of 1890 shows: The negro population is a little more than one-ninth of the entire population of the nation, yet it furnishes 37 per cent of its homicides."

[98] *"The Negro a Beast"; or "In the Image of God"* (St. Louis, 1900); *The Tempter of Eve; or the Criminality of Man's Social, Political, and Religious Equality with the Negro, and the Amalgamation to Which these Crimes Inevitably Lead* (St. Louis, 1902).

[99] This pamphlet seems to have had several editions, the first, a brief one of 48 pages privately printed in Cincinnati in 1867, and the longer one of 172 pages also privately published in Cincinnati in 1872. Payne also published a *Reply to the Rev. John A. Seiss* (Nashville, Tenn., 1876).

[100] "The Unity of the Human Race Disproved by the Hebrew Bible," *DeBow's Review*, XXIX (1860), 130; W. S. Jenkins, *Pro-Slavery Thought*, p. 254.

[101] *The Tempter of Eve*, pp. 170-171.

to all Negro crime as a deliberate campaign against the Negro in an attempt to justify white supremacy and Negro exploitation in the eyes of the world.[102] George Henry White, the last Negro to represent North Carolina in Congress, paid his respects to this propaganda of hate in 1900 on the floor of the House.

Possibly at no time in the history of our freedom has the effort been made to mould public sentiment against us and our progress so strongly as it is now being done. The forces have been set in motion and we must have sufficient manhood and courage to overcome all resistance that obstructs our progress....
It is easy for these gentlemen to taunt us with our inferiority, at the same time not mentioning the causes of this inferiority. It is rather hard to be accused of shiftlessness and idleness when the accuser of his own motion closes the avenues for labor and industrial pursuits to us. It is hardly fair to accuse us of ignorance when it was made a crime under the former order of things to learn enough about letters even to read the Word of God.
While I offer no extenuation for any immorality that may exist among my people, it comes with rather poor grace from those who forced it upon us for two hundred and fifty years to taunt us with that shortcoming.[103]

White supremacy had come now to be accepted as an absolute. It found respectable advocates in the North as well as in the South, in Europe as well as in the United States, in scholarship and in public opinion. But the Fourteenth and Fifteenth Amendments had thrown—and still continue to throw—the South upon the defensive by upsetting the legality of the status which the whites had assigned to the Negro during the more than two hundred years of slavery. With the principle of equality incorporated into the government as a part of the organic law, it was necessary for those who found the old status of inferiority, degradation, and exploitation disrupted to begin a new period of justification. All of the old assumptions used to justify the legal enslavement of the Negro were used to defend his civil enslavement. The work of justification was considerably speeded up by the appearance and widespread acceptance of the theory of positivism as expressed by Comte, the theory of evolution as expressed by Darwin, the theory of progress developed by Spencer, and by the continued acceptance of the theory of *laissez faire* in government and in business.

In the South itself little argument was needed to justify white supremacy. The controversy during the slavery regime had silenced opposition for almost thirty years before the conflict at arms. Occasionally during the Civil War[104] and for almost twenty years thereafter it was possible to protest against the lowly status assigned the Negro, but, after the emotions aroused during the controversies of the agrarian revolt, it became increasingly difficult to question the wisdom of caste relationships. The taboos of race relations which had been established during slavery were the taboos of freedom. The Negro had a definite and inferior place to

---

[102] See, for example, Kelly Miller, *Race Adjustment*.
[103] George Henry White, *Defence of the Negro Race—Charges Answered ... Speech in House of Representatives Jan. 29, 1901* (Washington, 1901).
[104] Bell Irvin Wiley, *Southern Negroes, 1861-1865* (New Haven, 1938), p. 170.

keep; so long as he kept that place he was acceptable. But he must never aspire to rise outside his own racial structure; no white man who wished to retain his superior caste position among other white men must ever suggest that the Negro deserved a higher status than that assigned him. As in the late ante-bellum period so in the period following Reconstruction there was little tolerance of debate upon "this delicate situation." When Walter Hines Page in 1909 made his plea for the intellectual freedom of the South in his novel, *The Southerner,* he felt obliged to write under the nom de plume of Nicholas Worth. Thomas P. Bailey, professor in the University of Mississippi, writing of *Race Orthodoxy in the South* in 1914, thought this stultification of southern thinking to be the worst aspect of the situation.[105]

The period between 1876 and 1910 had written the name of the Negro off the registration books and removed the Negro as a minority pressure group in southern politics. By means of state laws the caste status of the Negro was established in public as well as private relationships. There were few voices of protest throughout the land. When the caste position of the Negro was challenged, the points at issue were fundamentally the same as those of the slavery period: the status and capacities of the Negro Three groups of thinkers in the South—the romanticists, the paternalists, and those who accepted the theory of progress through education—held out some hope to the Negro, although they either neglected to define what this future higher status should be or they exhibited considerable confusion of thought on the subject. All tended alike to measure the Negro upon the Malthusian scale of personality traits and to find, when the Negro fell short of the ideal, that the black man had serious character defects in comparison to his Caucasian brother. The Negro was, in other words, still considered to be a "peculiar" type of man, and the negrophobists would declare that he always would remain so. White supremacy was, from this point of view, the determination of the dominant race "to ward off political ruin and to save society from destruction."[106]

[105] P. 346.
[106] P. A. Bruce, *The Plantation Negro as a Freeman,* p. 259.